THE ENCYCLOPEDIA OF

SEASONING

THE ENCYCLOPEDIA OF
SEASONING

500 MARINADES, RUBS, GLAZES, SAUCES, BASTES & BUTTERS FOR EVERY MEAL

CIDER MILL PRESS

BOOK PUBLISHERS

The Encyclopedia of Seasoning

• 13-Digit ISBN: 978-1-64643-374-2 • 10-Digit ISBN: 1-64643-374-2 • This book may be ordered by mail from the publisher. Please include $5.99 for postage and handling. Please support your local bookseller first! • Books published by Cider Mill Press Book Publishers are available at special discounts for bulk purchases in the United States by corporations, institutions, and other organizations. For more information, please contact the publisher. • Cider Mill Press Book Publishers • "Where good books are ready for press" • 501 Nelson Place, Nashville, TN 37214 • Typography: Hansief, Freight Sans, Freight Serif • Image credits: Pages 53, 54, 58, 69, 158, 180, 188, 202, 208, 258, 278, 304, 317, 324, 365, 379, 380, 388, 392–393, 395, 413, 423, 451, 479, 483, 508, 515, 536, and 543 courtesy of Cider Mill Press. All other images used under official license from Shutterstock • Printed in China

• 23 24 25 26 27 TYC 5 4 3 2 1 •

First Edition

CONTENTS

INTRODUCTION

The modern world keeps us ignorant of many miraculous things. Our trips to the airport are more focused on getting through security and possible missed connections than they are with our fortune to participate in the astounding phenomena of flight. Instead of engaging with the life-changing information available to us, our time online is mostly spent getting frustrated by the opinions of trolls or distracted by the tireless content cycle. In the supermarket, we push our carts around in a daze, looking to get through as quickly as possible, never recognizing the incredible bounty that has been gathered for us.

And nowhere is this grocery store lack of gratitude more true than in the spice aisle. To put it plainly, someone who lived five centuries ago would be as gob smacked by this collection of seasonings and their affordability as they would be an airplane in the sky or the phone/camera/computer in your pocket. In their day, one would either have to spend a lifetime traveling to encounter such an array of spices, or have considerable resources to procure them from those who ferried these exotic flavors back from the far-flung corners of the globe.

While their astonishment would seem comical to us, it's safe to say that their reaction is closer to correct than our indifference. After all, those spices and seasoning blends are the elements that make or break a meal. So great is their power that seasonings managed to revolutionize the way human civilization conducted itself, serving as a catalyst for the opening of trade routes and lines of communication between cultures.

Though the commercial incentive to trade in spices is not what it once was, their power in the kitchen has not dwindled in the slightest. A memorable meal depends on many factors, but proper seasoning stands as the biggest. So often, a preparation fails to fulfill its potential due to a cook not understanding how bold they can be with salt, lime juice, or paprika, while others are sunk by ham-fisted sorts who incorporated too much fish sauce or nutmeg into a dish.

While a faultless touch when it comes to seasoning can only be developed over time, the information in this book will help you avoid any of the above-mentioned disasters, and result in so many enjoyable meals that your journey to becoming a spice savant will seem effortless.

The second half of this introduction gets you acquainted with the components you will be employing in your endeavors, providing a solid foundation that will allow you to engage effectively with the other preparations in the book, both to determine where they will be at their best, and also imagine how they can be tweaked. From there, you will find rubs and marinades that effortlessly add complexity and depth to a preparation, sauces that enhance the flavor and texture of everything they touch, vinaigrettes that transform ho-hum ingredients into something vibrant, spreads that allow you to keep things simple without sacrificing enjoyment, and so much more.

The basis for every taste and texture you could ever imagine are contained in these pages, ensuring that this book is one you will turn to time and again, as your palate, passion, and abilities grow.

THE ELEMENTS OF SEASONING

SPICES

Allspice: This is the dried, unripe fruit of the *Peimenta dioica*, a tree native to Mexico and Central America. It has the flavor of cinnamon, nutmeg, and cloves.

Caraway seeds: Its anise-like flavor makes it a useful addition to traditionally bland foods like bread or cabbage.

Cardamom: This floral, aromatic spice may be expensive, but it is worth every penny. Toss a few pods in the pot the next time you make rice, and you'll see why.

Cayenne pepper: This chile packs a serious amount of heat but don't be afraid to use it—the spice it provides can take a dish to the next level.

Red pepper flakes: Also known as crushed red pepper, the spice these flakes provide is as potent as what you get from the cayenne. They are most commonly used in Italian cooking, but will come in handy in dishes from a number of cuisines.

Chili powder: A combination of paprika, garlic powder, cayenne, onion powder, dried oregano, and cumin.

Cinnamon: Functional in both sweet and savory preparations, every recipe gets a bit cozier when this ingredient is added.

Clove: A very aromatic spice that is primarily used in Asian, African, and Middle Eastern cuisine.

Coriander: When ground, the floral qualities you'd expect from the seeds of the cilantro plant give way to nuttiness.

Cumin: Popular in Mexican and Indian cuisines, this earthy spice also carries a pungent aroma.

Curry powder: Traditionally, a blend of coriander, turmeric, cumin, fenugreek, and chile peppers. Sometimes spices such as ginger, garlic, fennel seeds, cinnamon, caraway, cardamom, nutmeg, and black pepper are added.

Fennel pollen: Dried, small flowers from wild fennel, they have notes of anise, citrus, and vanilla. Though fennel pollen can carry a very hefty price tag and can also be difficult to find, the aroma it adds to a dish makes it worth seeking out.

Fennel seeds: An extremely aromatic, anise-flavored spice that lends warmth to any dish it is utilized in.

Five-spice powder: Most commonly used in Asian cuisine, this combination of star anise, cloves, cinnamon, Sichuan peppercorns, and fennel seeds provides each of the five basic flavors: sour, bitter, sweet, salty, and umami.

Mustard seeds: Often used in pickling, mustard seed is also a prominent spice in Indian cuisine. The tangy element it lends to a dish is too much for most of us to resist.

Nutmeg: A sweet spice often used in desserts. However, it is able to stand on its own, and pairs wonderfully with vegetables, creamy sauces, and gamy meats. Just be aware: a little goes a long way.

Old Bay: A seasoning mixture made from celery salt, black pepper, and crushed red pepper flakes, it is most at home in seafood dishes.

Paprika: A ground spice commonly made from red bell peppers, the smoked version adds depth to any soup, sauce, or vinaigrette it touches.

Pepper: Usually referring to ground black peppercorns; however, white peppercorns are often used in fine dining establishments so that the prepared food doesn't look "dirty."

Poppy seeds: Nutty and sometimes fruity, these seeds are most often used in pastries and breads.

Saffron: The world's most expensive spice, which is due in part to it being hand picked. Its spicy, pungent, bitter flavor features in a number of classic Mediterranean dishes, from bouillabaisse to paella.

Salt: There is much debate about which version of this staple is best for cooking. In this book, kosher salt, which has a larger grain and does not contain iodine—which can lend salt a slight bitterness—is recommended most of the time. However, a flaky sea salt such as Maldon, and a good-quality fine sea salt should also be in your pantry.

Sichuan peppercorn: Its name makes it seem as though it would be spicy, but it's actually not. Instead, it has slightly citrusy notes, allowing other spices to come to the fore.

Star anise: The product of an evergreen shrub native to Southwest China, this spice is beloved for both its flavor and the health benefits it provides.

Turmeric: A popular spice in Indian cuisine, it brings an earthy warmth to whatever dish it is added to, and the golden hue it inevitably produces is a treat for the eyes.

Vanilla bean: This one's an old standby when something sweet is being prepared. Keep in mind that both the seeds and the pod are aromatic, meaning you'll want to scrape out the seeds before using both to infuse whatever preparation you are utilizing it in.

HERBS

Basil: Initially peppery, basil rapidly escalates into a sweet, aromatic flavor that has just a hint of anise. When cooking with it, make sure to add it only during the final stages, since too much heat will ruin its flavor.

Chives: A delicate onion flavor makes them a wonderful garnish.

Bay leaf: An aromatic that changes with its surroundings, at times lending a pleasing bitter taste, at others an almost minty freshness.

Cilantro: Also known as coriander, this herb is a

true divider. Those who like it can't get enough of its citrusy taste, while those who don't like it bemoan its soapy flavor.

Dill: The extremely aromatic leaves of this herb make it perfect for those dishes with a strong taste, such as smoked salmon or borscht.

Marjoram: It has the pine and citrus flavors of oregano, but is sweeter and more delicate.

Mint: The leaves of this aromatic can be used in both savory and sweet preparations, and its refreshing aftertaste ensures that your mouth is always ready for the next bite.

Oregano: An intense, slightly bitter herb that spices up any dish.

Parsley: A slightly bitter herb that provides balance when added to savory dishes. There are two popular varieties, flat leaf and curly, with the former being more flavorful.

Rosemary: This hardy herb has been known to flower in early December, and its fragrant nettles are famous for the wonders they work with poultry.

Sage: Used more often in Europe than it is in the United States, this herb has an astringent but warm flavor, and is particularly good at cutting through the richness in a cream- or butter-based sauce.

Tarragon: One of the fines herbes in traditional French cuisine, it is best known for its role in béarnaise sauce. Tarragon also goes beautifully with a variety of seafood.

Thyme: The slightly minty flavor of this herb makes it a natural for both poultry and soups. If you just want to use the leaves in a dish, use the back of a knife to remove them easily from the woody stem.

VINEGARS

Apple cider: Made from fermented apple cider. For cooking, make sure you're using an unfiltered version.

Balsamic: This black, intensely flavored vinegar is made from grape must, and is traditionally aged in a series of wooden barrels.

Champagne: Produced with the same grapes used to make the famous bubbly beverage, this vinegar carries a lighter and brighter flavor than white wine vinegar.

Red wine: Red wine that is fermented until it turns sour, the flavor of this vinegar becomes muted as it ages.

Rice: Produced by fermenting the sugars in rice, this is less acidic than most vinegars and carries a mild, sweet flavor. It will be called for primarily in those dishes associated with Asian cuisine.

Sherry: Don't hesitate to be seduced by thehandsome, dark mahogany color of this vinegar—at around $10 a bottle, it is typically a better bet than similarly priced balsamic vinegars.

White distilled: The vinegar itself is not distilled, but produced by the fermentation of distilled alcohol. Its lower acidity makes it ideal for cooking.

White wine: Its flavor is not as potent as its brethren, but this makes it more versatile—it adds a clean fruitiness to any dish.

OILS

Extra-virgin olive oil: The go-to oil for sautéing and making vinaigrettes. When using it to cook, be aware of the temperature—the taste will deteriorate once it exceeds 210°F.

Peanut oil: Often used in American and Asian cuisines, this oil has a high smoke point, making it ideal for use in frying.

Sesame oil: A very flavorful, aromatic oil with a high smoke point. Often used in Indian, African, and Asian cuisines.

Truffle oil: Infused with the famous mushroom, it is used to finish dishes rather than cook them. Beware, there are many artificial impostors out there.

Canola oil: A neutral-flavored derived from the rapeseed that is low in saturated fat, high in Omega-6 fatty acids. Its high smoke point makes it perfect for normal cooking procedures and frying.

Avocado oil: When you need something that has a higher smoke point than olive oil, but are wary of the health concerns that swirl around canola and other seed oils, go with this oil. It also has a relatively mild flavor that will not affect the flavor of the other ingredients.

ALCOHOL

Brandy: A spirit that results from distilled wine. In cooking, it is typically used to intensify the flavor of a soup or sauce.

Calvados: A dry, apple-flavored brandy produced in the Normandy region in France. In the kitchen, it can find its way into pan sauces, soups, and pastries.

Kirsch: A clear, fermented cherry–flavored brandy that is often used in making desserts.

Madeira: A sweet, fortified wine produced in Portugal's Madeira Islands.

Mirin: A low-alcohol rice wine that is similar in flavor to sake. In Japanese cuisine, it is commonly used as a condiment.

Pernod: A green, anise-flavored liqueur from France that became popular after absinthe was banned in the early twentieth century.

Port: Both Madeira and white Port are utilized in this book.

Red wine: For the purposes of this book, Cabernet Sauvignon is a good go-to. But really, any dry red wine will do. Just don't go overboard and use an expensive bottle. Whatever bottle you've had lying around for a few days will work.

Riesling: A sweet wine with a strong, flowery aroma.

Sambuca: An anise-flavored liqueur from Italy.

Sherry: Fortified wine made from white grapes. It comes in a number of varieties, and is probably used in cooking as much as it is imbibed.

White wine: For the recipes in this book, Chardonnay is a good option, as its fruitiness comes through pleasantly in a dish. Again, stick to dry wines here, and make sure you don't break the bank when you're using it for cooking.

DAIRY & OTHER CHEESES

Butter: Typically, it consists of 80 to 85 percent butterfat, and carries a melting point of 90°F to 95°F. For the purpose of this book, almost every preparation calls for butter that is unsalted, since this will ensure that it is both fresh and provides a predictable flavor.

Buttermilk: The liquid remaining after the butter has been churned. Buttermilk has a slightly sour taste that can transform a dish.

Crème fraîche: A thick cream that is slightly sour and has the consistency of sour cream. It is traditionally made by leaving unpasteurized cream at room temperature. There are pasteurized versions available at the grocery store, which typically have buttermilk added in order to provide flavor and thickness.

Blue cheese: Cashel, a semi-soft pasteurized cheese made from cow's milk, is a good option when blue cheese is called for, as its flavor is round and full, while still providing the pleasant funk one expects. For a stronger-flavored option, go with Stilton.

Feta cheese: Made from sheep's or goat's milk, it is rich and salty. Most of the feta that is made in North America and Greece has been pasteurized.

Fontina: A nutty, delicate semi-soft cheese from Italy. Made from cow's milk, it features a dark brown rind and is typically unpasteurized.

Greek yogurt: Yogurt is the result of milk that yogurt cultures have been added to, heated, and then cooled before fermenting for several hours. Greek yogurt is the result of yogurt that has been strained to remove the whey. It has a slightly sour, zesty, and rich taste.

Gruyère: An unpasteurized, semi-soft cheese from Switzerland that is famous for its sweet, slightly salty flavor.

Heavy cream: Milk with a fat content of 36 to 40 percent. Also referred to as whipping cream, it is used frequently as an ingredient in this book.

Mascarpone: An Italian cream cheese thickened by the addition of citric acid. It is known for its creamy, mild flavor.

Monterey Jack: One of the few famed American cheeses, it is produced on the central California coast from pasteurized cow's milk.

Parmesan: Properly known as Parmigiano-Reggiano, this unpasteurized cheese is famed for its bold aroma and strong, slightly nutty taste.

Queso fresco: A Mexican cheese that is made from cow's milk or a combination of goat's and cow's milk. It resembles feta, but lacks feta's saltiness.

Sharp cheddar: Made from cow's milk, this is originally from Somerset, a village in England. It is typically pasteurized and aged 3 to 24 months.

Sour cream: Made by adding lactic acid to heavy cream, it has a similar texture to yogurt, but lacks yogurt's zest. The two are interchangeable, depending on what one wants to emphasize or soften in a dish.

RUBS & SEASONING BLENDS

Three-Pepper Rub

YIELD: ½ CUP | **ACTIVE TIME:** 5 MINUTES | **TOTAL TIME:** 5 MINUTES

1 TABLESPOON BLACK PEPPER

⅓ CUP KOSHER SALT

2 TEASPOONS DRY MUSTARD

1 TABLESPOON SMOKED PAPRIKA

2 TEASPOONS RED PEPPER FLAKES

2 TEASPOONS DRIED PARSLEY

2 TEASPOONS DRIED THYME

2 TEASPOONS GARLIC POWDER

1. Place all of the ingredients in a bowl, stir to combine, and use immediately or store in an airtight container.

Spicy Poultry Rub

YIELD: ¾ CUP | **ACTIVE TIME:** 5 MINUTES | **TOTAL TIME:** 5 MINUTES

⅓ CUP KOSHER SALT

2 TABLESPOONS BLACK PEPPER

1 TABLESPOON SWEET PAPRIKA

1 TABLESPOON CAYENNE PEPPER

1 TABLESPOON RED PEPPER FLAKES

4 GARLIC CLOVES, CHOPPED

1 TABLESPOON MINCED FRESH GINGER

1 TABLESPOON HOT SAUCE

1 TABLESPOON DIJON MUSTARD

1. Place all of the ingredients in a bowl, stir to combine, and use immediately or store in an airtight container.

BBQ Poultry Rub

YIELD: 1½ CUPS | **ACTIVE TIME:** 5 MINUTES | **TOTAL TIME:** 5 MINUTES

⅓ CUP KOSHER SALT

½ CUP BROWN SUGAR

¼ CUP SMOKED PAPRIKA

1 TABLESPOON CAYENNE PEPPER

1 TABLESPOON CHILI POWDER

2 TEASPOONS CUMIN

1 TABLESPOON ONION POWDER

2 TABLESPOONS GARLIC POWDER

1 TABLESPOON BLACK PEPPER

1 TABLESPOON GROUND FENNEL SEEDS

1 TABLESPOON CORIANDER

1 TABLESPOON DRY MUSTARD

1. Place all of the ingredients in a bowl, stir to combine, and use immediately or store in an airtight container.

Smoked Lemon Zest Rub

YIELD: ¾ CUP | **ACTIVE TIME:** 5 MINUTES | **TOTAL TIME:** 5 MINUTES

¼ CUP LEMON ZEST

1 TABLESPOON CORIANDER

2 TABLESPOONS BLACK PEPPER

⅓ CUP KOSHER SALT

2 TEASPOONS SUGAR

¼ CUP CHOPPED FRESH PARSLEY

4 GARLIC CLOVES, CHOPPED

1 TABLESPOON CHOPPED FRESH OREGANO

1. Place all of the ingredients in a bowl, stir to combine, and use immediately or store in an airtight container.

San Sebastian Rub

YIELD: ½ CUP | **ACTIVE TIME:** 5 MINUTES | **TOTAL TIME:** 5 MINUTES

¼ CUP SMOKED PAPRIKA

5 TEASPOONS ONION POWDER

1 TABLESPOON GARLIC POWDER

4 TEASPOONS CAYENNE PEPPER

2 TEASPOONS BLACK PEPPER

2 TEASPOONS FINE SEA SALT

2 TEASPOONS DRIED OREGANO

2 TEASPOONS DRIED THYME

1. Place all of the ingredients in a bowl, stir to combine, and use immediately or store in an airtight container.

Lemon-Pepper Poultry Rub

YIELD: ¾ CUP | **ACTIVE TIME:** 5 MINUTES | **TOTAL TIME:** 5 MINUTES

⅓ CUP KOSHER SALT

3 TABLESPOONS LEMON-PEPPER SEASONING

1 TABLESPOON ONION POWDER

2 TABLESPOONS GARLIC POWDER

1. Place all of the ingredients in a bowl, stir to combine, and use immediately or store in an airtight container.

Lemon-Pepper Poultry Rub
SEE PAGE 23

Sweet & Spicy Rub

YIELD: ½ CUP | **ACTIVE TIME:** 5 MINUTES | **TOTAL TIME:** 5 MINUTES

⅓ CUP LIGHT BROWN SUGAR

1 TEASPOON CAYENNE PEPPER

1 TEASPOON CHILI POWDER

1½ TEASPOONS PAPRIKA

2 TEASPOONS FINE SEA SALT

1 TEASPOON GARLIC POWDER

1 TEASPOON ONION POWDER

1 TEASPOON CUMIN

1 TEASPOON BLACK PEPPER

½ TEASPOON DRY MUSTARD

¼ TEASPOON DRIED OREGANO

1. Place all of the ingredients in a bowl, stir to combine, and use immediately or store in an airtight container.

Sachet D'Epices

YIELD: 1 SACHET | **ACTIVE TIME:** 5 MINUTES | **TOTAL TIME:** 5 MINUTES

3 SPRIGS OF FRESH PARSLEY

1 SPRIG OF FRESH THYME

½ BAY LEAF

¼ TEASPOON CRACKED BLACK PEPPERCORNS

½ GARLIC CLOVE

1. Place all of the ingredients in a 4-inch square of cheesecloth and fold the corners together to make a purse. Tie the sachet closed with a length of kitchen twine, tie the other end of the twine to the handle of your saucepan, and drop the sachet into the preparation when you desire.

Masala Rub

YIELD: ¾ CUP | **ACTIVE TIME:** 5 MINUTES | **TOTAL TIME:** 5 MINUTES

2 TABLESPOONS CUMIN

2 TABLESPOONS CORIANDER

2 TABLESPOONS CURRY POWDER

1 TEASPOON TURMERIC

2 TEASPOONS GARAM MASALA

1 TEASPOON KASHMIRI CHILI POWDER

6 TABLESPOONS EXTRA-VIRGIN OLIVE OIL

SALT, TO TASTE

1. Place all of the ingredients in a bowl, stir to combine, and use immediately or store in an airtight container.

Tom Yum Paste

YIELD: 1 CUP | **ACTIVE TIME:** 10 MINUTES | **TOTAL TIME:** 25 MINUTES

1 LEMONGRASS STALK, PEELED

2-INCH PIECE OF FRESH GALANGAL ROOT, PEELED AND MINCED

3 MAKRUT LIME LEAVES, SLICED THIN

1 TABLESPOON THAI CHILI PASTE

4 RED CHILE PEPPERS, STEMS AND SEEDS REMOVED

2 TABLESPOONS FISH SAUCE

JUICE OF 2 LIMES

2 SHALLOTS, CHOPPED

2 TEASPOONS SUGAR

3 TABLESPOONS CHOPPED FRESH CILANTRO

1. Place all of the ingredients in a food processor, blitz until smooth, and use immediately or store in the refrigerator.

Lemon & Herb Poultry Rub

YIELD: 1½ CUPS | **ACTIVE TIME:** 5 MINUTES | **TOTAL TIME:** 5 MINUTES

1 CUP SUGAR

2 TABLESPOONS KOSHER
SALT

2 TEASPOONS BLACK
PEPPER

2 TEASPOONS LEMON ZEST

1 TABLESPOON CHOPPED
FRESH ROSEMARY

1 TABLESPOON FRESH
THYME

1 TABLESPOON CHOPPED
FRESH PARSLEY

1. Place all of the ingredients in a bowl, stir to combine, and use immediately or store in an airtight container.

Nashville Hot Chicken Rub

YIELD: ½ CUP | **ACTIVE TIME:** 5 MINUTES | **TOTAL TIME:** 5 MINUTES

2 TABLESPOONS PAPRIKA

1 TEASPOON ONION SALT

1½ TEASPOONS FINE SEA SALT

1½ TEASPOONS BLACK PEPPER

2 TEASPOONS GARLIC POWDER

1 TEASPOON CHILI POWDER

1 TEASPOON GROUND THYME

1 TEASPOON GROUND SAGE

1 TEASPOON GROUND OREGANO

1 TEASPOON GROUND BASIL

3 TABLESPOONS CAYENNE PEPPER

1 TABLESPOON BROWN SUGAR

1. Place all of the ingredients in a bowl, stir to combine, and use immediately or store in an airtight container.

Maple Poultry Rub

YIELD: 1½ CUPS | **ACTIVE TIME:** 5 MINUTES | **TOTAL TIME:** 5 MINUTES

¾ CUP MAPLE SUGAR

2 TABLESPOONS KOSHER SALT

2 TEASPOONS PEPPER

2 TEASPOONS LEMON ZEST

2 TEASPOONS PAPRIKA

½ TEASPOON CINNAMON

½ TEASPOON NUTMEG

1. Place all of the ingredients in a bowl, stir to combine, and use immediately or store in an airtight container.

Acapulco Gold Rub

YIELD: 4 CUPS | **ACTIVE TIME:** 5 MINUTES | **TOTAL TIME:** 5 MINUTES

1 CUP BROWN SUGAR

½ CUP KOSHER SALT

½ CUP CHILI POWDER

¼ CUP HUNGARIAN PAPRIKA

¼ CUP CORIANDER

1 TABLESPOON GROUND GINGER

¼ CUP CUMIN

⅓ CUP GARLIC POWDER

⅓ CUP ONION POWDER

1 TABLESPOON LEMON ZEST

¼ CUP DUTCH COCOA POWDER

1. Place all of the ingredients in a bowl, stir to combine, and use immediately or store in an airtight container.

Colombian Gold Rub

YIELD: 4⅓ CUPS | **ACTIVE TIME:** 5 MINUTES | **TOTAL TIME:** 5 MINUTES

1½ CUPS DARK BROWN SUGAR

1 CUP KOSHER SALT

1 CUP GROUND ESPRESSO BEANS

¼ CUP BLACK PEPPER

¼ CUP GARLIC POWDER

2 TABLESPOONS CINNAMON

2 TABLESPOONS CUMIN

2 TABLESPOONS CAYENNE PEPPER

1. Place all of the ingredients in a bowl, stir to combine, and use immediately or store in an airtight container.

Nashville Hot Chicken Rub
SEE PAGE 30

Garlic & Sage Dry Brine

YIELD: ¾ CUP | **ACTIVE TIME:** 5 MINUTES | **TOTAL TIME:** 5 MINUTES

1 TEASPOON BLACK PEPPER

⅓ CUP KOSHER SALT

2 TABLESPOONS SUGAR

¼ CUP CHOPPED FRESH SAGE

6 GARLIC CLOVES, CHOPPED

2 TEASPOONS DRIED PARSLEY

1. Place all of the ingredients in a bowl, stir to combine, and use immediately or store in an airtight container.

Cajun Turkey Rub

YIELD: 1 CUP | **ACTIVE TIME:** 5 MINUTES | **TOTAL TIME:** 5 MINUTES

½ CUP KOSHER SALT

2 TABLESPOONS ONION POWDER

2 TABLESPOONS PAPRIKA

1 TABLESPOON CAYENNE PEPPER

1 TABLESPOON GARLIC POWDER

1 TABLESPOON DRIED OREGANO

1 TABLESPOON DRIED THYME

1 TABLESPOON BLACK PEPPER

1 TABLESPOON FINE SEA SALT

1. Place all of the ingredients in a small bowl, stir to combine, and use immediately or store in an airtight container.

Orange & Thyme Dry Brine

YIELD: ¾ CUP | **ACTIVE TIME:** 5 MINUTES | **TOTAL TIME:** 5 MINUTES

1 TEASPOON BLACK PEPPER

⅓ CUP KOSHER SALT

¼ CUP BROWN SUGAR

5 TABLESPOONS ORANGE ZEST

1 TABLESPOON DRIED THYME

1. Place all of the ingredients in a bowl, stir to combine, and use immediately or store in an airtight container.

Mole Rub

YIELD: ¼ CUP | **ACTIVE TIME:** 5 MINUTES | **TOTAL TIME:** 5 MINUTES

1 TABLESPOON ALLSPICE

1½ TEASPOONS GROUND CLOVES

1½ TEASPOONS CINNAMON

1½ TEASPOONS CUMIN

1 TABLESPOON CORIANDER

1 TABLESPOON GROUND GINGER

1. Place all of the ingredients in a small bowl, stir to combine, and use immediately or store in an airtight container.

Indian Kush Rub

YIELD: 4 CUPS | **ACTIVE TIME:** 5 MINUTES | **TOTAL TIME:** 5 MINUTES

1 CUP BROWN SUGAR

½ CUP KOSHER SALT

½ CUP CHILI POWDER

¼ CUP HUNGARIAN PAPRIKA

¼ CUP CORIANDER

1 TABLESPOON GROUND GINGER

¼ CUP CUMIN

⅓ CUP GARLIC

⅓ CUP ONION POWDER

1 TABLESPOON LEMON ZEST

¼ CUP GROUND MINT TEA

1. Place all of the ingredients in a bowl, stir to combine, and use immediately or store in an airtight container.

Garam Masala

YIELD: ½ CUP | **ACTIVE TIME:** 5 MINUTES | **TOTAL TIME:** 5 MINUTES

3 TABLESPOONS CUMIN

1½ TEASPOONS CORIANDER

1½ TEASPOONS CARDAMOM

1½ TEASPOONS BLACK PEPPER

1 TEASPOON CINNAMON

½ TEASPOON GROUND CLOVES

½ TEASPOON TURMERIC

½ TEASPOON FRESHLY GRATED NUTMEG

1. Place all of the ingredients in a mixing bowl, stir until well combined, and use immediately or store in an airtight container.

Orange & Thyme Dry Brine

SEE PAGE 38

Chicken 65 Wet Rub

YIELD: ½ CUP | **ACTIVE TIME:** 5 MINUTES | **TOTAL TIME:** 5 MINUTES

1 TEASPOON GRATED FRESH GINGER

1 TEASPOON GRATED GARLIC

1 TEASPOON CINNAMON

1 TEASPOON GROUND ANISE SEEDS

½ TEASPOON CHILI POWDER

1 TEASPOON FRESH LEMON JUICE

½ TEASPOON BLACK PEPPER

⅛ TEASPOON TURMERIC

SALT, TO TASTE

½ TEASPOON SUGAR

2 TABLESPOONS PLAIN YOGURT

1 TABLESPOON UNSALTED BUTTER

3 CURRY LEAVES, MINCED

2 GREEN CHILE PEPPERS, STEMS AND SEEDS REMOVED, CHOPPED

½ TEASPOON CUMIN

1. Place all of the ingredients in a small bowl, stir to combine, and use immediately or store in an airtight container in the refrigerator.

Togarashi

YIELD: ¾ CUP | **ACTIVE TIME:** 5 MINUTES | **TOTAL TIME:** 5 MINUTES

¼ CUP CAYENNE PEPPER

2 TABLESPOONS GROUND
DRIED ORANGE PEEL

2 TABLESPOONS SESAME
SEEDS

2 TEASPOONS HEMP SEEDS

2 TEASPOONS GROUND
SANSHO PEPPERCORNS

2 TEASPOONS MINCED NORI

1 TEASPOON GROUND
GINGER

1. Place all of the ingredients in a mixing bowl, stir until well combined, and use immediately or store in an airtight container.

Red Thai Curry Paste

YIELD: 1 CUP | **ACTIVE TIME:** 5 MINUTES | **TOTAL TIME:** 5 MINUTES

1 SHALLOT, FINELY DICED

2-INCH PIECE OF
LEMONGRASS, TRIMMED
AND GRATED

1-INCH PIECE OF GALANGAL
ROOT, GRATED

4 GARLIC CLOVES, MINCED

2 BIRD'S EYE CHILI PEPPERS

2 TABLESPOONS FISH SAUCE

2 TABLESPOONS FRESH
LIME JUICE

1 TEASPOON SHRIMP PASTE

1 TEASPOON SUGAR

1 TEASPOON CUMIN

¾ TEASPOON CORIANDER

¼ TEASPOON WHITE
PEPPER

¼ TEASPOON CINNAMON

1. Place all of the ingredients in a food processor, blitz until smooth, and use immediately or store in the refrigerator.

Laksa Curry Paste

YIELD: 1 CUP | **ACTIVE TIME:** 5 MINUTES | **TOTAL TIME:** 5 MINUTES

2 TEASPOONS CORIANDER SEEDS

½ TEASPOON FENNEL SEEDS

1 TEASPOON TURMERIC

1-INCH PIECE OF FRESH GINGER, PEELED AND MINCED

1 GREEN CHILE PEPPER, STEM AND SEEDS REMOVED, CHOPPED

½ TEASPOON CAYENNE PEPPER

1 LEMONGRASS STALK, TRIMMED AND GRATED

2 GARLIC CLOVES

2 TABLESPOONS CASHEWS, SOAKED IN WARM WATER FOR 10 MINUTES

½ CUP CHOPPED FRESH CILANTRO

1 TABLESPOON FRESH LIME JUICE

1 TABLESPOON WATER

SALT AND PEPPER, TO TASTE

1. Place the coriander seeds and fennel seeds in a small skillet and toast them over medium heat until they are fragrant, about 2 minutes, shaking the pan occasionally.

2. Transfer the toasted seeds to a food processor, add the remaining ingredients, and blitz until smooth. Use immediately or store in the refrigerator.

Crayfish Boil Blend

YIELD: 1 CUP | **ACTIVE TIME:** 5 MINUTES | **TOTAL TIME:** 5 MINUTES

¼ CUP PICKLING SPICES

¼ CUP KOSHER SALT

2 TABLESPOONS MUSTARD SEEDS

2 TABLESPOONS BLACK PEPPERCORNS

2 TABLESPOONS RED PEPPER FLAKES

1 TABLESPOON CELERY SEEDS

2 TABLESPOONS GROUND GINGER

2 TEASPOONS DRIED OREGANO

1. Place all of the ingredients in a mixing bowl, stir until well combined, and use immediately or store in an airtight container.

Everything Seasoning

YIELD: ½ CUP | **ACTIVE TIME:** 5 MINUTES | **TOTAL TIME:** 5 MINUTES

2 TABLESPOONS POPPY SEEDS

1 TABLESPOON FENNEL SEEDS

1 TABLESPOON ONION FLAKES

1 TABLESPOON GARLIC FLAKES

2 TABLESPOONS SESAME SEEDS

1. Place all of the ingredients in a small bowl, stir to combine, and use immediately or store in an airtight container.

Cajun Seafood Rub

YIELD: ¾ CUP | **ACTIVE TIME:** 5 MINUTES | **TOTAL TIME:** 5 MINUTES

2 TABLESPOONS PAPRIKA

1 TABLESPOON ONION POWDER

3 TABLESPOONS GARLIC POWDER

2 TABLESPOONS CAYENNE PEPPER

1½ TEASPOONS WHITE PEPPER

1½ TEASPOONS CELERY SALT

1½ TABLESPOONS BLACK PEPPER

1 TABLESPOON DRIED THYME

1 TABLESPOON DRIED OREGANO

1 TABLESPOON CHIPOTLE CHILE POWDER

1. Place all of the ingredients in a mixing bowl, stir until well combined, and use immediately or store in an airtight container.

Bouquet Garni

YIELD: 1 BOUQUET | **ACTIVE TIME:** 2 MINUTES | **TOTAL TIME:** 2 MINUTES

2 BAY LEAVES

3 SPRIGS OF FRESH THYME

3 SPRIGS OF FRESH PARSLEY

1. Cut a 6-inch section of kitchen twine. Tie one side of the twine around the herbs and knot it tightly.

2. To use, attach the other end of the twine to one of the pot's handles and slip the herbs into the broth. Remove before serving.

Blackening Spice

YIELD: ¼ CUP | **ACTIVE TIME:** 5 MINUTES | **TOTAL TIME:** 5 MINUTES

1½ TABLESPOONS PAPRIKA

1 TABLESPOON CHILI POWDER

1 TABLESPOON CUMIN

1½ TEASPOONS CORIANDER

½ TEASPOON CAYENNE PEPPER

1 TABLESPOON ONION POWDER

2 TEASPOONS GARLIC POWDER

2 TEASPOONS BLACK PEPPER

1. Place all of the ingredients in a mixing bowl, stir to combine, and use immediately or store in an airtight container.

Everything Seasoning
SEE PAGE 46

Furikake

YIELD: 1 CUP | **ACTIVE TIME:** 10 MINUTES | **TOTAL TIME:** 10 MINUTES

1 CUP TOASTED SESAME SEEDS

6 NORI SHEETS

½ TABLESPOON FINE SEA SALT

½ TABLESPOON SUGAR

1 TEASPOON RED PEPPER FLAKES

1 TABLESPOON MINCED BONITO FLAKES (OPTIONAL)

1. Using a mortar and pestle or spice grinder, grind the sesame seeds until they are partially broken down. Place them in a bowl.

2. Cut the nori sheets into small, thin strips and use your hands to crumble them. Add them to the bowl containing the sesame seeds.

3. Add the remaining ingredients and stir until well combined. Use immediately or store in an airtight container.

Roasted Fall Vegetable Blend

YIELD: ½ CUP | **ACTIVE TIME:** 5 MINUTES | **TOTAL TIME:** 5 MINUTES

2 TABLESPOONS KOSHER SALT

1 TABLESPOON BLACK PEPPER

1 TABLESPOON PAPRIKA

1 TABLESPOON DRIED PARSLEY

1 TABLESPOON DRIED BASIL

1½ TEASPOONS DRIED THYME

1½ TEASPOONS DRIED SAGE

1. Place all of the ingredients in a bowl, stir to combine, and use immediately or store in an airtight container.

Spicy Roasted Vegetable Blend

YIELD: ½ CUP | **ACTIVE TIME:** 5 MINUTES | **TOTAL TIME:** 5 MINUTES

1 TABLESPOON TOASTED
SESAME SEEDS

1 TABLESPOON CHILI
POWDER

1 TABLESPOON CUMIN

1½ TEASPOONS SICHUAN
PEPPER

1 TABLESPOON LIGHT
BROWN SUGAR

1 TABLESPOON SMOKED
PAPRIKA

1½ TEASPOONS KOSHER
SALT

5 GARLIC CLOVES, MINCED

1-INCH PIECE OF FRESH
GINGER, PEELED AND
GRATED

1. Place all of the ingredients in a bowl, stir to combine, and use immediately or store in an airtight container.

New Mexico Rub

YIELD: ½ CUP | **ACTIVE TIME:** 5 MINUTES | **TOTAL TIME:** 5 MINUTES

2 TABLESPOONS NEW
MEXICO CHILE POWDER

2 TABLESPOONS PAPRIKA

1 TABLESPOON CAYENNE
PEPPER

1 TABLESPOON CUMIN

1 TABLESPOON CORIANDER

1 TABLESPOON GRATED
GARLIC

1 TABLESPOON KOSHER
SALT

1 TABLESPOON BLACK
PEPPER

1. Place all of the ingredients in a mixing bowl, stir to combine, and use immediately or store in an airtight container.

Walnut Dukkah

YIELD: ½ CUP | **ACTIVE TIME:** 5 MINUTES | **TOTAL TIME:** 5 MINUTES

SALT, TO TASTE

2 TABLESPOONS CHOPPED
WALNUTS

2 TABLESPOONS CHOPPED
HAZELNUTS

2 TEASPOONS BLACK
PEPPER

2 TEASPOONS POPPY SEEDS

2 TEASPOONS BLACK
SESAME SEEDS

1 TEASPOON CINNAMON

1. Place all of the ingredients in a small bowl, stir to combine, and use immediately or store in an airtight container.

Ras el Hanout

YIELD: ½ CUP | **ACTIVE TIME:** 5 MINUTES | **TOTAL TIME:** 5 MINUTES

1 TEASPOON TURMERIC

1 TEASPOON GROUND GINGER

1 TEASPOON CUMIN

¾ TEASPOON CINNAMON

1 TEASPOON BLACK PEPPER

½ TEASPOON CORIANDER

½ TEASPOON CAYENNE PEPPER

½ TEASPOON ALLSPICE

½ TEASPOON FRESHLY GRATED NUTMEG

¼ TEASPOON GROUND CLOVES

1 TEASPOON FINE SEA SALT

1. Place all of the ingredients in a bowl, stir to combine, and use immediately or store in an airtight container.

Jerk Rub

YIELD: ¼ CUP | **ACTIVE TIME:** 5 MINUTES | **TOTAL TIME:** 5 MINUTES

½ TEASPOON CAYENNE PEPPER

1 TEASPOON CHILI POWDER

2 TEASPOONS GRATED FRESH GINGER

1 TEASPOON CINNAMON

1 TEASPOON FRESHLY GRATED NUTMEG

2 TEASPOONS ALLSPICE

1 TEASPOON DRIED THYME

1 TEASPOON CAYENNE PEPPER

¼ TEASPOON GROUND CLOVES

2 TEASPOONS BLACK PEPPER

2 TEASPOONS KOSHER SALT

1. Place all of the ingredients in a bowl and stir until well combined. Use immediately or store in an airtight container.

Spicy Southwestern Rub

YIELD: ½ CUP | **ACTIVE TIME:** 5 MINUTES | **TOTAL TIME:** 5 MINUTES

2 TABLESPOONS CHILI POWDER

2 TABLESPOONS PAPRIKA

1 TABLESPOON CAYENNE PEPPER

1 TABLESPOON MINCED HABANERO PEPPER

1 TABLESPOON CUMIN

1 TABLESPOON CORIANDER

1 TABLESPOON GRATED GARLIC

1 TABLESPOON KOSHER SALT

1 TABLESPOON BLACK PEPPER

1. Place all of the ingredients in a mixing bowl, stir to combine, and use immediately or store in an airtight container.

Smoky Southwestern Rub

YIELD: ½ CUP | **ACTIVE TIME:** 5 MINUTES | **TOTAL TIME:** 5 MINUTES

2 TABLESPOONS CHILI POWDER

2 TABLESPOONS PAPRIKA

1 TABLESPOON CAYENNE PEPPER

1 TABLESPOON CUMIN

1 TABLESPOON CORIANDER

1 TABLESPOON GRATED GARLIC

1 TABLESPOON LIQUID SMOKE

1 TABLESPOON KOSHER SALT

1 TABLESPOON BLACK PEPPER

1. Place all of the ingredients in a bowl, stir to combine, and use immediately or store in an airtight container.

Rustic Steak Rub

YIELD: ½ CUP | **ACTIVE TIME:** 5 MINUTES | **TOTAL TIME:** 5 MINUTES

6 GARLIC CLOVES, MINCED

2 TABLESPOONS THYME

2 TABLESPOONS KOSHER SALT

1½ TABLESPOONS BLACK PEPPER

1½ TABLESPOONS WHITE PEPPER

1 TABLESPOON RED PEPPER FLAKES

1 TABLESPOON SWEET PAPRIKA

1½ TEASPOONS ONION POWDER

1. Place all of the ingredients in a bowl, stir to combine, and use immediately or store in an airtight container.

Dukkah

YIELD: ¾ CUP | **ACTIVE TIME:** 5 MINUTES | **TOTAL TIME:** 5 MINUTES

2 TABLESPOONS PUMPKIN
SEEDS

2 TABLESPOONS
HAZELNUTS OR PISTACHIOS

2 TABLESPOONS PEANUTS

1 TEASPOON BLACK
PEPPERCORNS

1 TABLESPOON SESAME
SEEDS

1 TEASPOON DRIED MINT

2 TABLESPOONS FRESH
THYME

1 TEASPOON CORIANDER
SEEDS

1 TEASPOON CUMIN SEEDS

2 TEASPOONS KOSHER SALT

1. Place a large, dry cast-iron skillet over medium heat and add all of the ingredients, except for the salt. Toast the mixture, stirring continually, until the seeds and nuts are lightly browned.

2. Remove the pan from heat and use a mortar and pestle to grind the mixture until it has broken down but still has some texture—you don't want it to be a paste.

3. Add the salt and stir to combine. Use immediately or store in an airtight container.

Shawarma Rub

YIELD: 1 CUP | **ACTIVE TIME:** 5 MINUTES | **TOTAL TIME:** 5 MINUTES

2 TABLESPOONS CUMIN SEEDS

2 TEASPOONS CARAWAY SEEDS

2 TEASPOONS CORIANDER SEEDS

2 RED CHILE PEPPERS, STEMS AND SEEDS REMOVED, FINELY DICED

4 GARLIC CLOVES, GRATED

½ CUP AVOCADO OIL

1 TABLESPOON PAPRIKA

½ TEASPOON CINNAMON

1 TEASPOON KOSHER SALT

1 TEASPOON BLACK PEPPER

1. Use a mortar and pestle to grind the cumin, caraway, and coriander seeds into a fine powder.

2. Transfer the powder to a small bowl, add the remaining ingredients, and stir to combine. Use immediately or store in an airtight container.

St. Louis Rub

YIELD: ¾ CUP | **ACTIVE TIME:** 5 MINUTES | **TOTAL TIME:** 5 MINUTES

¼ CUP PAPRIKA

3 TABLESPOONS GARLIC POWDER

2 TABLESPOONS BLACK PEPPER

2 TABLESPOONS KOSHER SALT

2 TABLESPOONS ONION POWDER

1 TABLESPOON DARK BROWN SUGAR

1 TABLESPOON GROUND GINGER

1 TABLESPOON DRY MUSTARD

1 TEASPOON CELERY SALT

1. Place all of the ingredients in a bowl, stir to combine, and use immediately or store in an airtight container.

Mediterranean Steak Rub

YIELD: ¼ CUP | **ACTIVE TIME:** 5 MINUTES | **TOTAL TIME:** 5 MINUTES

1 TABLESPOON BLACK PEPPER

1 TEASPOON CUMIN

1 TABLESPOON KOSHER SALT

1 TEASPOON DRIED THYME

1 TEASPOON SUMAC

1 TEASPOON SESAME SEEDS

½ TEASPOON HEMP SEEDS

1 TEASPOON DRIED OREGANO

1 TEASPOON CHOPPED FRESH BASIL

1. Place all of the ingredients in a small bowl, stir to combine, and use immediately or store in an airtight container.

Classic Seafood Rub

YIELD: ½ CUP | **ACTIVE TIME:** 5 MINUTES | **TOTAL TIME:** 5 MINUTES

2 TABLESPOONS SWEET PAPRIKA

2 TABLESPOONS GARLIC POWDER

1 TABLESPOON DRY MUSTARD

1 TABLESPOON ANCHO CHILE POWDER

1 TABLESPOON ONION POWDER

1 TABLESPOON BLACK PEPPER

1 TABLESPOON FINE SEA SALT

1 TEASPOON CINNAMON

1 TEASPOON CUMIN

1. Place all of the ingredients in a bowl, stir to combine, and use immediately or store in an airtight container.

Shawarma Rub
SEE PAGE 60

Coffee Brisket Rub

YIELD: 1 CUP | **ACTIVE TIME:** 5 MINUTES | **TOTAL TIME:** 5 MINUTES

¼ CUP GROUND COFFEE

1 TEASPOON CORIANDER

2 TEASPOONS BLACK PEPPER

PINCH OF RED PEPPER FLAKES

1 TEASPOON CUMIN

2 TEASPOONS DRY MUSTARD

2 TEASPOONS CHIPOTLE CHILE POWDER

1 TEASPOON PAPRIKA

6 TABLESPOONS KOSHER SALT

6 TABLESPOONS LIGHT BROWN SUGAR

1. Place all of the ingredients in a mixing bowl, stir to combine, and use immediately or store in an airtight container.

Smoked Paprika Rub

YIELD: ¾ CUP | **ACTIVE TIME:** 5 MINUTES | **TOTAL TIME:** 5 MINUTES

¼ CUP SMOKED PAPRIKA

4 TEASPOONS CORIANDER

4 TEASPOONS CUMIN

2 TEASPOONS CAYENNE PEPPER

2 TABLESPOONS BLACK PEPPER

2 TABLESPOONS KOSHER SALT

1. Place all of the ingredients in a bowl, stir to combine, and use immediately or store in an airtight container.

Amarillo Rub

YIELD: ½ CUP | **ACTIVE TIME:** 5 MINUTES | **TOTAL TIME:** 5 MINUTES

2 DRIED CHIPOTLE PEPPERS, STEMS AND SEEDS REMOVED, MINCED

1 TABLESPOON DRIED OREGANO

1 TABLESPOON DRIED CILANTRO

1 TABLESPOON BLACK PEPPER

2 TEASPOONS CUMIN

1 TEASPOON ONION POWDER

½ TEASPOON DRY MUSTARD

1 TEASPOON FINE SEA SALT

1. Place all of the ingredients in a bowl, stir to combine, and use immediately or store in an airtight container.

San Antonio Rub

YIELD: 1½ CUPS | **ACTIVE TIME:** 5 MINUTES | **TOTAL TIME:** 5 MINUTES

1 CUP ANCHO CHILE POWDER

2 TABLESPOONS PAPRIKA

1 TABLESPOON BLACK PEPPER

1 TABLESPOON FINE SEA SALT

2 TEASPOONS CUMIN

1 TEASPOON CAYENNE PEPPER

1 TEASPOON DRY MUSTARD

1 TEASPOON DRIED OREGANO

1. Place all of the ingredients in a bowl, stir to combine, and use immediately or store in an airtight container.

Coffee Brisket Rub

SEE PAGE 64

Za'atar

YIELD: 1½ CUPS | **ACTIVE TIME:** 5 MINUTES | **TOTAL TIME:** 5 MINUTES

1 TABLESPOON CUMIN

1 TABLESPOON SUMAC

1 TABLESPOON THYME

2 TEASPOONS HEMP SEEDS

2 TEASPOONS CRUSHED, TOASTED SUNFLOWER SEEDS

2 TABLESPOONS SESAME SEEDS

2 TABLESPOONS KOSHER SALT

1 TABLESPOON BLACK PEPPER

2 TABLESPOONS CHOPPED FRESH OREGANO

2 TABLESPOONS CHOPPED FRESH BASIL

2 TABLESPOONS CHOPPED FRESH PARSLEY

1 TABLESPOON GARLIC POWDER

1 TABLESPOON ONION POWDER

1. Place all of the ingredients in a bowl, stir to combine, and use immediately or store in an airtight container.

Surefire Steak Rub

YIELD: ½ CUP | **ACTIVE TIME:** 5 MINUTES | **TOTAL TIME:** 5 MINUTES

2 TABLESPOONS BLACK PEPPER

2 TABLESPOONS SWEET PAPRIKA

1 TABLESPOON KOSHER SALT

1 TABLESPOON ONION POWDER

1 TABLESPOON GARLIC POWDER

2 TEASPOONS CUMIN

1. Place all of the ingredients in a bowl, stir to combine, and use immediately or store in an airtight container.

Baharat

YIELD: ⅓ CUP | **ACTIVE TIME:** 5 MINUTES | **TOTAL TIME:** 5 MINUTES

1 TABLESPOON CUMIN SEEDS

1 TABLESPOON CORIANDER SEEDS

1 TEASPOON BLACK PEPPERCORNS

2 CINNAMON STICKS, BROKEN INTO PIECES

2 TEASPOONS GREEN CARDAMOM PODS

1½ TEASPOONS ALLSPICE BERRIES

1 TEASPOON WHOLE CLOVES

1 TEASPOON FRESHLY GRATED NUTMEG

4 BAY LEAVES

1. Use a mortar and pestle to grind all of the ingredients into a fine powder. Use immediately or store in an airtight container.

Autumn Baking Blend

YIELD: ¼ CUP | **ACTIVE TIME:** 5 MINUTES | **TOTAL TIME:** 5 MINUTES

2 CINNAMON STICKS, BROKEN INTO PIECES

1 TABLESPOON GREEN CARDAMOM PODS

¾ TEASPOON ALLSPICE BERRIES

½ TEASPOON WHITE PEPPERCORNS

½ TEASPOON FRESHLY GRATED NUTMEG

1. Place a large, dry cast-iron skillet over medium heat and add all of the ingredients, except for the nutmeg. Toast the mixture, stirring continually, until it is fragrant.

2. Remove the pan from heat and use a mortar and pestle to grind the mixture into a fine powder.

3. Add the nutmeg and stir to combine. Use immediately or store in an airtight container.

Sazón

YIELD: ½ CUP | **ACTIVE TIME:** 5 MINUTES | **TOTAL TIME:** 5 MINUTES

2 TABLESPOONS FINE SEA SALT

2 TABLESPOONS GROUND ANNATTO

1 TABLESPOON GARLIC POWDER

1 TABLESPOON ONION POWDER

1 TABLESPOON CUMIN

1 TABLESPOON TURMERIC

½ TEASPOON BLACK PEPPER

1. Place all of the ingredients in a bowl, stir to combine, and use immediately or store in an airtight container.

Taco Seasoning Blend

YIELD: ½ CUP | **ACTIVE TIME:** 5 MINUTES | **TOTAL TIME:** 5 MINUTES

¼ CUP ANCHO CHILE POWDER

1 TABLESPOON CUMIN

2 TEASPOONS KOSHER SALT

2 TEASPOONS BLACK PEPPER

2 TEASPOONS SMOKED PAPRIKA

½ TEASPOON GARLIC POWDER

½ TEASPOON ONION POWDER

1 TEASPOON RED PEPPER FLAKES

1. Place all of the ingredients in a bowl, stir to combine, and use immediately or store in an airtight container.

Smoky St. Louis Rub

YIELD: ¾ CUP | **ACTIVE TIME:** 5 MINUTES | **TOTAL TIME:** 5 MINUTES

¼ CUP PAPRIKA

3 TABLESPOONS GARLIC POWDER

2 TABLESPOONS BLACK PEPPER

2 TABLESPOONS KOSHER SALT

2 TABLESPOONS ONION POWDER

1 TABLESPOON DARK BROWN SUGAR

1 TABLESPOON GROUND GINGER

1 TABLESPOON DRY MUSTARD

2 TEASPOONS LIQUID SMOKE

1 TEASPOON CELERY SALT

1. Place all of the ingredients in a bowl, stir to combine, and use immediately or store in an airtight container.

Smoky Cajun Rub

YIELD: ½ CUP | **ACTIVE TIME:** 5 MINUTES | **TOTAL TIME:** 5 MINUTES

¼ CUP FINE SEA SALT

2 TEASPOONS LIQUID SMOKE

2 TABLESPOONS BLACK PEPPER

2 TEASPOONS SMOKED PAPRIKA

2 TEASPOONS GARLIC POWDER

1 TEASPOON ONION POWDER

1 TEASPOON CAYENNE PEPPER

1 TEASPOON DRIED THYME

1. Place all of the ingredients in a bowl, stir to combine, and use immediately or store in an airtight container.

Herbal Wet Rub

YIELD: 1 CUP | **ACTIVE TIME:** 5 MINUTES | **TOTAL TIME:** 5 MINUTES

¼ CUP FRESH PARSLEY, CHOPPED

¼ CUP FRESH ROSEMARY, CHOPPED

6 GARLIC CLOVES, MINCED

1 TABLESPOON BLACK PEPPER

2 TABLESPOONS FINE SEA SALT

¼ CUP EXTRA-VIRGIN OLIVE OIL

1. Place all of the ingredients, except for the olive oil, in a bowl and stir to combine.

2. While whisking continually, add the olive oil in a slow stream until the mixture is a smooth paste.

3. Let the rub rest for 30 minutes before applying to any food.

Spicy Coffee Rub

YIELD: 1 CUP | **ACTIVE TIME:** 5 MINUTES | **TOTAL TIME:** 5 MINUTES

¼ CUP FINELY GROUND COFFEE

2 TABLESPOONS DARK BROWN SUGAR

1 TABLESPOON CAYENNE PEPPER

1 TABLESPOON ANCHO CHILE POWDER

2 TABLESPOONS GARLIC POWDER

2 TABLESPOONS PAPRIKA

2 TABLESPOONS ONION POWDER

1 TABLESPOON CUMIN

1 TABLESPOON KOSHER SALT

1. Place all of the ingredients in a bowl, stir to combine, and use immediately or store in an airtight container.

Smoky Seafood Rub

YIELD: ⅓ CUP | **ACTIVE TIME:** 5 MINUTES | **TOTAL TIME:** 5 MINUTES

1 TABLESPOON SMOKED PAPRIKA

1 TABLESPOON BLACK PEPPER

1 TEASPOON DRIED BASIL

1 TEASPOON DRIED TARRAGON

1 GARLIC CLOVE, MINCED

1 TEASPOON LEMON ZEST

½ TEASPOON CHILI POWDER

½ TEASPOON ONION POWDER

1. Place all of the ingredients in a bowl, stir to combine, and use immediately or store in an airtight container.

Ancho Chile Rub

YIELD: ½ CUP | **ACTIVE TIME:** 5 MINUTES | **TOTAL TIME:** 5 MINUTES

2 TABLESPOONS SWEET PAPRIKA

1 TABLESPOON ANCHO CHILE POWDER

1 TABLESPOON CORIANDER

1 TABLESPOON CUMIN

2 TEASPOONS DRIED OREGANO

1 TABLESPOON ALLSPICE

1 TEASPOON ONION POWDER

½ TEASPOON CINNAMON

1. Place all of the ingredients in a bowl, stir to combine, and use immediately or store in an airtight container.

Madras Curry Blend

YIELD: ⅓ CUP | **ACTIVE TIME:** 5 MINUTES | **TOTAL TIME:** 5 MINUTES

2 TABLESPOONS MADRAS CURRY POWDER

1 TABLESPOON SMOKED PAPRIKA

1 TABLESPOON GROUND GINGER

2 TEASPOONS CUMIN

2 TEASPOONS ALLSPICE

2 TEASPOONS BLACK PEPPER

1 TEASPOON FINE SEA SALT

1. Place all of the ingredients in a bowl, stir to combine, and use immediately or store in an airtight container.

Dill & Coriander Rub

YIELD: ¾ CUP | **ACTIVE TIME:** 5 MINUTES | **TOTAL TIME:** 5 MINUTES

3 TABLESPOONS BLACK PEPPER

3 TABLESPOONS CORIANDER SEEDS, CRUSHED

2 TABLESPOONS CHOPPED FRESH DILL

2 GARLIC CLOVES, MINCED

2 TABLESPOONS FINE SEA SALT

1. Place all of the ingredients in a bowl, stir to combine, and use immediately or store in an airtight container.

Oregano & Garlic Rub

YIELD: ¾ CUP | **ACTIVE TIME:** 5 MINUTES | **TOTAL TIME:** 5 MINUTES

3 TABLESPOONS CHOPPED FRESH OREGANO

4 GARLIC CLOVES, MINCED

2 TABLESPOONS FRESH THYME

2 TABLESPOONS BLACK PEPPER

1 TABLESPOON KOSHER SALT

1 TABLESPOON CUMIN

1 TABLESPOON CORIANDER

1. Place all of the ingredients in a bowl, stir to combine, and use immediately or store in an airtight container.

Toasted Fennel Seed Rub

YIELD: ⅓ CUP | **ACTIVE TIME:** 5 MINUTES | **TOTAL TIME:** 5 MINUTES

¼ CUP FENNEL SEEDS

1 TABLESPOON CORIANDER SEEDS

2 TEASPOONS BLACK PEPPERCORNS

2 TEASPOONS KOSHER SALT

1. Place the fennel seeds and coriander seeds in a small skillet and toast them over medium heat until fragrant, about 2 minutes, shaking the pan occasionally.

2. Remove the seeds from the pan and let them cool.

3. Combine the toasted seeds, peppercorns, and salt and use a mortar and pestle to grind them into a fine powder. Use immediately or store in an airtight container.

Kashmiri Chili Rub

YIELD: ½ CUP | **ACTIVE TIME:** 5 MINUTES | **TOTAL TIME:** 5 MINUTES

3 TABLESPOONS KASHMIRI CHILI POWDER

3 TABLESPOONS SMOKED PAPRIKA

1 TABLESPOON DRIED OREGANO

2 TEASPOONS CUMIN

2 TEASPOONS BLACK PEPPER

2 TEASPOONS FINE SEA SALT

1 TEASPOON DRIED THYME

1. Place all of the ingredients in a bowl, stir to combine, and use immediately or store in an airtight container.

Kashmiri Chili Rub
SEE PAGE 85

Mediterranean Rub

YIELD: ½ CUP | **ACTIVE TIME:** 5 MINUTES | **TOTAL TIME:** 5 MINUTES

2 GARLIC CLOVES, MINCED

2 TABLESPOONS CHOPPED FRESH ROSEMARY

1 TABLESPOON THYME

1 TABLESPOON BLACK PEPPER

1 TABLESPOON KOSHER SALT

1 TEASPOON LEMON ZEST

1. Place all of the ingredients in a bowl, stir to combine, and use immediately or store in an airtight container.

Horseradish Crust

YIELD: 2 CUPS | **ACTIVE TIME:** 5 MINUTES | **TOTAL TIME:** 5 MINUTES

½ CUP UNSALTED BUTTER, SOFTENED

6 GARLIC CLOVES, CHOPPED

¾ CUP FRESHLY GRATED HORSERADISH

¼ CUP THYME

2 TABLESPOONS ROSEMARY, MINCED

3 TABLESPOONS BLACK PEPPER

2 TABLESPOONS FINE SEA SALT

1. Place the butter, garlic, and horseradish in a food processor and pulse until combined. Transfer the mixture to a medium bowl.

2. Add the remaining ingredients, stir to combine, and let the mixture rest for 30 minutes. Use immediately or store in the refrigerator.

Chinese Five-Spice Rub

YIELD: ½ CUP | **ACTIVE TIME:** 5 MINUTES | **TOTAL TIME:** 5 MINUTES

1 TABLESPOON GROUND STAR ANISE

1 TABLESPOON CINNAMON

1 TABLESPOON GROUND SICHUAN PEPPER

1 TABLESPOON GROUND FENNEL SEEDS

1 TABLESPOON GROUND CLOVES

1 TABLESPOON GARLIC POWDER

1 TABLESPOON GROUND GINGER

1 TABLESPOON FINE SEA SALT

1. Place all of the ingredients in a bowl, stir to combine, and use immediately or store in an airtight container.

Five-Alarm Rub

YIELD: ½ CUP | **ACTIVE TIME:** 5 MINUTES | **TOTAL TIME:** 5 MINUTES

½ HABANERO CHILE PEPPER, STEM AND SEEDS REMOVED, MINCED

1 TABLESPOON GROUND STAR ANISE

1 TABLESPOON CINNAMON

1 TABLESPOON GROUND SICHUAN PEPPER

1 TABLESPOON GROUND FENNEL SEEDS

1 TABLESPOON GROUND CLOVES

1 TABLESPOON GARLIC POWDER

1 TABLESPOON GROUND GINGER

1 TABLESPOON FINE SEA SALT

1. Place all of the ingredients in a bowl, stir to combine, and use immediately or store in an airtight container.

Pastrami Rub

YIELD: ¾ CUP | **ACTIVE TIME:** 5 MINUTES | **TOTAL TIME:** 5 MINUTES

2 TABLESPOONS CORIANDER

¼ CUP BLACK PEPPER

1 TABLESPOON DRY MUSTARD

2 TABLESPOONS FINE SEA SALT

2 TEASPOONS GARLIC POWDER

2 TEASPOONS ONION POWDER

1 TABLESPOON DARK BROWN SUGAR

2 TABLESPOONS PAPRIKA

1. Place all of the ingredients in a bowl, stir to combine, and use immediately or store in an airtight container.

Buffalo Dry Rub

YIELD: 1 CUP | **ACTIVE TIME:** 5 MINUTES | **TOTAL TIME:** 5 MINUTES

½ CUP LIGHT BROWN SUGAR

1 TABLESPOON CHILI POWDER

1 TABLESPOON SMOKED PAPRIKA

1 TABLESPOON CUMIN

1 TEASPOON CAYENNE PEPPER

2 TABLESPOONS GARLIC POWDER

2 TABLESPOONS KOSHER SALT

1 TABLESPOON BLACK PEPPER

1 TEASPOON ONION POWDER

1 TEASPOON DRY MUSTARD

1. Place all of the ingredients in a bowl, stir to combine, and use immediately or store in an airtight container.

Charleston Rub

YIELD: ¾ CUP | **ACTIVE TIME:** 5 MINUTES | **TOTAL TIME:** 5 MINUTES

¼ CUP PAPRIKA

3 TABLESPOONS BLACK PEPPER

1 TABLESPOON CHIPOTLE CHILE POWDER

1 TABLESPOON CHILI POWDER

2 TEASPOONS CAYENNE PEPPER

1 TEASPOON GROUND CUMIN

1 TEASPOON DRIED OREGANO

1 TEASPOON FINE SEA SALT

1. Place all of the ingredients in a bowl, stir to combine, and use immediately or store in an airtight container.

Spicy Steak Rub

YIELD: 1 CUP | **ACTIVE TIME:** 5 MINUTES | **TOTAL TIME:** 5 MINUTES

3 TABLESPOONS SMOKED PAPRIKA

2 TABLESPOONS LIGHT BROWN SUGAR

2 TABLESPOONS BLACK PEPPER

1 TABLESPOON CHILI POWDER

1 TABLESPOON FINE SEA SALT

1 TABLESPOON GARLIC POWDER

1 TABLESPOON ONION POWDER

2 TEASPOONS DRIED OREGANO

1 TEASPOON CUMIN

½ TEASPOON CAYENNE PEPPER

½ TEASPOON CHIPOTLE POWDER

1. Place all of the ingredients in a bowl, stir to combine, and use immediately or store in an airtight container.

Smoky & Spicy Poultry Rub

YIELD: ½ CUP | **ACTIVE TIME:** 5 MINUTES | **TOTAL TIME:** 5 MINUTES

JUICE OF ½ LIME

3 GARLIC CLOVES, MINCED

2 TABLESPOONS CHOPPED FRESH PARSLEY

1 TABLESPOON CUMIN

2 TEASPOONS PAPRIKA

1 TEASPOON CINNAMON

1 TEASPOON TURMERIC

1 TEASPOON RED PEPPER FLAKES

½ TEASPOON ONION POWDER

SALT AND PEPPER, TO TASTE

1. Place all of the ingredients in a bowl, stir to combine, and use immediately or store in an airtight container.

BBQ Shrimp Rub

YIELD: ½ CUP | **ACTIVE TIME:** 5 MINUTES | **TOTAL TIME:** 5 MINUTES

2 TABLESPOONS PAPRIKA

2 TABLESPOONS ANCHO CHILE POWDER

2 TEASPOONS GARLIC POWDER

2 TABLESPOONS BLACK PEPPER

1 TABLESPOON FINE SEA SALT

2 TEASPOONS DRIED OREGANO

2 TEASPOONS RED PEPPER FLAKES

1. Place all of the ingredients in a bowl, stir to combine, and use immediately or store in an airtight container.

Sweet & Spicy Coffee Rub

YIELD: ¾ CUP | **ACTIVE TIME:** 5 MINUTES | **TOTAL TIME:** 5 MINUTES

2 TABLESPOONS BLACK PEPPER

2 TABLESPOONS FINE SEA SALT

¼ CUP FINELY GROUND COFFEE

3 TABLESPOONS FRESH THYME

2 TABLESPOONS DARK BROWN SUGAR

2 TEASPOONS DRY MUSTARD

1 TEASPOON SMOKED PAPRIKA

1. Place all of the ingredients in a bowl, stir to combine, and use immediately or store in an airtight container.

MARINADES, BRINES, BASTES & GLAZES

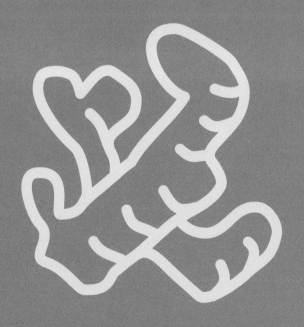

Tomatillo & Poblano Marinade

YIELD: 1½ CUPS | **ACTIVE TIME:** 5 MINUTES | **TOTAL TIME:** 5 MINUTES

1 TOMATILLO, HUSKED, RINSED, AND HALVED

1 PLUM TOMATO, HALVED

2 GARLIC CLOVES, MINCED

1 SHALLOT, PEELED AND HALVED

1 POBLANO PEPPER, HALVED AND SEEDED

½ CUP EXTRA-VIRGIN OLIVE OIL

1 TABLESPOON KOSHER SALT

1 TABLESPOON CUMIN

1. Place all of the ingredients in a food processor, blitz to combine, and use immediately or store in the refrigerator.

Garlic & Saffron Marinade

YIELD: 1 CUP | **ACTIVE TIME:** 10 MINUTES | **TOTAL TIME:** 30 MINUTES

¾ CUP EXTRA-VIRGIN OLIVE OIL

4 GARLIC CLOVES, MINCED

2 TEASPOONS KOSHER SALT

2 TEASPOONS BLACK PEPPER

2 TEASPOONS SUGAR

2 TEASPOONS PAPRIKA

1 TABLESPOON CHOPPED FRESH ROSEMARY

¼ TEASPOON SAFFRON

3 TABLESPOONS WHITE WINE VINEGAR

1. Place 1 tablespoon of the olive oil in a large, clean saucepan and warm it over medium heat. Add the garlic and cook, stirring continually, for 1 minute. Add the salt, pepper, sugar, paprika, rosemary, and remaining olive oil and cook, stirring continually, for 1 minute.

2. Remove the pan from heat, stir in the saffron and vinegar, and let the marinade cool before using or storing in an airtight container.

Sesame & Honey Marinade

YIELD: 1¾ CUPS | **ACTIVE TIME:** 5 MINUTES | **TOTAL TIME:** 5 MINUTES

¾ CUP KECAP MANIS

½ CUP RICE VINEGAR

¼ CUP SESAME OIL

¼ CUP HONEY

1 TEASPOON CINNAMON

1 TEASPOON BLACK PEPPER

1 TEASPOON SESAME SEEDS

1. Place all of the ingredients in a bowl, whisk to combine, and use immediately or store in the refrigerator.

Honey Mustard & Soy Seafood Baste

YIELD: 2½ CUPS | **ACTIVE TIME:** 5 MINUTES | **TOTAL TIME:** 5 MINUTES

6 TABLESPOONS DIJON MUSTARD

6 TABLESPOONS SOY SAUCE

6 TABLESPOONS HONEY

4 GARLIC CLOVES, MINCED

½ CUP EXTRA-VIRGIN OLIVE OIL

2 TEASPOONS SESAME SEEDS

1. Place all of the ingredients in a bowl, whisk to combine, and store in the refrigerator for 1 hour before using.

Sesame & Honey Marinade

SEE PAGE 101

Pomegranate & Fennel Glaze

YIELD: ½ CUP | **ACTIVE TIME:** 20 MINUTES | **TOTAL TIME:** 1 HOUR

2 CUPS POMEGRANATE JUICE

1 TEASPOON FENNEL SEEDS

1 TEASPOON BLACK PEPPERCORNS

1 BAY LEAF

PINCH OF KOSHER SALT

1. Place all of the ingredients in a small saucepan and simmer the mixture over medium-high heat until the liquid has been reduced to ½ cup.

2. Strain and let the glaze cool completely before using or storing in the refrigerator.

North Carolina Baste

YIELD: 2½ CUPS | **ACTIVE TIME:** 5 MINUTES | **TOTAL TIME:** 5 MINUTES

2 CUPS APPLE CIDER VINEGAR

2 TABLESPOONS DARK BROWN SUGAR

1 TABLESPOON EXTRA-VIRGIN OLIVE OIL

2 TEASPOONS WORCESTERSHIRE SAUCE

2 TEASPOONS RED PEPPER FLAKES

1 TEASPOON PAPRIKA

1 TEASPOON BLACK PEPPER

1 TEASPOON KOSHER SALT

1. Place all of the ingredients in a bowl, whisk to combine, and store in the refrigerator for 1 hour before using.

Garlic & Dill Marinade

YIELD: 1 CUP | **ACTIVE TIME:** 5 MINUTES | **TOTAL TIME:** 5 MINUTES

½ CUP EXTRA-VIRGIN OLIVE OIL

4 GARLIC CLOVES, MINCED

1 TABLESPOON CHOPPED FRESH DILL

1 TABLESPOON CHOPPED FRESH BASIL

1 TABLESPOON KOSHER SALT

½ CUP WHITE VINEGAR

1. Place all of the ingredients in a food processor, blitz until combined, and use immediately or store in an airtight container.

Citrus & Sage Marinade

YIELD: 1 CUP | **ACTIVE TIME:** 5 MINUTES | **TOTAL TIME:** 5 MINUTES

3 GARLIC CLOVES

⅓ CUP FRESH SAGE

ZEST AND JUICE OF 1 ORANGE

1 TABLESPOON CORIANDER

1½ TEASPOONS BLACK PEPPER

½ TEASPOON RED PEPPER FLAKES

¼ CUP EXTRA-VIRGIN OLIVE OIL

1. Place all of the ingredients in a food processor, blitz until combined, and use immediately or store in an airtight container.

Orange & Buckwheat Honey Glaze

YIELD: ½ CUP | **ACTIVE TIME:** 20 MINUTES | **TOTAL TIME:** 20 MINUTES

4 TABLESPOONS UNSALTED BUTTER

⅓ CUP ORANGE JUICE

1 TABLESPOON BUCKWHEAT HONEY

1½ TEASPOONS KOSHER SALT

2 TABLESPOONS FRESH LEMON JUICE

⅛ TEASPOON CAYENNE PEPPER

1. Place all of the ingredients in a saucepan and cook the mixture over medium heat until it has reduced by half, about 20 minutes. Use immediately or store in the refrigerator.

South Asian BBQ Marinade

YIELD: 1 CUP | **ACTIVE TIME:** 5 MINUTES | **TOTAL TIME:** 5 MINUTES

1 LEMONGRASS STALK, TRIMMED AND FINELY MINCED

2 GARLIC CLOVES

1 TABLESPOON GRATED FRESH GINGER

1 SCALLION, TRIMMED

¼ CUP BROWN SUGAR

2 TABLESPOONS GOCHUJANG

1 TABLESPOON SESAME OIL

1 TABLESPOON RICE VINEGAR

2 TABLESPOONS FISH SAUCE

1 TABLESPOON BLACK PEPPER

1. Place all of the ingredients in a food processor, blitz until combined, and use immediately or store in an airtight container.

Balsamic Glaze

YIELD: ½ CUP | **ACTIVE TIME:** 10 MINUTES | **TOTAL TIME:** 25 MINUTES

1 CUP BALSAMIC VINEGAR

¼ CUP BROWN SUGAR

1. Place the vinegar and sugar in a small saucepan and bring the mixture to a boil.

2. Reduce the heat to medium-low and simmer for 8 to 10 minutes, stirring frequently, until the mixture has thickened.

3. Remove the pan from heat and let the glaze cool for 15 minutes before using.

BBQ Glaze

YIELD: 1 CUP | **ACTIVE TIME:** 10 MINUTES | **TOTAL TIME:** 25 MINUTES

1½ CUPS LIGHT BROWN SUGAR

3 TABLESPOONS APPLE CIDER VINEGAR

3 TABLESPOONS WATER

1 TEASPOON RED PEPPER FLAKES

1 TEASPOON DIJON MUSTARD

1 TEASPOON BLACK PEPPER

1 TEASPOON KOSHER SALT

1. Place all of the ingredients in a saucepan and cook the mixture over medium heat until it has reduced by half, about 20 minutes. Use immediately or store in the refrigerator.

Bourbon & Brown Sugar Glaze

YIELD: 1 CUP | **ACTIVE TIME:** 10 MINUTES | **TOTAL TIME:** 25 MINUTES

4 TABLESPOONS BUTTER

½ CUP BOURBON

½ CUP BROWN SUGAR

¼ CUP APPLE CIDER VINEGAR

1 TEASPOON DIJON MUSTARD

1 TEASPOON BLACK PEPPER

1 TEASPOON KOSHER SALT

1. Place all of the ingredients in a saucepan and cook the mixture over medium heat until it has reduced by half, about 20 minutes. Use immediately or store in the refrigerator.

Balsamic Glaze

SEE PAGE 108

Amalfi Marinade

YIELD: 1 CUP | **ACTIVE TIME:** 5 MINUTES | **TOTAL TIME:** 5 MINUTES

½ CUP EXTRA-VIRGIN OLIVE OIL

½ SMALL WHITE ONION, DICED

¼ CUP FRESH PARSLEY

1 TABLESPOON CHOPPED FRESH ROSEMARY

2 GARLIC CLOVES, CRUSHED

2 TABLESPOONS RED WINE VINEGAR

JUICE OF ½ LEMON

2 TABLESPOONS DIJON MUSTARD

1. Place all of the ingredients in a food processor, blitz until combined, and use immediately or store in an airtight container.

Pomegranate & Honey Glaze

YIELD: 4 CUPS | **ACTIVE TIME:** 20 MINUTES | **TOTAL TIME:** 30 MINUTES

2 TABLESPOONS AVOCADO OIL

1 LARGE ONION, CHOPPED

3 GARLIC CLOVES, MINCED

½ CUP POMEGRANATE MOLASSES

½ CUP POMEGRANATE JUICE

½ CUP HONEY

2 CUPS VEGETABLE STOCK (SEE PAGE 303)

1 TEASPOON CUMIN

½ TEASPOON GROUND GINGER

⅛ TEASPOON ALLSPICE

½ TEASPOON TURMERIC

1. Place the avocado oil in a large skillet and warm it over medium-high heat. Add the onion and cook, stirring occasionally, until it is soft and translucent, about 3 minutes.

2. Add the garlic and cook, stirring continually, until it is fragrant, about 1 minute. Stir in the remaining ingredients and bring the mixture to a boil. Lower the heat and simmer the glaze until it has reduced by half, about 20 minutes. Taste the glaze, adjust the seasoning as necessary, and use immediately or store in the refrigerator.

Aloo Gobi Marinade

YIELD: 1 CUP | **ACTIVE TIME:** 10 MINUTES | **TOTAL TIME:** 10 MINUTES

1 CUP PLAIN YOGURT

½ TEASPOON CHILI POWDER

½ TEASPOON CHAAT MASALA POWDER

½ TEASPOON CUMIN

½ TEASPOON TURMERIC

1. Place all of the ingredients in a bowl, stir to combine, and use immediately or store in the refrigerator.

Beer Brine

YIELD: 4 CUPS | **ACTIVE TIME:** 5 MINUTES | **TOTAL TIME:** 5 MINUTES

3 (12 OZ.) BOTTLES OF DARK BEER

½ CUP KOSHER SALT

1 CUP DARK BROWN SUGAR

4 BAY LEAVES

3 SPRIGS OF FRESH THYME

1 ONION, QUARTERED

3 SPRIGS OF FRESH ROSEMARY

1 TABLESPOON PEPPERCORNS

1. Place all of the ingredients in a large pot, stir to combine, and use immediately or store in the refrigerator.

Apple Glaze

YIELD: 1 CUP | **ACTIVE TIME:** 10 MINUTES | **TOTAL TIME:** 25 MINUTES

2 TABLESPOONS EXTRA-VIRGIN OLIVE OIL

2 GARLIC CLOVES, MINCED

2 CUPS APPLE CIDER

1 TEASPOON DIJON MUSTARD

1 TEASPOON CHOPPED FRESH ROSEMARY

1 TEASPOON BLACK PEPPER

2 TEASPOONS KOSHER SALT

1. Place the olive oil in a saucepan and warm it over medium heat. Add the garlic and cook, stirring frequently, for 1 minute.

2. Add the remaining ingredients and cook until the mixture has reduced by half, about 15 minutes. Use immediately or store in the refrigerator.

Red Wine & Basil Marinade

YIELD: 5 CUPS | **ACTIVE TIME:** 5 MINUTES | **TOTAL TIME:** 5 MINUTES

2 CUPS FRESH BASIL LEAVES

2 LARGE CARROTS, PEELED AND DICED

2 LARGE ONIONS, DICED

2 GARLIC CLOVES, CHOPPED

1 SCALLION, TRIMMED AND CHOPPED

1 TEASPOON FRESH THYME

1 TABLESPOON CHOPPED FRESH ROSEMARY

1 TEASPOON DRIED OREGANO

3 TABLESPOONS EXTRA-VIRGIN OLIVE OIL

3 CUPS DRY RED WINE

1. Place all of the ingredients in a food processor, blitz until smooth, and use immediately or store in an airtight container.

Sweet Maple BBQ Glaze

YIELD: 1 CUP | **ACTIVE TIME:** 10 MINUTES | **TOTAL TIME:** 25 MINUTES

1 TABLESPOON EXTRA-VIRGIN OLIVE OIL

2 GARLIC CLOVES, MINCED

¾ CUP KETCHUP

1 CUP APPLE CIDER

¼ CUP REAL MAPLE SYRUP

2 TABLESPOONS APPLE CIDER VINEGAR

1 TEASPOON PAPRIKA

1 TEASPOON WORCESTERSHIRE SAUCE

1 TEASPOON BLACK PEPPER

1 TEASPOON SEA SALT

1. Place the olive oil in a saucepan and warm it over medium heat. Add the garlic and cook, stirring frequently, for 1 minute.

2. Add the remaining ingredients and cook until the mixture has reduced by half, about 15 minutes. Use immediately or store in the refrigerator.

Beef & Pork Brine

YIELD: 10 CUPS | **ACTIVE TIME:** 20 MINUTES | **TOTAL TIME:** 2 HOURS

1½ CUPS KOSHER SALT

½ CUP SUGAR

1 CUP BROWN SUGAR

8 TEASPOONS PINK CURING SALT

1 CUP PICKLING SPICE

¼ CUP HONEY

5 GARLIC CLOVES, CRUSHED

8 CUPS WATER

1. Place all of the ingredients in a large stockpot and bring the mixture to a boil.

2. Remove the pan from heat and let the brine cool completely before using or storing in the refrigerator.

Seafood Marinade

YIELD: 1 CUP | **ACTIVE TIME:** 5 MINUTES | **TOTAL TIME:** 5 MINUTES

JUICE OF 2 LEMONS

½ CUP EXTRA-VIRGIN OLIVE OIL

4 GARLIC CLOVES, MINCED

1 TABLESPOON FRESH OREGANO

1 TABLESPOON BLACK PEPPER

1 TABLESPOON FINE SEA SALT

1. Place all of the ingredients in a food processor, blitz until smooth, and use immediately or store in an airtight container.

Sweet Maple BBQ Glaze

SEE PAGE 116

Garlic & Dijon Marinade

YIELD: ¾ CUP | **ACTIVE TIME:** 5 MINUTES | **TOTAL TIME:** 5 MINUTES

8 GARLIC CLOVES, GRATED

1 TABLESPOON CHOPPED FRESH OREGANO

½ CUP DIJON MUSTARD

½ CUP CABERNET SAUVIGNON

1 TABLESPOON KOSHER SALT

1 TABLESPOON BLACK PEPPER

1. Place all of the ingredients in a bowl, stir to combine, and use immediately or store in the refrigerator.

Red Wine & Herb Marinade

YIELD: 2½ CUPS | **ACTIVE TIME:** 5 MINUTES | **TOTAL TIME:** 5 MINUTES

2 CUPS RED WINE

2 TABLESPOONS RED WINE VINEGAR

2 GARLIC CLOVES, MINCED

1 TABLESPOON CHOPPED FRESH ROSEMARY

1 TEASPOON FRESH THYME

½ SMALL WHITE ONION, FINELY DICED

1 TEASPOON FRESH LEMON JUICE

½ TEASPOON DRIED OREGANO

1 TEASPOON BLACK PEPPER

1 TEASPOON FINE SEA SALT

1. Place all of the ingredients in a bowl, whisk to combine, and use immediately or store in an airtight container.

Classic Kebab Marinade

YIELD: 1½ CUPS | **ACTIVE TIME:** 5 MINUTES | **TOTAL TIME:** 5 MINUTES

½ CUP EXTRA-VIRGIN OLIVE OIL

¼ CUP FRESH MINT LEAVES

2 TEASPOONS CHOPPED FRESH ROSEMARY

2 GARLIC CLOVES, SMASHED

1 TEASPOON KOSHER SALT

ZEST AND JUICE OF 1 LEMON

¼ TEASPOON BLACK PEPPER

1. Place all of the ingredients in a food processor, blitz until combined, and use immediately or store in an airtight container.

Harissa Glaze

YIELD: 1½ CUPS | **ACTIVE TIME:** 5 MINUTES | **TOTAL TIME:** 5 MINUTES

1 CUP HARISSA

½ CUP AGAVE NECTAR

2 TEASPOONS FRESH
LEMON JUICE

1. Place all of the ingredients in a bowl, stir to combine, and use immediately or store in an airtight container.

Maple & Chipotle Glaze

YIELD: 1½ CUPS | **ACTIVE TIME:** 5 MINUTES | **TOTAL TIME:** 5 MINUTES

¾ CUP REAL MAPLE SYRUP

1 CHIPOTLE CHILE,
CHOPPED

3 TABLESPOONS
FERMENTED CHILE ADOBO
(SEE PAGE 371)

2 TABLESPOONS KETCHUP

1½ TABLESPOONS DIJON
MUSTARD

1 TABLESPOON APPLE CIDER
VINEGAR

1. Place all of the ingredients in a bowl, stir to combine, and use immediately or store in an airtight container.

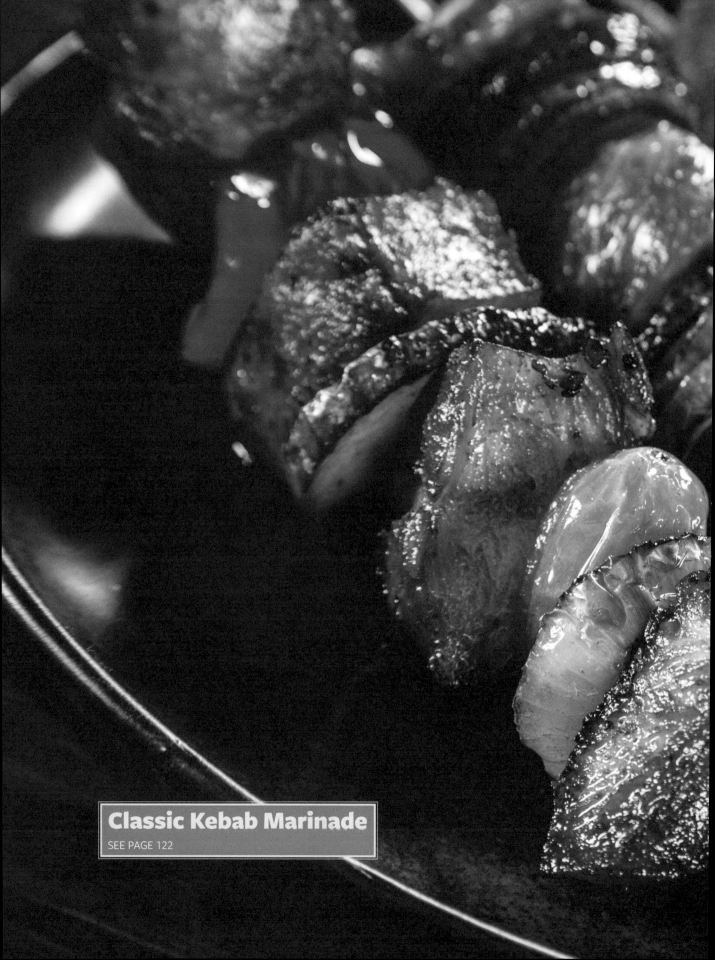

Classic Kebab Marinade

SEE PAGE 122

Blood Orange & Bourbon Brine

YIELD: 10 CUPS | **ACTIVE TIME:** 45 MINUTES | **TOTAL TIME:** 2 HOURS

12 CUPS HOT WATER

¾ CUP KOSHER SALT

½ CUP BROWN SUGAR

5 BLOOD ORANGES, HALVED

2 CINNAMON STICKS

2 STAR ANISE PODS

3 WHOLE CLOVES

2 CUPS BOURBON

1. Place all of the ingredients, except for the bourbon, in a stockpot and bring the mixture to a boil, stirring occasionally.

2. Remove the pan from heat, stir in the bourbon, and let the brine cool completely before using or storing.

Holiday Turkey Brine

YIELD: 8 CUPS | **ACTIVE TIME:** 15 MINUTES | **TOTAL TIME:** 2 HOURS

¾ CUP SUGAR

½ CUP KOSHER SALT

5 BAY LEAVES

3 CINNAMON STICKS

4 GARLIC CLOVES

3 SPRIGS OF FRESH THYME

3 SPRIGS OF FRESH ROSEMARY

2 TEASPOONS WHOLE CLOVES

2 TEASPOONS FRESHLY GRATED NUTMEG

8 CUPS WATER

1. Place all of the ingredients in a large stockpot and bring the mixture to a boil.

2. Reduce the heat and simmer the brine for 20 minutes.

3. Remove the pan from heat and let the brine cool completely before using or storing in the refrigerator.

Recado Negro

YIELD: 1½ CUPS | **ACTIVE TIME:** 10 MINUTES | **TOTAL TIME:** 30 MINUTES

12 ANCHO CHILE PEPPERS, STEMS AND SEEDS REMOVED

4 OZ. GARLIC, UNPEELED

1 OZ. ACHIOTE SEEDS

1 OZ. FRESH MEXICAN OREGANO

5 ALLSPICE BERRIES

¼ OZ. CUMIN SEEDS

½ OZ. KOSHER SALT

½ OZ. BLACK PEPPER

½ CUP WHITE VINEGAR

1. Place the chiles in a bowl, cover them with hot water, and let them soak for 20 minutes.

2. Place the garlic in a dry skillet and cook it over high heat until the peel is charred, about 5 minutes. Remove the garlic from the pan and set it aside.

3. Reduce the heat to medium and toast the achiote and oregano for about 30 seconds, shaking the pan occasionally.

4. Place the chiles, soaking liquid, garlic, achiote, oregano, and remaining ingredients in a food processor and blitz until the mixture is smooth. Use immediately or store in the refrigerator.

Apple Cider & Honey Glaze

YIELD: 1¼ CUPS | **ACTIVE TIME:** 5 MINUTES | **TOTAL TIME:** 15 MINUTES

1 CUP APPLE CIDER

1 TABLESPOON HONEY

¼ CUP CLARIFIED BUTTER (SEE PAGE 318)

1. Place all of the ingredients in a saucepan, bring the mixture to a boil, and cook until it has reduced by half, about 15 minutes.

2. Use immediately or store in the refrigerator.

Holiday Turkey Brine
SEE PAGE 126

Marley's Collie

YIELD: 1½ CUPS | **ACTIVE TIME:** 5 MINUTES | **TOTAL TIME:** 5 MINUTES

1 MEDIUM ONION, CHOPPED

3 SCALLIONS, TRIMMED AND CHOPPED

2 SCOTCH BONNET CHILES, CHOPPED

2 GARLIC CLOVES, CHOPPED

CHINESE FIVE-SPICE POWDER, TO TASTE

1 TABLESPOON CRACKED ALLSPICE BERRIES

1 TABLESPOON CRACKED BLACK PEPPER

1 TEASPOON DRIED THYME

1 TEASPOON FRESHLY GRATED NUTMEG

1 TEASPOON KOSHER SALT

½ CUP SOY SAUCE

1 TABLESPOON AVOCADO OIL

1. Place the onion, scallions, chiles, garlic, five-spice powder, allspice, pepper, thyme, nutmeg, and salt in a food processor and blitz until the mixture is a smooth paste.

2. With the machine running, add the soy sauce and the avocado oil in a slow, steady stream until they have been incorporated. Use immediately or store in the refrigerator.

Recado Blanco

YIELD: 1½ CUPS | **ACTIVE TIME:** 10 MINUTES | **TOTAL TIME:** 10 MINUTES

½ TEASPOON ALLSPICE BERRIES

½ TEASPOON WHOLE CLOVES

3½ OZ. BLACK PEPPERCORNS

1 CINNAMON STICK

1 TEASPOON DRIED OREGANO

1 TEASPOON DRIED MARJORAM

8 GARLIC CLOVES

14 TABLESPOONS WHITE VINEGAR

SALT, TO TASTE

1. Place the allspice berries, cloves, peppercorns, and cinnamon stick in a dry skillet and toast until fragrant, shaking the pan so that they do not burn. Remove the mixture from the pan and use a mortar and pestle to grind it into a fine powder.

2. Place the spice powder, oregano, marjoram, garlic, and three-quarters of the vinegar in a blender and puree until the mixture is a thick paste. Add the remaining vinegar as needed to get the desired consistency. Season the rub with salt and either use immediately or store in the refrigerator.

Recado Rojo

YIELD: 3 CUPS | **ACTIVE TIME:** 20 MINUTES | **TOTAL TIME:** 20 MINUTES

3½ OZ. YUCATECA ACHIOTE PASTE

14 TABLESPOONS FRESH LIME JUICE

14 TABLESPOONS ORANGE JUICE

7 TABLESPOONS GRAPEFRUIT JUICE

1 TEASPOON DRIED OREGANO

1 TEASPOON DRIED MARJORAM

1 HABANERO CHILE PEPPER, STEMS AND SEEDS REMOVED

5 GARLIC CLOVES

1 CINNAMON STICK, GRATED

SALT, TO TASTE

1. Place the achiote paste and juices in a bowl and let the mixture sit for 15 minutes.

2. Place the mixture and the remaining ingredients in a blender and puree until smooth.

3. Taste, adjust the seasoning as needed, and use as desired.

Rosemary, Lemon & Olive Oil Lamb Marinade

YIELD: 1½ CUPS | **ACTIVE TIME:** 5 MINUTES | **TOTAL TIME:** 5 MINUTES

¾ CUP EXTRA-VIRGIN OLIVE OIL

¼ CUP FRESH ROSEMARY, CHOPPED

JUICE OF 3 LEMONS

4 GARLIC CLOVES, MINCED

2 TEASPOONS KOSHER SALT

2 TEASPOONS BLACK PEPPER

1. Place all of the ingredients in a bowl, whisk to combine, and use immediately or store in an airtight container.

Dill & Coriander Marinade

YIELD: 1¾ CUPS | **ACTIVE TIME:** 5 MINUTES | **TOTAL TIME:** 5 MINUTES

1 CUP EXTRA-VIRGIN OLIVE OIL

3 TABLESPOONS BLACK PEPPER

3 TABLESPOONS CORIANDER SEEDS, CRUSHED

2 TABLESPOONS CHOPPED FRESH DILL

2 GARLIC CLOVES, MINCED

2 TABLESPOONS FINE SEA SALT

1. Place all of the ingredients in a bowl, stir to combine, and use immediately or store in an airtight container.

Bay Blend Marinade

YIELD: 1½ CUPS | **ACTIVE TIME:** 5 MINUTES | **TOTAL TIME:** 5 MINUTES

12 BAY LEAVES

1 ONION, CHOPPED

6 GARLIC CLOVES, CHOPPED

2 CELERY STALKS, CHOPPED

½ TEASPOON ALLSPICE

¼ TEASPOON CINNAMON

½ TEASPOON GROUND GINGER

2 TEASPOONS BLACK PEPPER

1 TABLESPOON KOSHER SALT

¼ CUP EXTRA-VIRGIN OLIVE OIL

1. Place all of the ingredients in a food processor, blitz until smooth, and use immediately or store in the refrigerator.

Agave & Sriracha Glaze

YIELD: 1½ CUPS | **ACTIVE TIME:** 5 MINUTES | **TOTAL TIME:** 5 MINUTES

1 CUP AGAVE NECTAR

¼ CUP GARLIC POWDER

¼ CUP SRIRACHA

1. Place all of the ingredients in a bowl, stir to combine, and use immediately or store in an airtight container.

Lemongrass Marinade

YIELD: 1½ CUPS | **ACTIVE TIME:** 5 MINUTES | **TOTAL TIME:** 5 MINUTES

½ CUP SOY SAUCE

½ CUP FISH SAUCE

4 GARLIC CLOVES, MINCED

1 TABLESPOON GRATED
FRESH GINGER

2 TABLESPOONS MINCED
LEMONGRASS

¼ CUP HONEY

ZEST AND JUICE OF 3 LIMES

1. Place all of the ingredients in a bowl, whisk to combine, and use immediately or store in the refrigerator.

Miso & Whisky Marinade

YIELD: 2 CUPS | **ACTIVE TIME:** 5 MINUTES | **TOTAL TIME:** 5 MINUTES

½ CUP SOY SAUCE

½ CUP RED MISO

½ CUP BROWN SUGAR

½ CUP SCOTCH WHISKY

1. Place all of the ingredients in a bowl, whisk to combine, and use immediately or store in the refrigerator.

Agave & Sriracha Glaze
SEE PAGE 134

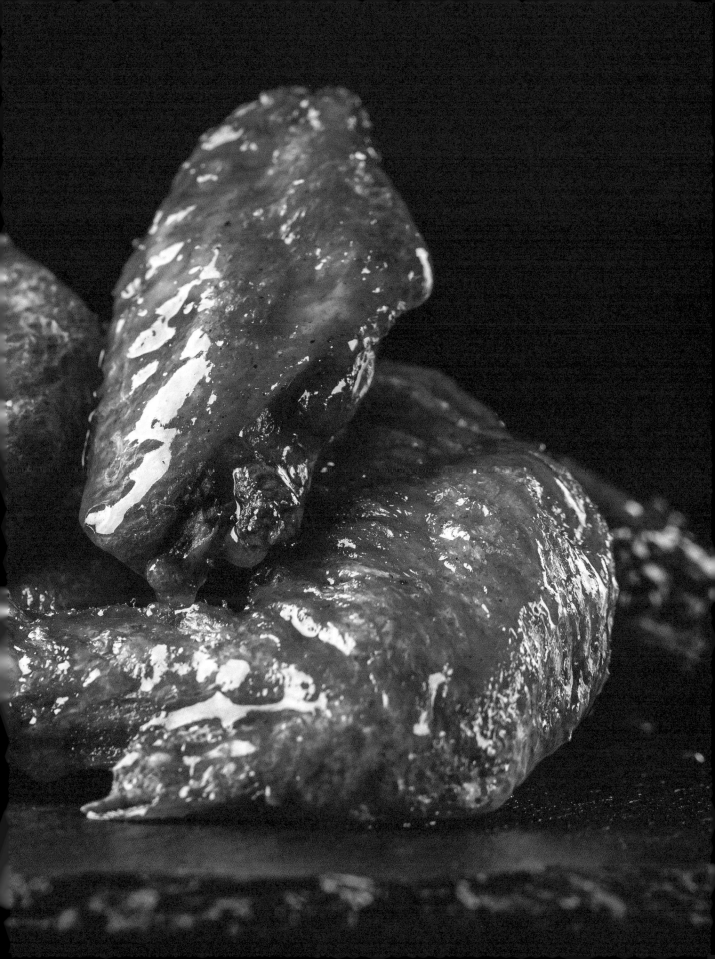

Barbacoa Marinade

YIELD: 2 CUPS | **ACTIVE TIME:** 10 MINUTES | **TOTAL TIME:** 35 MINUTES

1 TABLESPOON CORIANDER SEEDS

½ TEASPOON WHOLE CLOVES

½ TEASPOON ALLSPICE BERRIES

½ TEASPOON CUMIN SEEDS

1½ TABLESPOONS BLACK PEPPERCORNS

1 ANCHO CHILE PEPPER, STEM AND SEEDS REMOVED

1 GUAJILLO CHILE PEPPER, STEM AND SEEDS REMOVED

1 CHIPOTLE CHILE PEPPER, STEM AND SEEDS REMOVED

1 PASILLA CHILE PEPPER, STEM AND SEEDS REMOVED

5 GARLIC CLOVES

1 CUP ORANGE JUICE

1 CUP FRESH LIME JUICE

2 SMALL ONIONS, SLICED, PLUS MORE FOR SERVING

2 BAY LEAVES

SALT, TO TASTE

1. Place the coriander, cloves, allspice, cumin, and peppercorns in a dry skillet and toast until fragrant, shaking the pan frequently. Use a mortar and pestle to grind the mixture into a powder.

2. Place the chiles in the skillet and toast until they are fragrant and pliable, about 30 seconds. Transfer the chiles to a bowl of hot water and soak for 20 minutes.

3. Drain the chiles and reserve the soaking liquid. Place the chiles, garlic, and some of the soaking liquid in a food processor and blitz until smooth. Add the toasted spice powder and the remaining ingredients and pulse until incorporated. Use immediately or store in the refrigerator.

Citrus Brine

YIELD: 2½ CUPS | **ACTIVE TIME:** 5 MINUTES | **TOTAL TIME:** 5 MINUTES

1 CUP SUGAR

¾ CUP KOSHER SALT

2 LEMONS, SLICED

2 ORANGES, SLICED

2 LIMES, SLICED

5 BAY LEAVES

2 CINNAMON STICKS

4 GARLIC CLOVES

1. Place all of the ingredients in a bowl, stir to combine, and use immediately or store in the refrigerator.

Mojo Marinade

YIELD: 8 CUPS | **ACTIVE TIME:** 5 MINUTES | **TOTAL TIME:** 5 MINUTES

18 GARLIC CLOVES, CHOPPED

1½ CUPS MINCED YELLOW ONION

3 CUPS FRESH ORANGE JUICE

1½ CUPS FRESH LIME JUICE

1½ TEASPOONS CUMIN

1 TABLESPOON DRIED OREGANO

1½ TEASPOONS LEMON-PEPPER SEASONING

1½ TEASPOONS BLACK PEPPER

1 TABLESPOON KOSHER SALT

¾ CUP CHOPPED FRESH CILANTRO

1 TABLESPOON HOT SAUCE

3 CUPS EXTRA-VIRGIN OLIVE OIL

1. Place all of the ingredients, except for the olive oil, in a food processor and blitz until smooth.

2. With the food processor running, add the olive oil in a slow, steady stream until it has been emulsified. Use immediately or store in the refrigerator.

Grilled Poultry Marinade

YIELD: 1½ CUPS | **ACTIVE TIME:** 5 MINUTES | **TOTAL TIME:** 5 MINUTES

1 TABLESPOON ALLSPICE BERRIES

1 CINNAMON STICK

3 TABLESPOONS CORIANDER SEEDS

2 TABLESPOONS CUMIN SEEDS

½ TEASPOON WHOLE CLOVES

2 TABLESPOONS BLACK PEPPERCORNS

1½ TEASPOONS WHITE PEPPERCORNS

3 BAY LEAVES

1 TEASPOON DRIED MEXICAN OREGANO

1 TEASPOON DRIED MARJORAM

1 TABLESPOON ANCHO CHILE POWDER

3½ TABLESPOONS ORANGE JUICE

3½ TABLESPOONS FRESH LIME JUICE

2 TABLESPOONS EXTRA-VIRGIN OLIVE OIL

1. Place the allspice berries, cinnamon stick, coriander seeds, cumin seeds, cloves, peppercorns, and bay leaves in a dry skillet and toast the mixture until it is fragrant, shaking the pan to prevent it from burning. Grind the mixture into a fine powder with a mortar and pestle.

2. Place the toasted spice powder and the remaining ingredients in a food processor and blitz until combined. Use immediately or store in the refrigerator.

Roasted Chicken Brine

YIELD: 18 CUPS | **ACTIVE TIME:** 5 MINUTES | **TOTAL TIME:** 5 MINUTES

16 CUPS WARM WATER

1 CUP FINE SEA SALT

1 CUP LIGHT BROWN SUGAR

¼ CUP EXTRA-VIRGIN OLIVE OIL

JUICE OF ½ LEMON

4 GARLIC CLOVES, CRUSHED

1 TABLESPOON BLACK PEPPER

1. Place all of the ingredients in a stockpot and stir to combine. Use immediately or cover until ready to use.

Pierna de Puerco Marinade

YIELD: 1½ CUPS | **ACTIVE TIME:** 10 MINUTES | **TOTAL TIME:** 35 MINUTES

2 ANCHO CHILE PEPPERS, STEMS AND SEEDS REMOVED

1 DRIED CASCABEL CHILE PEPPER, STEMS AND SEEDS REMOVED

1 CHIPOTLE MORITA CHILE PEPPER, STEMS AND SEEDS REMOVED

1 GUAJILLO CHILE PEPPER, STEMS AND SEEDS REMOVED

½ TEASPOON BLACK PEPPERCORNS

1½ TEASPOONS CORIANDER SEEDS

1 TEASPOON CUMIN SEEDS

½ TEASPOON CINNAMON

½ TEASPOON GROUND CLOVES

8 GARLIC CLOVES

½ CUP WHITE VINEGAR

1 CUP MEZCAL

SALT, TO TASTE

1. Place the chiles in a dry skillet and toast over medium heat until they become fragrant and pliable, about 30 seconds. Place the chiles in a bowl, cover them with hot water, and let them soak for 30 minutes.

2. Place the peppercorns, coriander seeds, and cumin seeds in the skillet and toast until fragrant, 1 to 2 minutes, shaking the pan frequently. Grind the mixture into a fine powder using a mortar and pestle.

3. Drain the chiles and reserve the soaking liquid. Place the chiles in a food processor along with the toasted spice powder and remaining ingredients and blitz until smooth, adding the reserved liquid as needed. Use immediately or store in the refrigerator.

Teriyaki Marinade

YIELD: 2 CUPS | **ACTIVE TIME:** 5 MINUTES | **TOTAL TIME:** 5 MINUTES

1 CUP SOY SAUCE

½ CUP BROWN SUGAR

¼ RICE VINEGAR

4 GARLIC CLOVES, MINCED

1 TABLESPOON GRATED FRESH GINGER

2 TEASPOONS BLACK PEPPER

1. Place all of the ingredients in a food processor, blitz until smooth, and use immediately or store in the refrigerator.

Teriyaki Marinade
SEE PAGE 141

Mixiotes Marinade

YIELD: 2½ CUPS | **ACTIVE TIME:** 10 MINUTES | **TOTAL TIME:** 35 MINUTES

4 ANCHO CHILE PEPPERS, STEMS AND SEEDS REMOVED

4 GUAJILLO CHILE PEPPERS, STEMS AND SEEDS REMOVED

½ TEASPOON ALLSPICE BERRIES

½ TEASPOON WHOLE CLOVES

2 BAY LEAVES

1 CINNAMON STICK

10 GARLIC CLOVES

7 TABLESPOONS APPLE CIDER VINEGAR

7 TABLESPOONS ORANGE JUICE

7 TABLESPOONS FRESH LIME JUICE

1. Place the chiles in a dry skillet and toast over medium heat until they become fragrant and pliable, about 30 seconds. Place the chiles in a bowl, cover them with hot water, and let them soak for 30 minutes.

2. Place the allspice berries, cloves, bay leaves, and cinnamon stick in the skillet and toast until fragrant, 1 to 2 minutes, shaking the pan frequently. Grind the mixture into a fine powder using a mortar and pestle.

3. Drain the chiles and reserve the soaking liquid. Place the chiles in a food processor along with the toasted spice powder and remaining ingredients and blitz until smooth, adding the reserved liquid as needed. Use immediately or store in the refrigerator.

Souvlaki Marinade

YIELD: 1½ CUPS | **ACTIVE TIME:** 5 MINUTES | **TOTAL TIME:** 5 MINUTES

10 GARLIC CLOVES, CRUSHED

4 SPRIGS OF FRESH OREGANO

1 SPRIG OF FRESH ROSEMARY

1 TEASPOON PAPRIKA

1 TEASPOON KOSHER SALT

1 TEASPOON BLACK PEPPER

¼ CUP EXTRA-VIRGIN OLIVE OIL

¼ CUP DRY WHITE WINE

2 TABLESPOONS FRESH LEMON JUICE

2 BAY LEAVES

1. Place all of the ingredients in a food processor, blitz to combine, and use immediately or store in the refrigerator.

Sweet Cilantro Glaze

YIELD: 1 CUP | **ACTIVE TIME:** 5 MINUTES | **TOTAL TIME:** 5 MINUTES

⅓ CUP HONEY

7 TABLESPOONS FRESH LIME JUICE

1 SHALLOT, CHOPPED

1 SMALL BUNCH OF FRESH CILANTRO

SALT AND PEPPER, TO TASTE

1. Place all of the ingredients in a food processor, blitz until smooth, and use immediately or store in an airtight container.

Garlic & Herb Marinade

YIELD: 3 CUPS | **ACTIVE TIME:** 5 MINUTES | **TOTAL TIME:** 5 MINUTES

12 GARLIC CLOVES, CRUSHED

2 TABLESPOONS FRESH ROSEMARY

1 TABLESPOON FRESH THYME

2½ CUPS EXTRA-VIRGIN OLIVE OIL

1 TABLESPOON BLACK PEPPER

1 TABLESPOON FINE SEA SALT

1. Place all of the ingredients in a food processor, blitz until smooth, and use immediately or store in an airtight container.

Chicken Satay Marinade

YIELD: 1 CUP | **ACTIVE TIME:** 5 MINUTES | **TOTAL TIME:** 5 MINUTES

¼ CUP KECAP MANIS

1 TABLESPOON KOSHER SALT

¼ CUP MINCED LEMONGRASS

2 TABLESPOONS MINCED SHALLOTS

4 GARLIC CLOVES, MINCED

1½ TEASPOONS CUMIN

1 TABLESPOON CORIANDER

1 TEASPOON FISH SAUCE

1. Place all of the ingredients in a bowl, whisk to combine, and use immediately or store in the refrigerator.

Red Wine & Dijon Marinade

YIELD: 1½ CUPS | **ACTIVE TIME:** 5 MINUTES | **TOTAL TIME:** 5 MINUTES

¾ CUP DRY RED WINE

¼ CUP EXTRA-VIRGIN OLIVE OIL

2 GARLIC CLOVES, MINCED

1 TABLESPOON DIJON MUSTARD

1 TABLESPOON BLACK PEPPER

1 TABLESPOON FINE SEA SALT

1 TEASPOON CHOPPED FRESH ROSEMARY

1. Place all of the ingredients in a bowl, whisk to combine, and use immediately or store in an airtight container.

Apple Cider Marinade

YIELD: 2½ CUPS | **ACTIVE TIME:** 5 MINUTES | **TOTAL TIME:** 5 MINUTES

2 CUPS APPLE CIDER

¼ CUP EXTRA-VIRGIN OLIVE OIL

JUICE OF ½ LEMON

1 TEASPOON FRESH THYME

1 TEASPOON CHOPPED FRESH ROSEMARY

2 GARLIC CLOVES, MINCED

1 TABLESPOON BLACK PEPPER

2 TEASPOONS FINE SEA SALT

1. Place all of the ingredients in a bowl, whisk to combine, and use immediately or store in an airtight container.

Lemon & Herb Marinade

YIELD: 2½ CUPS | **ACTIVE TIME:** 5 MINUTES | **TOTAL TIME:** 5 MINUTES

JUICE OF 4 LEMONS

6 GARLIC CLOVES

2 TEASPOONS FRESH THYME

1 TABLESPOON CHOPPED FRESH ROSEMARY

2 TEASPOONS GROUND FENNEL SEEDS

1 TABLESPOON BLACK PEPPER

1 TABLESPOON FINE SEA SALT

1. Place all of the ingredients in a bowl, whisk to combine, and use immediately or store in an airtight container.

Chicken Satay Marinade

SEE PAGE 146

Beef Bulgogi Marinade

YIELD: 1 CUP | **ACTIVE TIME:** 5 MINUTES | **TOTAL TIME:** 5 MINUTES

6 GARLIC CLOVES, MINCED

¼ CUP SOY SAUCE

2 TABLESPOONS GOCHUGARU

2 TABLESPOONS CHOPPED FRESH GINGER

2 TABLESPOONS LIGHT BROWN SUGAR

2 TABLESPOONS SESAME OIL

1. Place all of the ingredients in a bowl, whisk to combine, and use immediately or store in the refrigerator.

Char Siu Marinade

YIELD: 1 CUP | **ACTIVE TIME:** 5 MINUTES | **TOTAL TIME:** 5 MINUTES

1¼ CUP HOISIN SAUCE (SEE PAGE 282)

1 TABLESPOON DARK SOY SAUCE

2 TABLESPOONS SHAOXING WINE

2 TABLESPOONS KETCHUP

1 TABLESPOON OYSTER SAUCE

¼ CUP HONEY

2 TEASPOONS KOSHER SALT

3 PINCHES OF CURING SALT

1 TEASPOON CHINESE FIVE-SPICE POWDER

2 TO 3 DROPS OF RED GEL FOOD COLORING (OPTIONAL)

1. Place all of the ingredients in a bowl, whisk to combine, and use immediately or store in the refrigerator.

Mint Marinade

YIELD: 1½ CUPS | **ACTIVE TIME:** 5 MINUTES | **TOTAL TIME:** 5 MINUTES

½ CUP EXTRA-VIRGIN OLIVE OIL

½ CUP FRESH MINT LEAVES, FINELY CHOPPED

¼ CUP DRY RED WINE

4 GARLIC CLOVES, MINCED

1 TABLESPOON CHOPPED FRESH PARSLEY

1 TABLESPOON BLACK PEPPER

2 TEASPOONS FINE SEA SALT

1. Place all of the ingredients in a bowl, whisk to combine, and use immediately or store in an airtight container.

Cilantro & Lime Marinade

YIELD: 1½ CUPS | **ACTIVE TIME:** 5 MINUTES | **TOTAL TIME:** 5 MINUTES

JUICE OF 4 LIMES

½ CUP EXTRA-VIRGIN OLIVE OIL

½ CUP FRESH CILANTRO, FINELY CHOPPED

4 GARLIC CLOVES, MINCED

4 TEASPOONS BLACK PEPPER

4 TEASPOONS FINE SEA SALT

1 TEASPOON HONEY

1. Place all of the ingredients in a bowl, whisk to combine, and use immediately or store in an airtight container.

Ginger & Sesame Marinade

YIELD: 1½ CUPS | **ACTIVE TIME:** 5 MINUTES | **TOTAL TIME:** 5 MINUTES

1 CUP SOY SAUCE

2 TABLESPOONS GRATED FRESH GINGER

2 TABLESPOONS SESAME OIL

4 TEASPOONS SESAME SEEDS

4 SCALLIONS, TRIMMED AND CHOPPED

2 TEASPOONS BLACK PEPPER

1. Place all of the ingredients in a food processor, blitz until smooth, and use immediately or store in an airtight container.

Char Siu Marinade
SEE PAGE 152

Quick Adobo Marinade

YIELD: 1 CUP | **ACTIVE TIME:** 10 MINUTES | **TOTAL TIME:** 30 MINUTES

4 GUAJILLO CHILE PEPPERS, STEMS AND SEEDS REMOVED

6 GARLIC CLOVES

2 SMALL ROMA TOMATOES

3 TABLESPOONS CHOPPED CHIPOTLES IN ADOBO

SALT, TO TASTE

1. Place the chiles in a dry skillet and toast over medium heat until they darken and become fragrant and pliable, about 30 seconds. Transfer the chiles to a bowl, cover them with hot water, and let them soak for 15 to 20 minutes.

2. Drain the chiles and reserve the soaking liquid. Add the chiles to a food processor along with the garlic, tomatoes, chipotles, and a small amount of the soaking liquid and blitz until the mixture is a smooth paste. Season the marinade with salt and let it cool completely.

Cecina de Cerdo Marinade

YIELD: 2 CUPS | **ACTIVE TIME:** 5 MINUTES | **TOTAL TIME:** 5 MINUTES

7 OZ. GUAJILLO CHILE PEPPERS, STEMS AND SEEDS REMOVED

1 TEASPOON CUMIN SEEDS

1 TEASPOON CORIANDER SEEDS

1 BAY LEAF

2 TABLESPOONS EXTRA-VIRGIN OLIVE OIL

4 GARLIC CLOVES, MINCED

10 DRIED CHILES DE ÀRBOL, STEMS AND SEEDS REMOVED

7 TABLESPOONS APPLE CIDER VINEGAR

SALT, TO TASTE

1. Place the guajillo chiles in a dry skillet and toast over medium heat until they become fragrant and pliable, about 30 seconds. Place the chiles in a bowl, cover them with hot water, and let them soak for 30 minutes.

2. Place the seeds and bay leaf in the skillet and toast until fragrant, 1 to 2 minutes, shaking the pan frequently. Grind the mixture into a fine powder using a mortar and pestle.

3. Place the olive oil in a skillet and warm it over medium heat. Add the garlic, cook, stirring continually, for 1 minute and then add the chiles de àrbol. Stir-fry for 30 seconds and then remove the pan from heat.

4. Drain the guajillo peppers and reserve the soaking liquid. Place the guajillo chiles, chiles de àrbol, toasted spice powder, and garlic in a food processor and blitz until smooth, adding the vinegar and soaking liquid as needed to attain a "nappe" consistency, meaning smooth and thick. Season the marinade with salt and use immediately or store in the refrigerator.

Carne Asada

YIELD: 1½ CUPS | **ACTIVE TIME:** 5 MINUTES | **TOTAL TIME:** 5 MINUTES

1 JALAPEÑO CHILE PEPPER, STEMS AND SEEDS REMOVED, MINCED

3 GARLIC CLOVES, MINCED

½ CUP CHOPPED FRESH CILANTRO

¼ CUP EXTRA-VIRGIN OLIVE OIL

JUICE OF 1 SMALL ORANGE

2 TABLESPOONS APPLE CIDER VINEGAR

2 TEASPOONS CAYENNE PEPPER

1 TEASPOON ANCHO CHILE POWDER

1 TEASPOON GARLIC POWDER

1 TEASPOON PAPRIKA

1 TEASPOON KOSHER SALT

1 TEASPOON CUMIN

1 TEASPOON DRIED OREGANO

¼ TEASPOON BLACK PEPPER

1. Place all of the ingredients in a bowl, whisk to combine, and use immediately or store in the refrigerator.

Grilled Seafood Marinade

YIELD: ¾ CUP | **ACTIVE TIME:** 10 MINUTES | **TOTAL TIME:** 35 MINUTES

3 GUAJILLO CHILE PEPPERS, STEMS AND SEEDS REMOVED

2 ANCHO CHILE PEPPERS, STEMS AND SEEDS REMOVED

3 GARLIC CLOVES

2 TABLESPOONS WORCESTERSHIRE SAUCE

¼ CUP FRESH LIME JUICE

1. Place the chiles in a dry skillet and toast over medium heat until they become fragrant and pliable, about 30 seconds. Place the chiles in a bowl, cover them with hot water, and let them soak for 30 minutes.

2. Drain the chiles and reserve the soaking liquid. Place the chiles in a food processor, add the remaining ingredients, and blitz until smooth, adding the reserved liquid as needed to get the desired texture. Use immediately or store in the refrigerator.

Pineapple Marinade

YIELD: 2 CUPS | **ACTIVE TIME:** 5 MINUTES | **TOTAL TIME:** 5 MINUTES

1½ CUPS PINEAPPLE JUICE

¼ CUP BROWN SUGAR

¼ CUP SOY SAUCE

2 GARLIC CLOVES, MINCED

1 TEASPOON FINE SEA SALT

1. Place all of the ingredients in a food processor, blitz until smooth, and use immediately or store in an airtight container.

Balsamic Marinade

YIELD: 2 CUPS | **ACTIVE TIME:** 5 MINUTES | **TOTAL TIME:** 5 MINUTES

2 TABLESPOONS CHOPPED FRESH BASIL

2 TEASPOONS CHOPPED FRESH ROSEMARY

2 GARLIC CLOVES, CRUSHED

2 TEASPOONS DIJON MUSTARD

1 TEASPOON HONEY

1 CUP EXTRA-VIRGIN OLIVE OIL

¼ CUP BALSAMIC VINEGAR

1 TABLESPOON BLACK PEPPER

1 TABLESPOON FINE SEA SALT

1. Place all of the ingredients in a food processor, blitz until smooth, and use immediately or store in an airtight container.

Five-Spice Marinade

YIELD: 1½ CUPS | **ACTIVE TIME:** 5 MINUTES | **TOTAL TIME:** 5 MINUTES

¾ CUP SOY SAUCE

¼ CUP RICE VINEGAR

1 TABLESPOON GRATED FRESH GINGER

2 TEASPOONS SESAME OIL

2 TEASPOONS CHINESE FIVE-SPICE POWDER

¼ CUP EXTRA-VIRGIN OLIVE OIL

1 TEASPOON BLACK PEPPER

1. Place all of the ingredients in a bowl, whisk to combine, and use immediately or store in the refrigerator.

Grilled Seafood Marinade
SEE PAGE 162

Citrus & Herb Marinade

YIELD: 1½ CUPS | **ACTIVE TIME:** 5 MINUTES | **TOTAL TIME:** 5 MINUTES

¾ CUP ORANGE JUICE

JUICE OF 1 LIME

JUICE OF 1 LEMON

¼ CUP FRESH CILANTRO, CHOPPED

¼ CUP EXTRA-VIRGIN OLIVE OIL

2 TABLESPOONS CHOPPED FRESH ROSEMARY

4 GARLIC CLOVES, MINCED

1 TABLESPOON BLACK PEPPER

1 TABLESPOON FINE SEA SALT

1. Place all of the ingredients in a bowl, whisk to combine, and use immediately or store in the refrigerator.

Tandoori Marinade

YIELD: 2 CUPS | **ACTIVE TIME:** 10 MINUTES | **TOTAL TIME:** 10 MINUTES

2 TABLESPOONS EXTRA-VIRGIN OLIVE OIL

2 GARLIC CLOVES, MINCED

½ TEASPOON TURMERIC

2 TABLESPOONS CUMIN

1 TABLESPOON MINCED FRESH GINGER

1 TEASPOON PAPRIKA

½ TEASPOON CORIANDER

3 TABLESPOONS CHOPPED FRESH CILANTRO

JUICE OF ½ LIME

1½ CUPS FULL-FAT PLAIN YOGURT

1. Place the olive oil in a skillet and warm it over medium heat. Add all of the remaining ingredients, except for the lime juice and yogurt, to the skillet and cook, stirring continually, for 2 minutes.

2. Transfer the mixture to a bowl, stir in the lime juice and yogurt, and use immediately or store in the refrigerator.

Smoky Jerk Marinade

YIELD: 1½ CUPS | **ACTIVE TIME:** 5 MINUTES | **TOTAL TIME:** 5 MINUTES

1 MEDIUM ONION, FINELY DICED

¼ CUP SCALLIONS, TRIMMED AND FINELY DICED

1 SCOTCH BONNET PEPPER, CHOPPED

3 TABLESPOONS SOY SAUCE

1 TABLESPOON WHITE VINEGAR

3 TABLESPOONS EXTRA-VIRGIN OLIVE OIL

2 TEASPOONS FRESH THYME

2 TEASPOONS SUGAR

2 TEASPOONS LIQUID SMOKE

1 TEASPOON FINE SEA SALT

1 TEASPOON BLACK PEPPER

1 TEASPOON ALLSPICE

½ TEASPOON FRESHLY GRATED NUTMEG

½ TEASPOON CINNAMON

1. Place all of the ingredients in a food processor, blitz until smooth, and use immediately or store in an airtight container.

Chipotle & Adobo Marinade

YIELD: 1½ CUPS | **ACTIVE TIME:** 5 MINUTES | **TOTAL TIME:** 5 MINUTES

1 (7 OZ.) CAN OF CHIPOTLES IN ADOBO

2 GARLIC CLOVES, MINCED

JUICE OF ½ LIME

1 TEASPOON BLACK PEPPER

1 TEASPOON FINE SEA SALT

1. Place all of the ingredients in a food processor, blitz until smooth, and use immediately or store in an airtight container.

Jerk Marinade

YIELD: 1½ CUPS | **ACTIVE TIME:** 5 MINUTES | **TOTAL TIME:** 5 MINUTES

1 MEDIUM ONION, FINELY DICED

¼ CUP SCALLIONS, TRIMMED AND FINELY DICED

1 SCOTCH BONNET PEPPER, CHOPPED

3 TABLESPOONS SOY SAUCE

1 TABLESPOON WHITE VINEGAR

3 TABLESPOONS EXTRA-VIRGIN OLIVE OIL

2 TEASPOONS FRESH THYME

2 TEASPOONS SUGAR

1 TEASPOON FINE SEA SALT

1 TEASPOON BLACK PEPPER

1 TEASPOON ALLSPICE

½ TEASPOON FRESHLY GRATED NUTMEG

½ TEASPOON CINNAMON

1. Place all of the ingredients in a food processor, blitz until smooth, and use immediately or store in an airtight container.

Smoky Steak Marinade

YIELD: 1½ CUPS | **ACTIVE TIME:** 5 MINUTES | **TOTAL TIME:** 5 MINUTES

8 GARLIC CLOVES, MINCED

3 TABLESPOONS DIJON MUSTARD

3 TABLESPOONS SOY SAUCE

3 TABLESPOONS EXTRA-VIRGIN OLIVE OIL

3 TABLESPOONS WORCESTERSHIRE SAUCE

2 TABLESPOONS BLACK PEPPER

1 TABLESPOON FINE SEA SALT

2 TEASPOONS LIQUID SMOKE

1. Place all of the ingredients in a bowl, whisk to combine, and use immediately or store in an airtight container.

All-Purpose Marinade

YIELD: 1 CUP | **ACTIVE TIME:** 5 MINUTES | **TOTAL TIME:** 5 MINUTES

½ CUP SOY SAUCE

2 TABLESPOONS WORCESTERSHIRE SAUCE

2 GARLIC CLOVES, FINELY CHOPPED

¼ MEDIUM ONION, FINELY DICED

¼ CUP EXTRA-VIRGIN OLIVE OIL

JUICE OF ½ LIME

1. Place all of the ingredients in a bowl, whisk to combine, and use immediately or store in an airtight container.

Salt & Vinegar Marinade

YIELD: 1½ CUPS | **ACTIVE TIME:** 5 MINUTES | **TOTAL TIME:** 5 MINUTES

1 CUP WHITE VINEGAR

¼ CUP APPLE CIDER VINEGAR

3 TABLESPOONS FINE SEA SALT

½ TEASPOON GARLIC POWDER

½ TEASPOON ONION POWDER

1. Place all of the ingredients in a bowl, whisk to combine, and use immediately or store in an airtight container.

Jerk Marinade
SEE PAGE 168

Classic Steak Marinade

YIELD: 1½ CUPS | **ACTIVE TIME:** 5 MINUTES | **TOTAL TIME:** 5 MINUTES

8 GARLIC CLOVES, MINCED

3 TABLESPOONS DIJON MUSTARD

3 TABLESPOONS SOY SAUCE

3 TABLESPOONS EXTRA-VIRGIN OLIVE OIL

3 TABLESPOONS WORCESTERSHIRE SAUCE

2 TABLESPOONS BLACK PEPPER

1 TABLESPOON FINE SEA SALT

1. Place all of the ingredients in a bowl, whisk to combine, and use immediately or store in an airtight container.

Spicy Shrimp Marinade

YIELD: 1½ CUPS | **ACTIVE TIME:** 10 MINUTES | **TOTAL TIME:** 35 MINUTES

10 GUAJILLO CHILE PEPPERS

4 DRIED CHILES DE ÀRBOL

3 GARLIC CLOVES, CHOPPED

4 LARGE TOMATOES, QUARTERED

½ WHITE ONION, CHOPPED

1 TABLESPOON KOSHER SALT

1. Place the chiles in a dry skillet and toast over medium heat until they darken and become fragrant and pliable, about 30 seconds. Transfer the chiles to a bowl, cover them with hot water, and let them soak for 15 to 20 minutes.

2. Drain the chiles and reserve the soaking liquid. Add the chiles to a food processor along with the garlic, tomatoes, onion, and a small amount of the soaking liquid and blitz until the mixture is a smooth paste. Season the marinade with the salt and use immediately or store in the refrigerator.

Beer Marinade

YIELD: 3 CUPS | **ACTIVE TIME:** 5 MINUTES | **TOTAL TIME:** 5 MINUTES

3 TABLESPOONS BLACK PEPPER

2 TABLESPOONS FINE SEA SALT

4 GARLIC CLOVES, MINCED

¼ CUP EXTRA-VIRGIN OLIVE OIL

2 TABLESPOONS CHOPPED FRESH ROSEMARY

2 TEASPOONS FRESH THYME

2 TABLESPOONS SOY SAUCE

1 TEASPOON WORCESTERSHIRE SAUCE

2 CUPS DARK BEER

1 LARGE WHITE ONION, FINELY DICED

1. Place all of the ingredients in a bowl, whisk to combine, and use immediately or store in an airtight container.

Pork Shoulder Brine

YIELD: 17 CUPS | **ACTIVE TIME:** 5 MINUTES | **TOTAL TIME:** 5 MINUTES

16 CUPS WARM WATER

¼ CUP APPLE CIDER VINEGAR

¼ CUP LIGHT BROWN SUGAR

1 TEASPOON FRESH THYME

5 GARLIC CLOVES, CRUSHED

JUICE OF ½ LEMON

1 TABLESPOON BLACK PEPPER

2 TABLESPOONS FINE SEA SALT

1. Place all of the ingredients in a stockpot and stir to combine. Use immediately or cover until ready to use.

Rosemary & Dijon Marinade

YIELD: 1 CUP | **ACTIVE TIME:** 5 MINUTES | **TOTAL TIME:** 5 MINUTES

3 TABLESPOONS EXTRA-VIRGIN OLIVE OIL

¼ CUP CHOPPED FRESH ROSEMARY

¼ CUP DIJON MUSTARD

4 GARLIC CLOVES, MINCED

1 LARGE SHALLOT, MINCED

JUICE OF ½ LEMON

1 TABLESPOON CHOPPED FRESH PARSLEY

1 TEASPOON BLACK PEPPER

1 TEASPOON FINE SEA SALT

1. Place all of the ingredients in a bowl, whisk to combine, and use immediately or store in an airtight container.

Ginger & Sesame Marinade

YIELD: 1 CUP | **ACTIVE TIME:** 5 MINUTES | **TOTAL TIME:** 5 MINUTES

2-INCH PIECE OF FRESH GINGER, PEELED AND GRATED

2 SCALLIONS, TRIMMED AND MINCED

2 GARLIC CLOVES, MINCED

JUICE OF ½ LEMON

1 TEASPOON BLACK PEPPER

1 TEASPOON FINE SEA SALT

3 TABLESPOONS SESAME SEEDS

1. Place all of the ingredients in a food processor, blitz until combined, and use immediately or store in an airtight container.

Upper Peninsula Marinade

YIELD: 1 CUP | **ACTIVE TIME:** 5 MINUTES | **TOTAL TIME:** 5 MINUTES

½ CUP EXTRA-VIRGIN OLIVE OIL

4 GARLIC CLOVES, MINCED

2 TABLESPOONS WHITE WINE VINEGAR

JUICE OF ½ LEMON

2 TEASPOONS CHOPPED FRESH ROSEMARY

1 TEASPOON CHOPPED FRESH SAGE

½ TEASPOON FRESH THYME

1. Place all of the ingredients in a bowl, whisk to combine, and use immediately or store in an airtight container.

Al Pastor Marinade

YIELD: 1½ CUPS | **ACTIVE TIME:** 20 MINUTES | **TOTAL TIME:** 45 MINUTES

3 ALLSPICE BERRIES

2 WHOLE CLOVES

½ CINNAMON STICK

3 CHIPOTLE MORITA CHILE PEPPERS

2 DRIED CHILES DE ÀRBOL

7 GUAJILLO CHILE PEPPERS

2 TABLESPOONS FRESH LIME JUICE

2 TABLESPOONS ORANGE JUICE

2 TABLESPOONS GRAPEFRUIT JUICE

7 TABLESPOONS PINEAPPLE JUICE

½ CUP RECADO ROJO (SEE PAGE 132)

5 GARLIC CLOVES

⅛ TEASPOON DRIED OREGANO

SALT, TO TASTE

1. Place the allspice, cloves, and cinnamon stick in a dry skillet and toast until they are fragrant, 1 to 2 minutes, shaking the pan frequently. Grind the mixture into a fine powder using a mortar and pestle.

2. Place the chiles in the skillet and toast over medium heat until they darken and become fragrant and pliable, about 30 seconds. Transfer the chiles to a bowl, cover them with hot water, and let them soak for 30 minutes.

3. Drain the chiles and reserve the liquid. Place the chiles, toasted spice powder, juices, Recado Rojo, garlic cloves, and oregano in a food processor and blitz until smooth. Season the marinade with salt and use immediately or store in the refrigerator.

Artichoke Heart Marinade

YIELD: 2½ CUPS | **ACTIVE TIME:** 5 MINUTES | **TOTAL TIME:** 5 MINUTES

2 CUPS EXTRA-VIRGIN OLIVE OIL

JUICE OF 1 LEMON

6 GARLIC CLOVES

¼ TEASPOON RED PEPPER FLAKES

1 TEASPOON FRESH THYME

1 SHALLOT, SLICED THIN

1 TABLESPOON CHOPPED FRESH BASIL

1. Place all of the ingredients in a bowl, whisk to combine, and use immediately or store in an airtight container.

SAUCES & STOCKS

Teriyaki Sauce

YIELD: 1 CUP | **ACTIVE TIME:** 5 MINUTES | **TOTAL TIME:** 5 MINUTES

2 TEASPOONS GRATED
FRESH GINGER

3 GARLIC CLOVES, PEELED
AND MINCED

1 TABLESPOON RICE
VINEGAR

2 TABLESPOONS HONEY

¼ CUP SOY SAUCE

1 TABLESPOON TAPIOCA
STARCH OR CORNSTARCH

½ CUP WATER

1. Place all of the ingredients in a food processor, blitz to combine, and use immediately or store in the refrigerator.

Pea Shoot Pesto

YIELD: 2 CUPS | **ACTIVE TIME:** 15 MINUTES | **TOTAL TIME:** 15 MINUTES

2 CUPS PEA SHOOTS

1 CUP FRESH BASIL

2 TABLESPOONS FRESH LEMON JUICE

½ TEASPOON RED PEPPER FLAKES

¼ CUP PINE NUTS

¼ CUP FRESHLY GRATED PARMESAN CHEESE

¼ CUP EXTRA-VIRGIN OLIVE OIL

SALT AND PEPPER, TO TASTE

1. Place the pea shoots, basil, lemon juice, red pepper flakes, pine nuts, and Parmesan in a food processor and pulse until you have a rough paste.

2. With the food processor running, add the olive oil in a slow stream until it has emulsified. Season the sauce with salt and pepper and use immediately or store in the refrigerator.

Corn Stock

YIELD: 12 CUPS | **ACTIVE TIME:** 15 MINUTES | **TOTAL TIME:** 1 HOUR AND 30 MINUTES

8 CORN COBS, KERNELS REMOVED

1 BAY LEAF

1 SPRIG OF THYME

½ TEASPOON BLACK PEPPER

14 CUPS WATER

1. Place all of the ingredients in a stockpot and bring the mixture to a boil over medium-high heat. Reduce the heat and simmer the stock for 45 minutes.

2. Strain the stock, discard the solids, and let it cool completely before using or storing in the refrigerator.

Chipotle & Pistachio Pesto

YIELD: 2 CUPS | **ACTIVE TIME:** 5 MINUTES | **TOTAL TIME:** 5 MINUTES

4 CANNED CHIPOTLES IN ADOBO, SEEDS REMOVED

3 GARLIC CLOVES

⅔ CUP SALTED PISTACHIOS, SHELLS REMOVED

⅓ CUP EXTRA-VIRGIN OLIVE OIL

1 CUP FRESHLY GRATED MANCHEGO CHEESE

SALT, TO TASTE

1. Place the chipotles and garlic in a food processor and blitz until smooth. Add the pistachios and pulse until they are slightly crushed. Transfer the mixture to a medium bowl.

2. While whisking continually, add the olive oil in a slow, steady stream until it has emulsified.

3. Stir in the cheese, season the sauce with salt, and use immediately or store in the refrigerator.

Pork & Black Bean Sauce

YIELD: 4 CUPS | **ACTIVE TIME:** 25 MINUTES | **TOTAL TIME:** 40 MINUTES

½ LB. PORK TENDERLOIN, CUBED

2 TABLESPOONS SHAOXING WINE OR MIRIN

1-INCH PIECE OF FRESH GINGER, PEELED AND GRATED

SALT, TO TASTE

½ TEASPOON BLACK PEPPER

½ CUP BLACK BEAN PASTE

¼ CUP CANOLA OIL

2 TABLESPOONS SUGAR

1 LARGE ONION, DICED

1½ CUPS CHOPPED CABBAGE

1 LARGE ZUCCHINI, CUBED

2 CUPS CHICKEN STOCK (SEE PAGE 303)

2 TABLESPOONS CORNSTARCH

¼ CUP WATER

1. Place the pork, Shaoxing wine, ginger, salt, and pepper in a bowl and stir to combine. Let the mixture marinate at room temperature for 15 minutes.

2. Place the black bean paste, 2 tablespoons of the canola oil, and the sugar in a small saucepan and warm the mixture over medium heat, stirring constantly, for 2 minutes. Remove the pan from heat and set the mixture aside.

3. Warm a wok or a large skillet over medium heat. Add the pork and stir-fry until it begins to brown, 3 to 4 minutes. Transfer the pork to a bowl and cover it loosely with aluminum foil.

4. Add the onion, cabbage, and zucchini to the pan, season the mixture with salt, and cook, stirring occasionally, until the vegetables have softened, about 5 minutes.

5. Stir the pork and the black bean paste mixture into the pan and cook until the pork is cooked through, 3 to 4 minutes.

6. Place the cornstarch and water in a bowl, stir to combine, and then stir the slurry into the pan. Cook the sauce until it thickens, 1 to 2 minutes. Use immediately or store in the refrigerator.

Roasted Red Pepper, Corn & Herb Sauce

YIELD: 3 CUPS | **ACTIVE TIME:** 30 MINUTES | **TOTAL TIME:** 1 HOUR

2 LARGE RED BELL PEPPERS

2 TABLESPOONS UNSALTED BUTTER

5 SCALLIONS, TRIMMED AND SLICED THIN

SALT AND PEPPER, TO TASTE

KERNELS FROM 4 EARS OF CORN

ANCHO CHILE POWDER, TO TASTE

2 TABLESPOONS EXTRA-VIRGIN OLIVE OIL

2 HANDFULS OF FRESH PARSLEY, CHOPPED

2 HANDFULS OF FRESH CILANTRO, CHOPPED

¼ CUP HEAVY CREAM

¾ CUP CRUMBLED COTIJA CHEESE

1. Preheat the oven to 500°F. Place the peppers on a baking sheet, place them in the oven, and roast until they are charred all over, turning them as necessary. Remove the peppers from the oven, place them in a bowl, and cover it with plastic wrap. Let the peppers steam for 10 minutes.

2. Remove the stems, seeds, and skins from the peppers and chop the remaining flesh.

3. Place the butter in a large skillet and melt it over medium heat. Add the scallions, season them with salt, and cook, stirring occasionally, until the scallions are translucent, about 4 minutes.

4. Add two-thirds of the corn, season the mixture with ancho chile powder, and cook, stirring occasionally, until the corn is tender, about 4 minutes. Transfer the mixture to a food processor and pulse until it is a chunky puree.

5. Place the olive oil in a clean skillet and warm it over medium-high heat. Add the peppers and the remaining corn, season the mixture with salt and pepper, and cook, stirring occasionally, until the corn turns golden brown, about 6 minutes.

6. Stir in half of the parsley and half of the cilantro and cook for 30 seconds. Add the puree, cream, and cheese, reduce the heat to low, and bring the sauce to a gentle simmer.

7. Season the sauce with salt, pepper, and ancho chile powder and use immediately or store in the refrigerator.

Roasted Poblano & Caramelized Onion Sauce

YIELD: 3 CUPS | **ACTIVE TIME:** 1 HOUR | **TOTAL TIME:** 1 HOUR AND 30 MINUTES

3 POBLANO PEPPERS

3 TABLESPOONS EXTRA-VIRGIN OLIVE OIL, PLUS MORE AS NEEDED

2 LARGE ONIONS, SLICED THIN

SALT AND PEPPER, TO TASTE

KERNELS FROM 3 EARS OF CORN

1 CUP CREMA

¾ CUP FRESHLY GRATED MANCHEGO CHEESE

1. Preheat the oven to 500°F. Place the peppers on a baking sheet, place them in the oven, and roast until they are charred all over, turning them as necessary. Remove the peppers from the oven, place them in a bowl, and cover it with plastic wrap. Let the peppers steam for 10 minutes.

2. Remove the stems, seeds, and skins from the peppers and chop the remaining flesh.

3. Place the olive oil in a large skillet and warm it over medium-low heat. Add the onions, season them with salt, and cook, stirring occasionally, until the onions are caramelized and very tender, about 40 minutes.

4. Add the corn, raise the heat to medium, and cook, stirring occasionally, until the corn starts to brown, about 10 minutes. Remove the pan from heat.

5. Place the poblanos, crema, and cheese in a food processor and blitz until smooth. Transfer the mixture to a bowl and stir in the caramelized onion mixture. Use immediately or store in the refrigerator.

Brown Butter & Sage Sauce

YIELD: ¾ CUP | **ACTIVE TIME:** 5 MINUTES | **TOTAL TIME:** 10 MINUTES

¾ CUP UNSALTED BUTTER, CUT INTO SMALL PIECES

16 FRESH SAGE LEAVES

SALT AND PEPPER, TO TASTE

1. Place the butter in a large skillet and melt it over medium heat.

2. Add the sage leaves and cook, stirring occasionally, until the butter begins to brown and give off a nutty fragrance and the sage leaves become crispy. You will need to be very attentive during this step, as butter can burn in a blink of an eye.

3. Remove the pan from heat, remove the sage leaves from the butter, and season the sauce with salt and pepper. Use immediately or store in an airtight container.

Brown Butter & Sage Sauce

SEE PAGE 193

Gingery Red Pepper Sauce

YIELD: 2 CUPS | **ACTIVE TIME:** 10 MINUTES | **TOTAL TIME:** 30 MINUTES

2 RED BELL PEPPERS, STEMS AND SEEDS REMOVED, CHOPPED

1-INCH PIECE OF FRESH GINGER, PEELED AND CHOPPED

4 GARLIC CLOVES, MINCED

3 TABLESPOONS SUGAR

2 TABLESPOONS TOMATO PASTE

1 TABLESPOON EXTRA-VIRGIN OLIVE OIL

1 TABLESPOON APPLE CIDER VINEGAR

1 TABLESPOON SOY SAUCE

1. Place all of the ingredients in a food processor and blitz until smooth.

2. Transfer the mixture to a small saucepan and cook over medium heat, stirring occasionally, until it has reduced and thickened.

3. Taste, adjust the seasoning as necessary, and use immediately or store in the refrigerator.

Smoked Salmon & Asparagus Sauce

YIELD: 4 CUPS | **ACTIVE TIME:** 20 MINUTES | **TOTAL TIME:** 3 HOURS AND 45 MINUTES

4 OZ. SMOKED SALMON, SLICED

¾ CUP HEAVY CREAM

1 TEASPOON FRESHLY GRATED NUTMEG

SALT, TO TASTE

1 LB. ASPARAGUS, TRIMMED

1½ TABLESPOONS UNSALTED BUTTER

2 LEEKS, TRIMMED, RINSED WELL, AND SLICED THIN

1. Place the salmon, cream, and nutmeg in a small bowl, stir to combine, and let the mixture steep for 3 hours in the refrigerator.

2. Bring water to a boil in a large saucepan. Add salt and the asparagus and cook until the asparagus is just tender, about 3 minutes. Drain and let the asparagus cool slightly. When the asparagus is cool enough to handle, chop it.

3. Place the butter in a large skillet and warm it over medium heat. Add the asparagus and cook, stirring occasionally, until it is golden brown. Remove the asparagus from the pan and set it aside.

4. Add the leeks to the skillet, season them with salt, and cook, stirring occasionally, until they are very soft, about 15 minutes.

5. Add the asparagus and salmon-and-cream mixture to the pan, reduce the heat to low, and cook the sauce until it is warmed through, about 5 minutes. Use immediately or store in the refrigerator.

Broccoli Rabe & Ham Sauce

YIELD: 4 CUPS | **ACTIVE TIME:** 25 MINUTES | **TOTAL TIME:** 40 MINUTES

2 TABLESPOONS KOSHER SALT, PLUS MORE TO TASTE

1½ LBS. BROCCOLI RABE, TRIMMED

¼ CUP EXTRA-VIRGIN OLIVE OIL

1 SMALL YELLOW ONION, MINCED

3 GARLIC CLOVES, MINCED

1 TABLESPOON CAPERS

4 OZ. SLICED HAM, JULIENNED

1. Bring water to a boil in a large saucepan. Add the salt and broccoli rabe and cook until the broccoli rabe is tender, about 6 minutes. Drain and rinse it under cold water. Squeeze the broccoli rabe to remove as much excess water as possible, chop it, and set it aside.

2. Place the olive oil in a large skillet and warm it over medium heat. Add the onion and garlic and cook, stirring frequently, until the onion turns translucent, about 3 minutes. Stir in the capers and ham and cook until the mixture becomes very tender, about 6 minutes.

3. Add the broccoli rabe, season the sauce with salt, and cook it for 5 minutes. Use immediately or store in the refrigerator.

Sun-Dried Tomato Aioli

YIELD: 2½ CUPS | **TOTAL TIME:** 5 MINUTES | **ACTIVE TIME:** 5 MINUTES

1 CUP SUN-DRIED TOMATOES IN OLIVE OIL, DRAINED AND CHOPPED

1 CUP MAYONNAISE

1 TABLESPOON WHOLE-GRAIN MUSTARD

2 TABLESPOONS FINELY CHOPPED FRESH PARSLEY

2 TABLESPOONS MINCED SCALLIONS

1 TEASPOON WHITE BALSAMIC VINEGAR

1 GARLIC CLOVE, MINCED

2 TEASPOONS KOSHER SALT

1 TEASPOON BLACK PEPPER

1. Place all of the ingredients in a mixing bowl, stir until combined, and use immediately or store in the refrigerator.

Yakiniku Sauce

YIELD: 2 CUPS | **ACTIVE TIME:** 10 MINUTES | **TOTAL TIME:** 30 MINUTES

1 GARLIC CLOVE, CHOPPED

½ CUP YUZU JUICE

⅓ CUP SOY SAUCE

3 TABLESPOONS MIRIN

3 TABLESPOONS SUGAR

2 TEASPOONS HONEY

2 TEASPOONS SESAME OIL

1 TABLESPOON CORNSTARCH

1 TABLESPOON WATER

2 TEASPOONS TOASTED SESAME SEEDS, GROUND

1. Place all of the ingredients, except for the cornstarch, water, and sesame seeds, in a saucepan. Bring the mixture to a boil over medium heat. Reduce the heat so that it simmers and cook until it thickens slightly, about 5 minutes.

2. Strain the sauce into a small saucepan and bring it back to a simmer.

3. Place the cornstarch and water in a bowl and stir to combine. Stir the slurry and the sesame seeds into the saucepan and cook until the sauce has thickened. Use immediately or store in the refrigerator.

Sunchoke Aioli

YIELD: 2 CUPS | **ACTIVE TIME:** 10 MINUTES | **TOTAL TIME:** 30 MINUTES

2 SUNCHOKES

2 EGG YOLKS

½ GARLIC CLOVE, MINCED

½ TEASPOON DIJON MUSTARD

1 TEASPOON FRESH LEMON JUICE

½ CUP EXTRA-VIRGIN OLIVE OIL

SALT AND PEPPER, TO TASTE

1. Place the sunchokes in a small saucepan and cover them with water. Bring the water to a boil and cook the sunchokes until they are very tender, about 25 minutes.

2. Drain the sunchokes, cut them in half, and remove the flesh with a spoon. Place the sunchokes in a bowl and mash it until it is smooth.

3. Add the egg yolks, garlic, mustard, and lemon juice, and whisk vigorously until the mixture is nice and smooth.

4. While whisking continually, add the olive oil in a slow stream. Season the aioli with salt and pepper and use immediately or store in the refrigerator.

Creamy Leek Sauce

YIELD: 2 CUPS | **ACTIVE TIME:** 20 MINUTES | **TOTAL TIME:** 40 MINUTES

2½ TABLESPOONS UNSALTED BUTTER

4 LEEKS, TRIMMED, RINSED WELL, AND CHOPPED

SALT, TO TASTE

1 CUP HEAVY CREAM

¼ CUP WHOLE MILK

½ TEASPOON WHITE PEPPER

1. Warm a large skillet over low heat for 2 to 3 minutes. Add 2 tablespoons of the butter, raise the heat to medium, and melt the butter. Add the leeks and a few pinches of salt and cook until the leeks begin to gently sizzle. Reduce the heat to low, cover the pan, and cook the leeks, stirring occasionally, until they are very soft and turn a slightly darker shade of green, about 20 minutes.

2. Raise heat to medium-high, stir in the cream, milk, and white pepper, season the sauce with salt, and bring it to a boil. Reduce the heat to low and simmer the sauce until it has reduced slightly, about 5 minutes. Serve immediately.

Aromatic Béchamel Sauce

YIELD: 2 CUPS | **ACTIVE TIME:** 30 MINUTES | **TOTAL TIME:** 45 MINUTES

4 CUPS WHOLE MILK

2 BAY LEAVES

½ WHITE ONION

10 BLACK PEPPERCORNS

½ CUP UNSALTED BUTTER

⅓ CUP ALL-PURPOSE FLOUR

SALT AND WHITE PEPPER, TO TASTE

1. Place the milk, bay leaves, onion, and peppercorns in a medium saucepan and warm the mixture over low heat. Cook, stirring occasionally, until the mixture is just about to come to a boil, about 6 minutes. Remove the pan from heat, let the mixture steep for 20 minutes, and then strain. Discard the solids and set the liquid aside.

2. Place the butter in a medium saucepan and melt it over medium heat. Add the flour and stir until the mixture is smooth. Cook, stirring continually, until the mixture is golden brown, about 5 minutes.

3. Pour in ½ cup of the milk mixture and stir vigorously until you've thinned out the flour mixture. Add the remaining milk and cook, stirring continually, until the mixture thickens.

4. Season the sauce with salt and pepper and use immediately or store in the refrigerator.

Donair Sauce

YIELD: 1¼ CUPS | **ACTIVE TIME:** 5 MINUTES | **TOTAL TIME:** 5 MINUTES

7 OZ. SWEETENED CONDENSED MILK

¼ CUP WHITE VINEGAR

½ TEASPOON GARLIC POWDER

1. Place all of the ingredients in a bowl, whisk to combine, and use immediately or store in the refrigerator.

Fermented Hot Sauce

YIELD: 2 CUPS | **ACTIVE TIME:** 10 MINUTES | **TOTAL TIME:** 30 DAYS TO 6 MONTHS

2 LBS. CHILES DE ÀRBOL

1 LB. JALAPEÑO CHILE PEPPERS

5 GARLIC CLOVES

1 RED ONION, QUARTERED

3 TABLESPOONS KOSHER SALT, PLUS MORE TO TASTE

FILTERED WATER, AS NEEDED

1. Remove the tops of the peppers and split them down the middle.

2. Place the split peppers and the garlic, onion, and salt in a mason jar and cover the mixture with water. Cover the jar and shake well.

3. Place the jar away from direct sunlight and let stand for at least 30 days and up to 6 months—the flavor will improve the longer you let the mixture ferment. Occasionally unscrew the lid to release some of the gases that build up.

4. Once you are ready to make the sauce, reserve most of the brine, transfer the mixture to a blender, and puree to the desired thickness. If you want your sauce to be on the thin side, keep adding brine until you have the consistency you want. Season the sauce with salt, transfer it to an airtight container, and store it in the refrigerator for up to 3 months.

Chimichurri Redux

YIELD: 1 CUP | **ACTIVE TIME:** 5 MINUTES | **TOTAL TIME:** 5 MINUTES

1 CUP FRESH PARSLEY

1 GARLIC CLOVE

JUICE OF ¼ LEMON

1 TEASPOON CHOPPED FRESH ROSEMARY

1 TEASPOON KOSHER SALT

1 STRIP OF LEMON PEEL

1 TABLESPOON CAPERS

½ TEASPOON RED PEPPER FLAKES

BLACK PEPPER, TO TASTE

¼ CUP EXTRA-VIRGIN OLIVE OIL

1. Place all of the ingredients, except for the olive oil, in a food processor and blitz until the mixture is almost smooth, scraping down the work bowl as needed.

2. With the food processor running, add the oil in a slow stream and puree until emulsified. Use immediately or store in the refrigerator.

Pistachio Pesto

YIELD: 2 CUPS | **ACTIVE TIME:** 5 MINUTES | **TOTAL TIME:** 5 MINUTES

½ LB. UNSALTED PISTACHIOS, SHELLS REMOVED

2 OZ. PARMESAN CHEESE, GRATED

ZEST OF ½ LEMON

½ GARLIC CLOVE

½ CUP WATER

1 GENEROUS HANDFUL OF FRESH BASIL

SALT AND PEPPER, TO TASTE

½ CUP EXTRA-VIRGIN OLIVE OIL

1. Place the pistachio meats in a food processor and pulse until they are coarsely ground.

2. Add the remaining ingredients and pulse until the mixture is a slightly chunky paste. Use immediately or store in the refrigerator.

Zucchini Cream

YIELD: ½ CUP | **ACTIVE TIME:** 20 MINUTES | **TOTAL TIME:** 20 MINUTES

2 TABLESPOONS EXTRA-VIRGIN OLIVE OIL

1 ZUCCHINI, CHOPPED

½ ONION, CHOPPED

SALT AND PEPPER, TO TASTE

1. Coat the bottom of a large skillet with half of the olive oil and warm it over medium heat. Add the zucchini and onion and cook, stirring occasionally, until they are tender, about 10 minutes.

2. Season the vegetables with salt and pepper, raise the heat to medium-high, and cook until all of the liquid in the pan has evaporated.

3. Place the sautéed vegetables in a blender or food processor, add the remaining olive oil, and puree until smooth.

Parsley Pesto

YIELD: 1 CUP | **ACTIVE TIME:** 20 MINUTES | **TOTAL TIME:** 20 MINUTES

1 BUNCH OF FRESH PARSLEY

¼ CUP BREAD CRUMBS

6 TABLESPOONS EXTRA-VIRGIN OLIVE OIL, PLUS MORE TO TASTE

DASH OF WATER

3 ANCHOVIES IN OLIVE OIL, DRAINED

SALT, TO TASTE

1. Place all of the ingredients in a food processor, blitz until smooth, and use immediately or store in the refrigerator.

Chimichurri Redux
SEE PAGE 210

Balado Sauce

YIELD: 1 CUP | **ACTIVE TIME:** 5 MINUTES | **TOTAL TIME:** 5 MINUTES

2 TABLESPOONS AVOCADO OIL

2 SHALLOTS, CHOPPED

4 RED CHILE PEPPERS, STEMS AND SEEDS REMOVED, CHOPPED

1 LARGE TOMATO, CHOPPED

JUICE OF 1 LIME

1 TABLESPOON SUGAR

SALT, TO TASTE

1. Place the avocado oil in a large skillet and warm it over medium-high heat. Add the shallots, chiles, and tomato and stir-fry until the shallots have softened, about 4 minutes.

2. Stir in the lime juice, sugar, and salt and then transfer the sauce to a blender and blitz until pureed. If the sauce is too watery for your liking, place it in a saucepan and cook over medium-low heat until it has reduced to the desired consistency. Use immediately or store in the refrigerator.

Romanesco Broccoli Cream

YIELD: 4 CUPS | **ACTIVE TIME:** 15 MINUTES | **TOTAL TIME:** 25 MINUTES

SALT AND PEPPER, TO TASTE

1 LB. ROMANESCO BROCCOLI FLORETS

1 TABLESPOON EXTRA-VIRGIN OLIVE OIL, PLUS MORE AS NEEDED

½ SMALL ONION, SLICED THIN

1 OZ. PARMESAN CHEESE, GRATED

3 FRESH BASIL LEAVES

1. Bring salted water to a boil in a large saucepan and add the broccoli. Cook until it starts to feel tender, drain it, and pat it dry.

2. Coat the bottom of a skillet with olive oil and warm it over medium-high heat. Add the onion and broccoli and cook, stirring occasionally, until the onion starts to soften, about 5 minutes. Transfer the mixture to a food processor, add the remaining ingredients, and blitz until smooth.

3. If the sauce is not as thick as you would like, place it in a saucepan and cook over medium heat until it has reduced to the desired consistency. Use immediately or store in the refrigerator.

Béchamel Sauce

YIELD: 4 CUPS | **ACTIVE TIME:** 20 MINUTES | **TOTAL TIME:** 20 MINUTES

½ CUP UNSALTED BUTTER

½ CUP ALL-PURPOSE FLOUR

4 CUPS WHOLE MILK

½ TEASPOON FRESHLY GRATED NUTMEG

SALT AND PEPPER, TO TASTE

1. Place the butter in a medium saucepan and melt it over medium heat. Add the flour and cook, stirring continually, for 5 minutes, until the mixture turns golden brown.

2. Add ½ cup of the milk and stir vigorously until the mixture has thinned somewhat. Add the remaining milk and cook, stirring continually, until the mixture starts to thicken.

3. Stir in the nutmeg, season the sauce with salt and pepper, and use immediately or store in the refrigerator.

Sausage Ragù

YIELD: 4 CUPS | **ACTIVE TIME:** 30 MINUTES | **TOTAL TIME:** 4 TO 6 HOURS

2 LBS. ITALIAN SAUSAGE

2 TABLESPOONS EXTRA-VIRGIN OLIVE OIL

1 SWEET ONION, DICED

2 GREEN BELL PEPPERS, STEMS AND SEEDS REMOVED, DICED

1 (28 OZ.) CAN OF SAN MARZANO TOMATOES, WITH THEIR LIQUID

1 CUP CHOPPED FRESH BASIL

2 TEASPOONS RED PEPPER FLAKES

1 TABLESPOON ITALIAN SEASONING

1 CUP WATER, PLUS MORE AS NEEDED

SALT AND PEPPER, TO TASTE

1. Working in batches to avoid crowding the pan, place the sausage in a large saucepan and cook it over medium-high heat, stirring occasionally, until it is browned and cooked through. Remove the sausage from the pan and set it aside.

2. Add the olive oil and onion to the pan and cook the onion over medium heat, stirring occasionally, until it is translucent, about 3 minutes. Add the peppers and cook, stirring occasionally, for 5 minutes.

3. Chop the sausage and add it to the pan along with the remaining ingredients. Bring the sauce to a boil, reduce the heat, and partially cover the pan.

4. Simmer the sauce for 4 to 6 hours, until the flavor has developed to your liking. Add water as needed so that the sauce doesn't burn. Use immediately or store in the refrigerator.

Chipotle & Blue Cheese Sauce

YIELD: 1½ CUPS | **ACTIVE TIME:** 5 MINUTES | **TOTAL TIME:** 5 MINUTES

3 OZ. BLUE CHEESE, CRUMBLED

2 TABLESPOONS MINCED CHIPOTLE PEPPERS IN ADOBO

2 TABLESPOONS BUTTERMILK

¼ CUP SOUR CREAM

¼ CUP KEWPIE MAYO

1 TABLESPOON RICE VINEGAR

2 TEASPOONS SUGAR

SALT AND PEPPER, TO TASTE

1. Place all of the ingredients in a food processor, blitz until smooth, and use immediately or store in the refrigerator.

Habanero, Calabrian Chile & Pineapple Hot Sauce

YIELD: 1½ CUPS | **ACTIVE TIME:** 15 MINUTES | **TOTAL TIME:** 1 HOUR

6 GARLIC CLOVES, MINCED

2 TABLESPOONS MINCED FRESH GINGER

½ LB. HABANERO CHILE PEPPERS, STEMS REMOVED

4 OZ. CALABRIAN CHILE PEPPERS, STEMS REMOVED

1 LB. PINEAPPLE, CHOPPED

2 CARROTS, PEELED AND CHOPPED

1½ CUPS RICE VINEGAR

¼ CUP MAPLE SYRUP

2 TABLESPOONS KOSHER SALT

1. Place the garlic and ginger in a saucepan and cook, stirring continually, for 1 minute.

2. Add the remaining ingredients, cover the pan, reduce the heat to low, and cook until the carrots are tender, about 30 minutes.

3. Remove the pan from heat and let the sauce cool to room temperature.

4. Transfer the sauce to a food processor and puree until very smooth. Taste, adjust the seasoning as necessary, and use immediately or store in the refrigerator.

Rose Sauce

YIELD: 4 CUPS | **ACTIVE TIME:** 30 MINUTES | **TOTAL TIME:** 30 MINUTES

1 LB. CANNED TOMATOES, DRAINED

1 TABLESPOON UNSALTED BUTTER

2 TABLESPOONS CHOPPED WHITE ONION

SALT, TO TASTE

½ CUP HEAVY CREAM

1. Place the tomatoes in a food processor and blitz until smooth.

2. Place the butter in a saucepan and melt it over medium heat. Add the onion and a pinch of salt, stir, and cook until the onion begins to gently sizzle. Reduce the heat to low, cover the pan, and cook, stirring occasionally, until the onion has softened and is starting to brown, about 10 minutes.

3. Add the pureed tomatoes and a few pinches of salt. Bring the sauce to a boil, then reduce the heat to low and simmer for 20 minutes.

4. As the tomato sauce cooks, place the cream in a small saucepan and warm it over low heat until it has reduced by about half.

5. When the tomato sauce has thickened to the desired texture, stir in the reduced cream, season the sauce with salt, and use immediately or store in the refrigerator.

Peppercorn Cream Sauce

YIELD: 1 CUP | **ACTIVE TIME:** 20 MINUTES | **TOTAL TIME:** 20 MINUTES

2 TABLESPOONS PEPPERCORNS

1 CUP HEAVY CREAM

SALT, TO TASTE

1. Using a mortar and pestle, roughly grind the peppercorns. Place them in a dry skillet and toast for 1 minute, shaking the pan occasionally.

2. Add the cream and a pinch of salt, reduce the heat to medium-low, and cook the sauce, stirring constantly, for 2 minutes. Use the sauce immediately or store it in the refrigerator.

Traditional Turkey Gravy

YIELD: 6 CUPS | **ACTIVE TIME:** 15 MINUTES | **TOTAL TIME:** 30 MINUTES

½ CUP TURKEY FAT SKIMMED FROM DRIPPINGS

¼ CUP UNSALTED BUTTER

¼ CUP CHOPPED SHALLOTS

4 GARLIC CLOVES, MINCED

2 TABLESPOONS FRESH THYME

1 TABLESPOON CHOPPED FRESH SAGE

2 TEASPOONS CHOPPED FRESH ROSEMARY

¼ CUP WHITE WINE

½ CUP ALL-PURPOSE FLOUR, SIFTED

2 CUPS PAN DRIPPINGS, FAT SKIMMED OFF

4 CUPS CHICKEN STOCK (SEE PAGE 303)

SALT AND PEPPER, TO TASTE

1. After the turkey has been cooked, transfer it to a resting rack and pour the pan drippings into a heat-resistant measuring cup. Allow the fat to rise to the surface—placing the drippings in the refrigerator or freezer will speed up the process. Skim off the fat and reserve it.

2. Place a large skillet over medium heat. Add the butter and turkey fat and warm the mixture. Add the shallots and garlic and cook, stirring continually, until the shallots are translucent, about 3 minutes.

3. Add the herbs, cook for 30 seconds, and then deglaze the pan with the white wine, scraping up any browned bits from the bottom of the pan. Cook off the alcohol, add the flour, and cook, stirring continually. The mixture should have the consistency of wet sand, with a nutty aroma.

4. Slowly add the pan drippings, whisking continually to prevent the gravy from becoming lumpy.

5. Slowly whisk in 1 cup of stock. Slowly whisk in the remaining stock and let the gravy simmer until it has reduced to the desired consistency.

6. Taste the gravy, season it as necessary, and use immediately.

Traditional Chicken Gravy

YIELD: 6 CUPS | **ACTIVE TIME:** 15 MINUTES | **TOTAL TIME:** 30 MINUTES

½ CUP CHICKEN FAT SKIMMED FROM DRIPPINGS

¼ CUP UNSALTED BUTTER

¼ CUP CHOPPED SHALLOTS

4 GARLIC CLOVES, MINCED

2 TABLESPOONS FRESH THYME

1 TABLESPOON CHOPPED FRESH SAGE

2 TEASPOONS CHOPPED FRESH ROSEMARY

¼ CUP WHITE WINE

½ CUP ALL-PURPOSE FLOUR, SIFTED

2 CUPS PAN DRIPPINGS, FAT SKIMMED OFF

4 CUPS CHICKEN STOCK (SEE PAGE 303)

SALT AND PEPPER, TO TASTE

1. After the chicken has been cooked, transfer it to a resting rack and pour the pan drippings into a heat-resistant measuring cup. Allow the fat to rise to the surface—placing the drippings in the refrigerator or freezer will speed up the process. Skim off the fat and reserve it.

2. Place a large skillet over medium heat. Add the butter and chicken fat and warm the mixture. Add the shallots and garlic and cook, stirring continually, until the shallots are translucent, about 3 minutes.

3. Add the herbs, cook for 30 seconds, and then deglaze the pan with the white wine, scraping up any browned bits from the bottom of the pan. Cook off the alcohol, add the flour, and cook, stirring continually. The mixture should have the consistency of wet sand, with a nutty aroma.

4. Slowly add the pan drippings, whisking continually to prevent the gravy from becoming lumpy.

5. Slowly whisk in 1 cup of stock. Slowly whisk in the remaining stock and let the gravy simmer until it has reduced to the desired consistency.

6. Taste the gravy, season it as necessary, and use immediately.

Peppercorn Cream Sauce
SEE PAGE 222

Rabbit Ragù

YIELD: 5 CUPS | **ACTIVE TIME:** 30 MINUTES | **TOTAL TIME:** 2 HOURS

¼ CUP EXTRA-VIRGIN OLIVE OIL

3½ LB. RABBIT, CUT INTO 8 BONE-IN PIECES

SALT AND PEPPER, TO TASTE

1 CUP ALL-PURPOSE FLOUR

1 YELLOW ONION, DICED

2 CELERY STALKS, DICED

2 CARROTS, PEELED AND DICED

1 GARLIC CLOVE, MINCED

2 TABLESPOONS TOMATO PASTE

½ CUP RED WINE

1 (28 OZ.) CAN OF CRUSHED TOMATOES

1 CUP CHICKEN STOCK (SEE PAGE 303)

2 BAY LEAVES

2 SPRIGS OF FRESH ROSEMARY

4 SPRIGS OF FRESH THYME

1. Place the olive oil in a large cast-iron Dutch oven and warm it over medium heat. Season the pieces of rabbit with salt and pepper, dredge them in the flour, and shake to remove any excess.

2. Add the rabbit to the pot and cook, turning them as necessary, until the pieces are browned all over, 12 to 15 minutes.

3. Use a slotted spoon to remove the rabbit from the pot and set it aside. Add the onion, celery, carrots, and garlic and cook, stirring frequently, until browned.

4. Stir in the tomato paste and cook for 4 minutes.

5. Add the wine and let the mixture come to a boil. Reduce the heat and cook until the wine has reduced by half, about 10 minutes.

6. Add the tomatoes, stock, bay leaves, rosemary, and thyme and simmer for 2 minutes before adding the rabbit back to the pot. Simmer until the flavor has developed to your liking, about 1½ hours.

7. Remove the rabbit from the pot and set it aside. Remove the bay leaves, rosemary, and thyme from the sauce and discard them. When the rabbit is cool enough to handle, remove the meat from the bones and shred it. Discard the bones and return the meat to the sauce. Use immediately or store in the refrigerator.

Steak Sauce

YIELD: 1½ CUPS | **ACTIVE TIME:** 5 MINUTES | **TOTAL TIME:** 5 MINUTES

1¼ CUPS KETCHUP

2 TABLESPOONS YELLOW MUSTARD

2 TABLESPOONS WORCESTERSHIRE SAUCE

1½ TABLESPOONS APPLE CIDER VINEGAR

4 DROPS OF HOT SAUCE

½ TEASPOON KOSHER SALT

½ TEASPOON BLACK PEPPER

1. Place all of the ingredients in a bowl, whisk to combine, and use immediately or store in the refrigerator.

Chipotle & Cilantro Chimichurri

YIELD: ½ CUP | **ACTIVE TIME:** 5 MINUTES | **TOTAL TIME:** 15 MINUTES

1 CHIPOTLE IN ADOBO

1 CUP FRESH CILANTRO

2 GARLIC CLOVES

2 TABLESPOONS EXTRA-VIRGIN OLIVE OIL

JUICE OF 1 LIME

ZEST OF ½ LIME

SALT AND PEPPER, TO TASTE

1. Place all of the ingredients in a food processor, blitz until smooth, and use immediately or store in the refrigerator.

Chimichurri Sauce

YIELD: 2 CUPS | **ACTIVE TIME:** 10 MINUTES | **TOTAL TIME:** 10 MINUTES

1 CUP FRESH PARSLEY

2 LARGE GARLIC CLOVES, SMASHED

1 TEASPOON DRIED THYME

¼ TEASPOON RED PEPPER FLAKES

½ CUP WATER

¼ CUP WHITE WINE VINEGAR

¼ CUP EXTRA-VIRGIN OLIVE OIL

1 TEASPOON FINE SEA SALT

⅛ TEASPOON BLACK PEPPER

1. Use a mortar and pestle or a food processor to combine the ingredients until the sauce has the desired texture. Use immediately or store in the refrigerator.

Turkey Giblet Gravy

YIELD: 5 CUPS | **ACTIVE TIME:** 15 MINUTES | **TOTAL TIME:** 1 HOUR AND 30 MINUTES

2 TABLESPOONS EXTRA-VIRGIN OLIVE OIL

GIBLETS FROM 1 TURKEY (NECK, HEART, LIVER, GIZZARD)

1 CUP SLICED SHALLOTS

½ CUP CHOPPED CELERY

½ CUP CHOPPED CARROT

4 GARLIC CLOVES, SLICED

3 SPRIGS OF FRESH THYME

1 SPRIG OF FRESH ROSEMARY

5 CUPS WATER

½ CUP UNSALTED BUTTER

½ CUP ALL-PURPOSE FLOUR, SIFTED

SALT AND PEPPER, TO TASTE

1. Place the olive oil in a large saucepan and warm it over medium-high heat. Add the giblets and cook until browned all over, turning them as necessary.

2. Add the shallots, celery, carrot, and garlic and cook, stirring occasionally, until the shallots start to brown.

3. Add the thyme, rosemary, and water, cover the pan, and bring the mixture to a boil. Reduce the heat and simmer the mixture for about an hour so the flavors develop. There should be about 4 cups of liquid in the pan.

4. Strain the liquid and set it aside. Discard all of the solids, except for the turkey neck. Transfer the neck to a cutting board, remove the meat from it, and set it aside. Discard the neck bones.

5. Place the butter in the pan and melt it over medium heat. Add the flour and cook, stirring continually. The mixture should have the consistency of wet sand, with a nutty aroma.

6. Slowly add 1 cup of the reserved liquid, whisking continually. Slowly whisk in the remaining liquid and let the gravy simmer until it has reduced to the desired consistency.

7. Taste the gravy, season it as necessary, and use immediately.

Beef Gravy

YIELD: 2 CUPS | **ACTIVE TIME:** 20 MINUTES | **TOTAL TIME:** 30 MINUTES

1 CUP DRY RED WINE

1½ CUPS BEEF STOCK (SEE PAGE 306)

1 TABLESPOON UNSALTED BUTTER

1 TABLESPOON ALL-PURPOSE FLOUR

1 TABLESPOON FRESH THYME

SALT AND PEPPER, TO TASTE

1. After removing your roast from the oven, pour the juices from the roasting pan into a fat separator; discard the fat and return the juices to the original roasting pan. Note that there is still flavor blanketing the roasting pan, so be sure to use the same pan.

2. Set the roasting pan over high heat—it may be necessary to use two burners if the roasting rack is too large for one. Add the red wine and stock to the pan and bring the mixture to a gentle simmer, using a wooden spoon to scrape up any bits that are stuck to the bottom of the pan.

3. Stir in the butter and then the flour. Depending on how thick you want the gravy, add more butter and flour in incremental and equal proportions.

4. When the gravy has thickened to the desired consistency. Stir in the thyme, season the gravy with salt and pepper, and use immediately.

TIP: If you don't have a have fat separator, bring the roasting pan to the sink and tilt to one side. Next, with a large spoon or ladle, slowly skim off the fat that remains at the top of the dish.

Madeira Sauce

YIELD: 1½ CUPS | **ACTIVE TIME:** 20 MINUTES | **TOTAL TIME:** 25 MINUTES

2 TABLESPOONS UNSALTED BUTTER

1 SMALL SHALLOT, MINCED

1 TABLESPOON ALL-PURPOSE FLOUR

¼ CUP DRY RED WINE

¾ CUP MADEIRA

1 CUP BEEF STOCK (SEE PAGE 306)

1 TEASPOON FRESH THYME

1 TEASPOON CHOPPED FRESH ROSEMARY

SALT AND PEPPER, TO TASTE

1. Place the butter in a cast-iron skillet and melt it over medium heat. Add the shallot and cook, stirring occasionally, until it is translucent, about 3 minutes.

2. Add the flour to the pan and cook, stirring continually, for 1 minute. Reduce the heat to medium-low and then stir in the dry red wine, Madeira, stock, thyme, and rosemary.

3. Cook the sauce for about 15 to 20 minutes, until it has reduced to the desired consistency.

4. Season the sauce with salt and pepper and use immediately or store in the refrigerator.

Pizzaiola Sauce

YIELD: 4 CUPS | **ACTIVE TIME:** 35 MINUTES | **TOTAL TIME:** 45 MINUTES

¼ CUP EXTRA-VIRGIN OLIVE OIL

4 GARLIC CLOVES, MINCED

2 LBS. PLUM TOMATOES, CRUSHED

¼ CUP SUN-DRIED TOMATOES IN OLIVE OIL, DRAINED

1 TEASPOON FRESH OREGANO

1 TEASPOON FRESH THYME

1 TEASPOON RED PEPPER FLAKES

¼ CUP DRY WHITE WINE

SALT AND PEPPER, TO TASTE

½ CUP FRESH BASIL, CHOPPED

1. Place the extra-virgin olive oil in a cast-iron skillet and warm it over medium heat. Add the garlic and cook, stirring continually, for 1 minute.

2. Add the plum tomatoes, sun-dried tomatoes, oregano, thyme, and red pepper flakes and simmer the sauce for 15 minutes.

3. Stir in the the wine, season the sauce with salt and pepper, and simmer it for another 20 minutes.

4. Stir the basil into the sauce and use immediately or store in the refrigerator.

Beef Gravy
SEE PAGE 232

Sun-Dried Tomato Pesto

YIELD: 2 CUPS | **ACTIVE TIME:** 5 MINUTES | **TOTAL TIME:** 5 MINUTES

12 SUN-DRIED TOMATOES IN OLIVE OIL, DRAINED

½ CUP FRESH BASIL LEAVES

¼ SMALL SHALLOT

¼ CUP PINE NUTS

1 GARLIC CLOVE

1 TABLESPOON BLACK PEPPER

1 TEASPOON SEA SALT

½ CUP EXTRA-VIRGIN OLIVE OIL

1. Place all of the ingredients, except for the olive oil, in a food processor and pulse until the mixture is a thick paste.

2. With the food processor running, add the olive oil in a slow stream until it has emulsified. Use immediately or store in the refrigerator.

Garlic & Chive Steak Sauce

YIELD: 1 CUP | **ACTIVE TIME:** 5 MINUTES | **TOTAL TIME:** 5 MINUTES

½ CUP SOUR CREAM

¼ CUP CHOPPED FRESH CHIVES

3 GARLIC CLOVES, MINCED

JUICE OF ¼ SMALL LEMON

SALT AND PEPPER, TO TASTE

1. Place all of the ingredients in a bowl, stir to combine, and use immediately or store in the refrigerator.

Broccoli Rabe Pesto

YIELD: 3 CUPS | **ACTIVE TIME:** 10 MINUTES | **TOTAL TIME:** 25 MINUTES

SALT AND PEPPER, TO TASTE

1 BUNCH OF BROCCOLI RABE, TRIMMED

1 CUP PINE NUTS

4 GARLIC CLOVES

1 CUP FRESH BASIL

1 CUP FRESHLY GRATED PARMESAN CHEESE

ZEST OF 1 LEMON

1 CUP EXTRA-VIRGIN OLIVE OIL

1. Bring salted water to a boil in a large saucepan and prepare an ice bath. Add the broccoli rabe and cook for 1 minute. Drain the broccoli rabe and plunge it into the ice bath until it has cooled completely. Drain the broccoli rabe again and set it aside.

2. Preheat the oven to 325°F.

3. Place the pine nuts on a baking sheet, place them in the oven, and toast them until they are slightly browned, about 8 minutes.

4. Remove the pine nuts from the oven and transfer them to a food processor. Add the broccoli rabe and remaining ingredients and blitz until the pesto has the desired texture. Use immediately or store in the refrigerator.

Fontina Sauce

YIELD: 2 CUPS | **ACTIVE TIME:** 10 MINUTES | **TOTAL TIME:** 10 MINUTES

2 TABLESPOONS EXTRA-VIRGIN OLIVE OIL

SALT, TO TASTE

1 LARGE ONION, GRATED

½ CUP CHICKEN STOCK (SEE PAGE 303)

4 OZ. FONTINA CHEESE, GRATED

¾ CUP HEAVY CREAM

1½ TEASPOONS WORCESTERSHIRE SAUCE

1. Place the olive oil in a large skillet and warm it over medium heat. Add the onion and a couple pinches of salt and cook, stirring occasionally, for 2 minutes.

2. Reduce the heat to low, cover the pan, and cook the onion, stirring occasionally, until it becomes very soft, about 15 minutes.

3. Remove the cover from the pan, raise the heat to medium-high, and add the stock, cheese, and cream, and stir until the cheese has melted and the sauce is bubbly.

4. Stir in the Worcestershire sauce and use immediately or store in the refrigerator.

General Tso Sauce

YIELD: 3 CUPS | **ACTIVE TIME:** 5 MINUTES | **TOTAL TIME:** 30 MINUTES

2 TABLESPOONS CANOLA
OIL

1 TEASPOON RED PEPPER
FLAKES

3 GARLIC CLOVES, MINCED

2 TABLESPOONS MINCED
FRESH GINGER

¼ CUP CHOPPED SCALLIONS

1 JALAPEÑO CHILE PEPPER,
STEM AND SEEDS REMOVED,
MINCED

½ CUP SOY SAUCE

½ CUP HOISIN SAUCE (SEE
PAGE 282)

¼ CUP RICE VINEGAR

3 TABLESPOONS HONEY

1 CUP CHICKEN STOCK (SEE
PAGE 303)

2 TABLESPOONS
CORNSTARCH

¼ CUP WATER

1. Place the canola oil, red pepper flakes, garlic, ginger, scallions, and jalapeño in a medium saucepan and cook the mixture over medium heat, stirring frequently, until the scallions have softened, 3 to 5 minutes.

2. Stir in the soy sauce, Hoisin Sauce, rice vinegar, honey, and stock and simmer the sauce for 15 to 20 minutes.

3. Place the cornstarch and water in a bowl and whisk to combine. Stir the slurry into the simmering sauce and cook until the sauce has thickened, about 1 minute. Remove the pan from heat. Use immediately or store in the refrigerator.

Bulgogi Sauce

YIELD: 2 CUPS | **ACTIVE TIME:** 15 MINUTES | **TOTAL TIME:** 30 MINUTES

3 OZ. POTATO STARCH

½ CUP WATER

3 TABLESPOONS BROWN SUGAR

1 CUP SOY SAUCE

6 TABLESPOONS RICE VINEGAR

1 TABLESPOON OYSTER SAUCE

4 GARLIC CLOVES, MINCED

1 TABLESPOON SESAME OIL

1. Place the potato starch and water in a bowl, whisk to combine, and set the slurry aside.

2. Place the remaining ingredients in a saucepan and warm the mixture over medium heat. Stir in the slurry and cook until the sauce has thickened.

3. Taste, adjust the seasoning as necessary, and use immediately or store in an airtight container.

Ultimate XO Sauce

YIELD: 4 CUPS | **ACTIVE TIME:** 15 MINUTES | **TOTAL TIME:** 30 MINUTES

½ CUP DRIED SHRIMP

6 DRIED SHIITAKE MUSHROOM CAPS

½ CUP COOKED BACON

½ CUP CHINESE SAUSAGE OR SOPPRESSATA

2 CUPS CANOLA OIL

2 SHALLOTS, MINCED

¼ CUP THINLY SLICED GARLIC

¼ CUP MINCED FRESH GINGER

¼ CUP RED PEPPER FLAKES

4 STAR ANISE PODS

1 CINNAMON STICK

½ CUP DRIED PORK

½ CUP SHAOXING WINE

½ CUP SOY SAUCE

1 TABLESPOON FISH SAUCE

½ CUP SUGAR

½ CUP FRIED GARLIC

½ CUP FRIED SHALLOTS

1. Place the dried shrimp and mushrooms in separate bowls, cover them with hot water, and let them soak until they are soft but still slightly firm, 15 to 20 minutes. Drain the shrimp and mushrooms.

2. Working with one ingredient at a time and removing it when it is chopped, finely chop the shrimp, mushrooms, bacon, and Chinese sausage in a food processor. Set the ingredients aside.

3. Place 1½ cups of the canola oil in a large skillet and warm it over medium-high heat. Add the shallots and stir-fry for 1 minute. Add the garlic and ginger and stir-fry for 1 minute. Stir in the red pepper flakes, star anise, and cinnamon stick and stir-fry for another minute.

4. Add the remaining canola oil the and mushrooms and stir-fry for 1 minute. Add the sausage, shrimp, bacon, and dried pork and stir-fry for 1 minute.

5. Slowly add the wine all at once; please be careful as there may be some flames when adding the alcohol. Simmer for about 30 seconds, then stir in the soy sauce, fish sauce, and sugar and simmer for another 30 seconds. Add the fried garlic and fried shallots, giving the sauce a good stir, and turn off the heat.

6. Don't let the sauce cool for more than 5 minutes before using or storing in the refrigerator.

Arugula Pesto

YIELD: 1 CUP | **ACTIVE TIME:** 10 MINUTES | **TOTAL TIME:** 10 MINUTES

2 CUPS ARUGULA

1 GARLIC CLOVE, MINCED

½ TEASPOON KOSHER SALT

¼ CUP WALNUTS

1 TEASPOON LEMON ZEST

⅓ CUP EXTRA-VIRGIN OLIVE OIL

1 TEASPOON FRESH LEMON JUICE

1. Place the arugula, garlic, salt, walnuts, and lemon zest in a food processor and pulse until the mixture is pureed, scraping down the side of the work bowl as needed.

2. With the food processor running, drizzle in the olive oil until it has emulsified. Add the lemon juice and pulse to incorporate.

3. Taste, adjust the seasoning as necessary, and use immediately or store in the refrigerator.

Radicchio Cream Sauce

YIELD: 3 CUPS | **ACTIVE TIME:** 15 MINUTES | **TOTAL TIME:** 30 MINUTES

3 TABLESPOONS UNSALTED BUTTER

1 LARGE HEAD OF RADICCHIO, CORED AND GRATED

SALT AND WHITE PEPPER, TO TASTE

3 TABLESPOONS WARM WATER

1½ CUPS HEAVY CREAM

1. Warm a large skillet over medium heat for 2 to 3 minutes and then add the butter. When it melts and stops foaming, add the radicchio, a couple pinches of salt and white pepper, and cook, stirring occasionally, until the radicchio wilts, about 5 minutes.

2. Add the warm water and cook until the radicchio has softened, another 4 to 5 minutes. Using a slotted spoon, transfer the radicchio to a bowl and cover it to keep warm.

3. Add the cream to the skillet and bring it to a simmer. Reduce heat to low and cook until the cream has reduced, about 15 minutes.

4. Add the reduced cream to the bowl containing the radicchio and stir to combine. Use immediately or store in the refrigerator.

Arugula Pesto
SEE PAGE 243

Blender Hollandaise

YIELD: 1¼ CUPS | **ACTIVE TIME:** 10 MINUTES | **TOTAL TIME:** 10 MINUTES

6 LARGE EGG YOLKS

½ TEASPOON KOSHER SALT

¼ CUP FRESH LEMON JUICE

1 CUP UNSALTED BUTTER

1. Place the egg yolks, salt, and lemon juice in a food processor and blitz until smooth.

2. Place the butter in a small saucepan and melt it over medium-low heat, being careful not to let it brown.

3. While the butter is hot, turn on the food processor and slowly drizzle in the butter until it has emulsified. Taste, adjust the seasoning as necessary, and use immediately.

Sofrito

YIELD: 2 CUPS | **ACTIVE TIME:** 5 MINUTES | **TOTAL TIME:** 5 MINUTES

2 POBLANO PEPPERS, STEMS AND SEEDS REMOVED

1 WHITE ONION, QUARTERED

1 RED BELL PEPPER, STEMS AND SEEDS REMOVED

1 GREEN BELL PEPPER, STEMS AND SEEDS REMOVED

3 PLUM TOMATOES

2 GARLIC CLOVES, CHOPPED

1 TABLESPOON CUMIN

2 TABLESPOONS ADOBO SEASONING

1. Place all of the ingredients in a food processor, blitz until smooth, and use immediately or store in the refrigerator.

Tamarind Sauce

YIELD: 1½ CUPS | **ACTIVE TIME:** 20 MINUTES | **TOTAL TIME:** 20 MINUTES

¼ CUP TAMARIND PULP

¾ CUP HOT WATER

2 TABLESPOONS SOY SAUCE

3 TABLESPOONS REAL MAPLE SYRUP

1 TABLESPOON SESAME OIL

2 GARLIC CLOVES, MINCED

1 TABLESPOON MINCED FRESH GINGER

1. Place the tamarind pulp in a small bowl and add the hot water. Stir, breaking up the paste until it has thinned, and then push the mixture through a strainer to remove the seeds. Discard the seeds.

2. Add the soy sauce and maple syrup to the strained pulp and set the mixture aside.

3. Place the sesame oil in a large skillet and warm it over high heat. Add the garlic and ginger and cook, stirring continually, for 1 minute.

4. Add the tamarind mixture and cook, stirring occasionally, until the sauce is warmed through. Use immediately or store in the refrigerator.

Red Bell Pepper & Shallot Pesto

YIELD: 2 CUPS | **ACTIVE TIME:** 20 MINUTES | **TOTAL TIME:** 45 MINUTES

3 RED BELL PEPPERS

3 TABLESPOONS EXTRA-VIRGIN OLIVE OIL

3 SHALLOTS, DICED

SALT, TO TASTE

1 TABLESPOON WORCESTERSHIRE SAUCE

¾ CUP CRUMBLED FETA CHEESE

1. Preheat the oven to 500°F. Place the peppers on a baking sheet, place them in the oven, and roast the peppers until they are tender and charred all over. Remove the peppers from the oven, place them in a mixing bowl, and let them cool.

2. When the peppers are cool enough to handle, remove the skins, stems, and seeds and discard them. Set the roasted peppers aside.

3. Place the olive oil in a small skillet and warm it over medium heat. Add the shallots and cook, stirring occasionally, until they are browned, about 10 minutes.

4. Place the peppers, shallots, and the remaining ingredients in a food processor and blitz until very smooth. Use immediately or store in the refrigerator.

Mascarpone Sauce

YIELD: 2 CUPS | **ACTIVE TIME:** 15 MINUTES | **TOTAL TIME:** 30 MINUTES

3 TABLESPOONS PINE NUTS

⅛ TEASPOON KOSHER SALT

½ CUP WALNUT PIECES

2 BLACK GARLIC CLOVES

½ CUP MASCARPONE CHEESE

3½ TABLESPOONS WHOLE MILK

3 TABLESPOONS FRESHLY GRATED PARMESAN CHEESE

WHITE PEPPER, TO TASTE

1. Warm a small skillet over medium-low heat for 2 minutes. Add the pine nuts and cook, stirring frequently, until they begin to brown in spots, 3 to 4 minutes. Remove the pan from heat and stir in the salt. Set the pine nuts aside.

2. Place the walnuts and black garlic in a food processor and blitz until the mixture is coarse crumbs. Transfer the mixture to a small saucepan and add the mascarpone, milk, and Parmesan. Season with pepper and warm the mixture over medium-low heat until it comes to a simmer.

3. Remove the pan from heat, stir in the toasted pine nuts, and use immediately or store in the refrigerator.

Pico de Gallo

YIELD: 1 CUP | **ACTIVE TIME:** 10 MINUTES | **TOTAL TIME:** 25 MINUTES

2 LARGE TOMATOES, FINELY DICED

½ ONION, FINELY DICED

2 JALAPEÑO CHILE PEPPERS, STEMS AND SEEDS REMOVED, FINELY DICED

SALT, TO TASTE

1 CUP FRESH CILANTRO, CHOPPED

1. Place the tomatoes, onion, and chiles in a small mixing bowl and stir to combine. Season the pico de gallo with salt, stir in the cilantro, and refrigerate the salsa for 15 minutes before serving.

Tamarind Sauce
SEE PAGE 250

Gorgonzola Cream Sauce

YIELD: 3 CUPS | **ACTIVE TIME:** 15 MINUTES | **TOTAL TIME:** 15 MINUTES

2 CUPS HEAVY CREAM

4 OZ. GORGONZOLA DOLCE CHEESE, CHOPPED

⅔ CUP FRESHLY GRATED PARMESAN CHEESE

1 TEASPOON FRESHLY GRATED NUTMEG

SALT AND WHITE PEPPER, TO TASTE

1. Place the cream and cheeses in a medium saucepan and cook the mixture over medium heat, stirring occasionally, until it is gently simmering and the sauce is smooth, about 5 minutes. Continue to simmer the sauce until it is thick enough to coat the back of a wooden spoon, about 8 minutes.

2. Stir in the nutmeg, season the sauce with salt and white pepper, and use immediately or store in the refrigerator.

Mojo de Ajo

YIELD: 3 CUPS | **ACTIVE TIME:** 20 MINUTES | **TOTAL TIME:** 45 MINUTES

10 OZ. GARLIC CLOVES, UNPEELED

1 CUP UNSALTED BUTTER

2 TABLESPOONS GUAJILLO CHILE POWDER

2 TABLESPOONS FRESH EPAZOTE LEAVES

SALT, TO TASTE

1. Place the garlic cloves in a dry skillet and toast them over medium heat until lightly charred in spots, about 10 minutes, turning them occasionally. Remove the garlic from the pan and let it cool slightly. When the garlic is cool enough to handle, peel it and set it aside.

2. Place the butter in a skillet and melt it over medium heat. Add the garlic and cook until the butter begins to foam and brown slightly. Remove the pan from heat and let the mixture cool to room temperature.

3. Place the butter, garlic, guajillo powder, and epazote in a blender and puree until smooth. Season the sauce with salt and use immediately or store in the refrigerator.

Beginner's Mole

YIELD: 6 CUPS | **ACTIVE TIME:** 40 MINUTES | **TOTAL TIME:** 1 HOUR

½ CUP SESAME SEEDS

5 WHOLE CLOVES

1 CINNAMON STICK

½ TEASPOON ANISE SEEDS

¼ TEASPOON CORIANDER SEEDS

6 TABLESPOONS LARD

6 GUAJILLO CHILE PEPPERS, STEMS AND SEEDS REMOVED

4 ANCHO CHILE PEPPERS, STEMS AND SEEDS REMOVED

¼ CUP RAISINS

¼ CUP BLANCHED ALMONDS

¼ CUP PUMPKIN SEEDS

2 CORN TORTILLAS, TORN INTO PIECES

4 CUPS CHICKEN STOCK (SEE PAGE 303)

1 TABLET OF ABUELITA CHOCOLATE

SALT AND PEPPER, TO TASTE

1. Place the sesame seeds in a dry skillet and toast them over medium heat until they lightly browned, about 2 minutes, shaking the pan occasionally. Remove the sesame seeds from the pan and place them in a food processor.

2. Add the cloves, cinnamon stick, anise seeds, and coriander seeds to the skillet and toast until fragrant, shaking the pan so that they do not burn. Transfer to the food processor.

3. Place half of the lard in a skillet and warm it over medium heat. Add the chiles and fry until they are fragrant and pliable, about 1 minute. Transfer the chiles to a bowl, cover them with hot water, and soak for 20 minutes.

4. Place the raisins, almonds, pumpkin seeds, and tortillas in the skillet and cook, stirring frequently, until the seeds turn golden brown, about 3 minutes. Transfer the contents of the skillet to the blender, add the chiles and half of the stock, and puree until smooth.

5. Place the remaining lard in a stockpot and warm it over medium heat. Add the puree, cook for 3 minutes, and then stir in the remaining stock and the chocolate. Reduce the heat and simmer the sauce for 30 minutes, stirring frequently.

6. Season the sauce with salt and pepper and use immediately or store in the refrigerator.

Pipian Verde

YIELD: 6 CUPS | **ACTIVE TIME:** 20 MINUTES | **TOTAL TIME:** 50 MINUTES

¼ CUP EXTRA-VIRGIN OLIVE OIL

½ CUP RAW PEANUTS

½ CUP RAW ALMONDS

1 LB. GREEN PUMPKIN SEEDS

1 LB. TOMATILLOS, HUSKED, RINSED, AND QUARTERED

3 SERRANO CHILE PEPPERS, STEMS AND SEEDS REMOVED, CHOPPED

1 JALAPEÑO CHILE PEPPER, STEMS AND SEEDS REMOVED, CHOPPED

1 PASILLA CHILE PEPPER, STEMS AND SEEDS REMOVED, CHOPPED

1 CUP PACKED FRESH SPINACH

½ BUNCH OF FRESH CILANTRO, CHOPPED

1 CUP CHOPPED ROMAINE LETTUCE

3 SPRIGS OF FRESH EPAZOTE LEAVES

1 BUNCH OF SCALLIONS, TRIMMED AND CHOPPED

1 TABLESPOON CUMIN SEEDS

2 TABLESPOONS SESAME SEEDS

½ WHITE ONION, CHOPPED

3 GARLIC CLOVES, CHOPPED

SALT, TO TASTE

1. Place the olive oil in a large saucepan and warm it over medium heat. Add the peanuts and almonds and fry until fragrant and browned, about 4 minutes. Place the pumpkin seeds in the pan and cook, stirring frequently to make sure that they don't burn, until golden brown. Place the nuts and pumpkin seeds in a food processor. Leave the olive oil in the pan.

2. Working with one ingredient at a time, add the tomatillos, chile peppers, spinach, cilantro, lettuce, and epazote to the food processor and blitz until smooth. When all of these have been incorporated, add the scallions, cumin seeds, sesame seeds, onion, and garlic and blitz until the sauce is smooth.

3. Warm the olive oil in the skillet and pour the sauce into the pan. Season it with salt, bring the sauce to a boil, and cook for 5 minutes. Reduce the heat so that the sauce simmers gently and cook for another 30 minutes.

4. Use immediately or store in the refrigerator.

Chile Colorado

YIELD: 4 CUPS | **ACTIVE TIME:** 30 MINUTES | **TOTAL TIME:** 1 HOUR AND 30 MINUTES

7 OZ. GUAJILLO CHILE PEPPERS, STEMS AND SEEDS REMOVED

1¾ OZ. ANCHO CHILE PEPPERS, STEMS AND SEEDS REMOVED

⅓ OZ. CHILES DE ÀRBOL, STEMS AND SEEDS REMOVED

1 TABLESPOON CORIANDER SEEDS

1½ TEASPOONS ALLSPICE BERRIES

1¼ TABLESPOONS CUMIN SEEDS

1 TABLESPOON EXTRA-VIRGIN OLIVE OIL

1 WHITE ONION, SLICED

10 GARLIC CLOVES

1 TABLESPOON DRIED MARJORAM

1 TABLESPOON DRIED MEXICAN OREGANO

1 TABLESPOON DRIED THYME

3 TABLESPOONS LARD

2 BAY LEAVES

CHICKEN STOCK (SEE PAGE 303), AS NEEDED

SALT, TO TASTE

1. Place the chiles in a dry skillet and toast until they are pliable and fragrant, about 30 seconds. Place them in a bowl, cover them with hot water, and soak the chiles for 30 minutes.

2. Place the coriander seeds, allspice berries, and cumin seeds in the skillet and toast until fragrant, shaking the pan frequently to keep them from burning. Grind the toasted seeds to a fine powder with a mortar and pestle.

3. Place the olive oil in the skillet and warm it over medium heat. Add the onion, garlic, toasted spice powder, marjoram, oregano, and thyme and cook, stirring frequently, until the onion is translucent, about 3 minutes.

4. Drain the chiles and reserve the soaking liquid. Place the chiles and onion mixture in a food processor and blitz until smooth, adding the reserved liquid as necessary.

5. Place the lard in a Dutch oven and warm it over high heat. Carefully add the puree (it will splatter) and the bay leaves, reduce the heat to low, and simmer the sauce for 1 hour, adding stock as necessary to get the flavor and texture to your liking. Season the sauce with salt before using or storing.

Mole Negro

YIELD: 12 CUPS | **ACTIVE TIME:** 1 HOUR | **TOTAL TIME:** 4 HOURS

2–3 DRIED CHIHUACLE NEGRO CHILE PEPPERS, STEMS AND SEEDS REMOVED, SEEDS RESERVED

1 CHIPOTLE MECO CHILE PEPPER, STEMS AND SEEDS REMOVED, SEEDS RESERVED

2 ANCHO CHILE PEPPERS, STEMS AND SEEDS REMOVED, SEEDS RESERVED

2 PASILLA CHILE PEPPERS, STEMS AND SEEDS REMOVED, SEEDS RESERVED

3 GUAJILLO CHILE PEPPERS, STEMS AND SEEDS REMOVED, SEEDS RESERVED

3 TABLESPOONS SESAME SEEDS

¼ CUP BLANCHED ALMONDS

3 TABLESPOONS PECANS

1½ SMALL WHITE ONIONS, CUT INTO 12 PIECES

10 GARLIC CLOVES, UNPEELED

5 ROMA TOMATOES, HALVED

4 OZ. TOMATILLOS, HUSKED AND RINSED

2 CINNAMON STICKS (MEXICAN PREFERRED)

¼ TEASPOON BLACK PEPPERCORNS

¼ TEASPOON WHOLE CLOVES

1 AVOCADO LEAF

1 HOJA SANTA LEAF

1 BAY LEAF

16 CUPS CHICKEN STOCK (SEE PAGE 303)

½ CUP LARD

1¾ OZ. BRIOCHE BREAD

½ CUP CHOPPED OVERRIPE PLANTAIN

2 TABLESPOONS RAISINS

½ TEASPOON DRIED THYME

½ TEASPOON DRIED MEXICAN OREGANO

5⅓ OZ. MEXICAN CHOCOLATE

SALT, TO TASTE

1. Place 2 quarts of water in a saucepan and bring it to a simmer. Turn off the heat.

2. Warm a comal or cast-iron skillet over medium-high heat. Place all of the chiles in the pan and toast until they are charred all over. Using a spatula, press down on the chiles as they toast.

3. Place the chiles in the hot water and soak them for 30 minutes. Preheat the oven to 350°F.

4. Drain the chiles and reserve the soaking liquid. Place the chiles in a food processor and blitz until smooth, adding the reserved liquid as needed. Strain the puree into a bowl, pressing down to extract as much liquid as possible, and discard the solids, or dehydrate and use as a spice powder.

5. Place the sesame seeds, almonds, and pecans on a parchment-lined baking sheet and place them in the oven. Toast the mixture until it is dark brown, 10 to 12 minutes. Remove the baking sheet from the oven and let the mixture cool.

6. Place the onions, garlic, tomatoes, and tomatillos in the dry comal or skillet and toast until charred all over, turning them occasionally. Peel the garlic cloves, place the charred vegetables in the food processor, and blitz until smooth. Strain the puree into a bowl, pressing down to extract as much liquid as possible, and discard the solids.

7. Place the cinnamon sticks, peppercorns, cloves, avocado leaf, hoja santa leaf, and bay leaf in a dry skillet and toast them until fragrant, shaking the pan frequently to prevent them from burning. Remove the mixture from the pan and let it cool. When the mixture has cooled, use a mortar and pestle to grind it into a fine powder.

8. Place all of the chile seeds in a dry skillet and toast them over medium-high heat until thoroughly blackened. Make sure to open windows, turn on the kitchen fan, and wear a mask, as the toasted seeds will produce noxious fumes.

9. Use a long match or a kitchen torch to light the seeds on fire. When the fire burns out, place the seeds in a bowl of cold water. Soak the seeds in cold water, and change the water every 10 minutes for a total of three changes. After the final soak, drain the seeds, place them in the food processor with 1 cup of stock, and blitz until smooth. Strain the liquid into a bowl through a fine-mesh sieve.

10. Place half of the lard in a skillet and warm it over medium heat. Add the bread and fry until it is dark brown. Remove it from the pan and set it aside.

11. Add the plantain to the pan and fry until it is dark brown and caramelized, about 4 minutes. Remove it from the pan and set it aside.

12. Add the raisins to the pan and fry them until plump and caramelized, about 3 minutes. Remove them from the pan and set them aside.

13. Add the toasted nuts and sesame seeds to the pan and fry for about 1 minute. Place the nuts and seeds in the food processor with a small amount of stock and puree until the mixture is a smooth paste.

14. Add the vegetable puree, toasted chile puree, chile seed puree, spice powder, raisins, plantains, and bread and puree until smooth. Strain the puree into a bowl through a fine-mesh sieve, again pressing down to get as much liquid from the mixture as possible.

15. Place the remaining lard in a large saucepan and warm it over medium-high heat. Add the chile puree and cook until it bubbles vigorously, stirring with a whisk to prevent the mixture from scorching. Reduce the heat to a simmer and cook for 30 minutes.

16. Add the thyme and oregano and cook for 1 to 2 hours, adding the remaining stock as needed.

17. When the rawness of the ingredients has been completely cooked out, add the chocolate and stir to incorporate. Season with salt and let the mole cool, then taste and adjust the seasoning as necessary. As it sits, the mole will take on stronger, increasingly delicious flavors. When the flavor has developed to your liking, use the mole as desired or store it in the refrigerator.

Tip: If you cannot find the chihuacle chile pepper, substitute additional pasilla and/or ancho chiles.

Mole Negro
SEE PAGE 260

Mole Manchamanteles

YIELD: 6 CUPS | **ACTIVE TIME:** 30 MINUTES | **TOTAL TIME:** 2 HOURS AND 30 MINUTES

½ LB. PILONCILLO

1 CUP WATER

1 APPLE, PEELED, CORE REMOVED, SLICED

1 PEAR, PEELED, CORE REMOVED, SLICED

1 PEACH, HALVED, PIT REMOVED, SLICED

¾ CUP SESAME SEEDS

½ MEXICAN CINNAMON STICK

1¼ TABLESPOONS CORIANDER SEEDS

1½ TEASPOONS ALLSPICE BERRIES

1 TABLESPOON CUMIN SEEDS

2 STAR ANISE PODS

1 WHITE ONION, QUARTERED

5 GARLIC CLOVES, UNPEELED

7 TABLESPOONS LARD

6 ANCHO CHILE PEPPERS, STEMS AND SEEDS REMOVED

5 GUAJILLO CHILE PEPPERS, STEMS AND SEEDS REMOVED

2 CHIPOTLE MECO CHILE PEPPERS, STEMS AND SEEDS REMOVED

½ CUP GOLDEN RAISINS

1 RIPE PLANTAIN, PEELED AND SLICED

10½ OZ. ROMA TOMATOES, HALVED

CHICKEN STOCK (SEE PAGE 303), AS NEEDED

SALT, TO TASTE

1. Preheat the oven to 400°F. Place the piloncillo and water in a saucepan and bring to a boil, stirring to dissolve the piloncillo. Toss the apple, pear, and peach into the syrup, place the mixture in a baking dish, place them in the oven, and roast until they are caramelized, about 20 minutes. Remove the dish from the oven and let the mixture cool.

2. Place the sesame seeds in a dry skillet and toast until lightly browned, shaking the pan frequently to keep them from burning. Add the cinnamon, coriander seeds, allspice berries, cumin seeds, and star anise to the skillet and toast until fragrant, shaking the pan frequently to keep them from burning. Grind the mixture to a fine powder with a mortar and pestle.

3. Place the onion and garlic in the skillet and toast over medium heat until charred, about 10 minutes, turning occasionally. Remove them from the pan and let them cool. When cool enough to handle, peel the garlic cloves.

4. Place the lard in a Dutch oven and warm it over medium heat. Add the chiles and fry until pliable and fragrant, about 30 seconds. Remove the chiles, place them in a bowl, and cover them with hot water. Let the chiles soak for 20 minutes.

5. Drain the chiles and reserve the soaking liquid.

6. Place the raisins and plantain in the lard and fry until the raisins are puffy and the plantain has caramelized. Add all of the ingredients to the Dutch oven and cook for 1 to 2 hours, adding stock and the reserved soaking liquid as needed to get the desired flavor and texture.

6. Place the mixture in a food processor and blitz until smooth. Strain the sauce, season it with salt, and use immediately or store in the refrigerator.

Àrbol Macha

YIELD: 1 CUP | **ACTIVE TIME:** 10 MINUTES | **TOTAL TIME:** 15 MINUTES

3 TOMATILLOS, HUSKED AND RINSED

¼ CUP LIGHTLY SALTED PEANUTS, CRUSHED

2 TEASPOONS FISH SAUCE

8 CHILES DE ÀRBOL, STEMS AND SEEDS REMOVED

⅓ CUP FRESH LIME JUICE

¼ CUP CHOPPED FRESH CILANTRO

1. Place the tomatillos in a dry skillet and cook them over medium-high heat until they are charred all over, turning them as necessary. Remove the tomatillos from the pan, let them cool briefly, and then chop them.

2. Use a mortar and pestle to crush the charred tomatillos and the remaining ingredients until the mixture is a chunky paste. Use immediately or store in the refrigerator.

Gochujang & Scallion Sauce

YIELD: 2 CUPS | **ACTIVE TIME:** 25 MINUTES | **TOTAL TIME:** 40 MINUTES

CANOLA OIL, AS NEEDED

½ CUP GARLIC CLOVES

2-INCH PIECE OF FRESH GINGER, PEELED AND CHOPPED

5 SCALLIONS, TRIMMED AND FINELY DICED, WHITE AND GREEN PARTS SEPARATED

½ CUP BROWN SUGAR

3 TABLESPOONS GOCHUJANG PASTE

1 CUP SOY SAUCE

1 TABLESPOON GINGER JUICE

1. Add canola oil to a Dutch oven until it is about 1 inch deep and warm it to 300ºF.

2. Gently slip the garlic into the hot oil and fry until it is golden brown, 2 to 3 minutes. Remove the garlic with a slotted spoon and transfer it to a paper towel–lined plate to drain.

3. Add the ginger to the hot oil and fry until it is golden brown, 2 to 3 minutes. Remove the ginger with a slotted spoon and transfer it to the paper towel–lined plate to drain.

4. Add 1 tablespoon of the hot oil to a medium saucepan and warm it over medium-low heat. Add the scallion whites and cook, stirring occasionally, until they are very tender, about 15 minutes.

5. Stir in the brown sugar and cook until it is about to caramelize. Add the gochujang and stir until well combined.

6. Stir in the soy sauce and ginger juice and bring the sauce to a gentle simmer. Cook for 5 minutes, stirring frequently.

7. Remove the pan from heat, stir the fried garlic, fried ginger, and scallion greens into the sauce, and let it cool to room temperature before serving.

Mole Blanco

YIELD: 4 CUPS | **ACTIVE TIME:** 30 MINUTES | **TOTAL TIME:** 1 HOUR

1 TABLESPOON PINE NUTS, LIGHTLY TOASTED

1 TABLESPOON SUNFLOWER SEEDS, LIGHTLY TOASTED

1 TABLESPOON SESAME SEEDS, LIGHTLY TOASTED

3½ TABLESPOONS CHICKEN STOCK (SEE PAGE 303), PLUS MORE AS NEEDED

2 TABLESPOONS EXTRA-VIRGIN OLIVE OIL

1½ TOMATILLOS, HUSKED AND RINSED

1 GARLIC CLOVE

¼ WHITE ONION, CHOPPED

1 TABLESPOON CHOPPED HABANERO CHILE PEPPER

2 TABLESPOONS CHOPPED TURNIP

1 TABLESPOON CHOPPED FENNEL

1 TABLESPOON PEELED AND CHOPPED GREEN APPLE

1 TABLESPOON SOURDOUGH BREAD CRUMBS

1 TABLESPOON GOLDEN RAISINS

1 TABLESPOON MINCED PLANTAIN

3 TABLESPOONS MASA HARINA

⅛ TEASPOON WHITE PEPPER

⅛ TEASPOON ALLSPICE

PINCH OF GROUND FENNEL SEEDS

1 CORIANDER SEED, TOASTED AND GROUND

3½ TABLESPOONS MILK

1 TEASPOON GRATED WHITE CHOCOLATE

SALT, TO TASTE

1. Use a mortar and pestle to grind the pine nuts, sunflower seeds, and sesame seeds into a paste, adding stock as needed to get the desired texture.

2. Place the olive oil in a Dutch oven and warm it over medium heat. Add the tomatillos, garlic, onion, habanero, turnip, fennel, apple, bread crumbs, raisins, and plantain and cook until the onion is translucent, about 3 minutes, stirring continually so that the contents of the pan do not take on any color.

3. Add the seed paste, masa harina, white pepper, allspice, fennel seeds, and coriander seed and stir to incorporate. Add the milk and stock and simmer until the fruits and vegetables are tender.

4. Stir in the white chocolate. Taste and adjust the seasoning as necessary. Place the mixture in a food processor and blitz until smooth. Strain the sauce and use immediately or store in the refrigerator.

Tahini & Yogurt Sauce

YIELD: 1 CUP | **ACTIVE TIME:** 5 MINUTES | **TOTAL TIME:** 5 MINUTES

¾ CUP FULL-FAT GREEK YOGURT

1 GARLIC CLOVE, MINCED

2 TABLESPOONS TAHINI PASTE

JUICE OF 1 LEMON

½ TEASPOON CUMIN

SALT AND PEPPER, TO TASTE

1 TABLESPOON BLACK SESAME SEEDS

1 TABLESPOON EXTRA-VIRGIN OLIVE OIL

1. Place the yogurt, garlic, tahini, lemon juice, and cumin in a small bowl and whisk to combine.

2. Season the sauce with salt and pepper, add the sesame seeds and olive oil, and whisk until incorporated. Use immediately or store in the refrigerator until needed.

Peanut Sauce

YIELD: 1 CUP | **ACTIVE TIME:** 10 MINUTES | **TOTAL TIME:** 10 MINUTES

2 GARLIC CLOVES, MINCED

2 SHALLOTS, MINCED

2 TABLESPOONS AVOCADO OIL

½ CUP COCONUT MILK

¼ CUP CREAMY PEANUT BUTTER

1 TABLESPOON TAMARIND PASTE

1½ TABLESPOONS KECAP MANIS

2 TEASPOONS FISH SAUCE

2 TEASPOONS FRESH LIME JUICE

2 TEASPOONS SWEET CHILI DIPPING SAUCE (SEE PAGE 273)

1. Using a mortar and pestle, grind the garlic and shallots into a paste.

2. Place the paste and the avocado oil in a small saucepan and warm the mixture over low heat, stirring frequently, for 2 minutes.

3. Stir in the remaining ingredients and cook until the sauce starts to bubble. Remove the pan from heat, taste the sauce, and adjust the seasoning as necessary. Use immediately or store in the refrigerator.

Pot Sticker Dipping Sauce

YIELD: ½ CUP | **ACTIVE TIME:** 5 MINUTES | **TOTAL TIME:** 35 MINUTES

2 TABLESPOONS SOY SAUCE

1 TABLESPOON SAMBAL OELEK

1 TABLESPOON WHITE WINE VINEGAR

1 TABLESPOON CHINKIANG VINEGAR

1 TABLESPOON SUGAR

2 GARLIC CLOVES, MINCED

1 TABLESPOON MINCED SCALLION

1 TABLESPOON CHOPPED FRESH CILANTRO

1 TEASPOON SESAME OIL

1 TEASPOON CHILI OIL

1. Place all of the ingredients in a bowl and stir until well combined. Let the sauce marinate for 30 minutes before using or storing.

Pineapple & Plum Dipping Sauce

YIELD: 1 CUP | **ACTIVE TIME:** 5 MINUTES | **TOTAL TIME:** 5 MINUTES

⅔ CUP PINEAPPLE JUICE

¼ CUP PLUM SAUCE

2 TABLESPOONS SWEET CHILI DIPPING SAUCE (SEE PAGE 273)

1. Place all of the ingredients in a bowl and stir until well combined. Use immediately or store in the refrigerator.

Sweet Chili Dipping Sauce

YIELD: 1½ CUPS | **ACTIVE TIME:** 10 MINUTES | **TOTAL TIME:** 10 MINUTES

3 BIRD'S EYE CHILI PEPPERS, STEMS REMOVED

4 GARLIC CLOVES

⅓ CUP WHITE VINEGAR

½ CUP SUGAR

1 TEASPOON KOSHER SALT

1 CUP PLUS 2 TABLESPOONS WATER

1 TABLESPOON CORNSTARCH

1. Place the chilies, garlic, vinegar, sugar, salt, and 1 cup of the water in a blender and blend until the mixture is a chunky puree.

2. Place the puree in a small saucepan and bring it to a boil over medium-high heat. Reduce the heat and simmer, stirring frequently, until the garlic is tender, about 3 minutes.

3. Place the cornstarch and remaining water in a small bowl and stir until well combined. Stir the slurry into the sauce and simmer until the sauce has thickened, about 1minute.

4. Remove the pan from heat and let the sauce cool before using or storing in the refrigerator.

Salsa Borracha

YIELD: 1½ CUPS | **ACTIVE TIME:** 20 MINUTES | **TOTAL TIME:** 30 MINUTES

½ LB. TOMATILLOS, HUSKED AND RINSED

¾ SMALL WHITE ONION

5 GARLIC CLOVES, UNPEELED

2 TABLESPOONS LARD

3 PASILLA CHILE PEPPERS, STEMS AND SEEDS REMOVED

2 CHIPOTLE MORITA CHILE PEPPERS, STEMS AND SEEDS REMOVED

3½ OZ. MEXICAN LAGER

1 TEASPOON MEZCAL OR TEQUILA

1 TEASPOON MAGGI SEASONING SAUCE

SALT, TO TASTE

1. Warm a cast-iron skillet over medium-high heat. Add the tomatillos, onion, and garlic and toast until charred all over, turning them as needed. Remove the vegetables from the pan and let them cool. When cool enough to handle, peel the garlic cloves and place the mixture in a blender.

2. Place half of the lard in the skillet and warm it over medium heat. Add the chiles and fry until they are fragrant and pliable. Place the chiles in the blender.

3. Add the beer, mezcal, and Maggi and puree until smooth.

4. Place the remaining lard in a saucepan and warm it over medium heat. Add the puree and fry for 5 minutes. Season the salsa with salt and let it cool before enjoying.

Sweet Chili Dipping Sauce

SEE PAGE 273

Salsa de Chiltomate

YIELD: 1½ CUPS | **ACTIVE TIME:** 20 MINUTES | **TOTAL TIME:** 1 HOUR

8½ OZ. ROMA TOMATOES, HALVED

2 HABANERO CHILE PEPPERS

1 SMALL WHITE ONION, QUARTERED

4 GARLIC CLOVES, UNPEELED

2 TABLESPOONS EXTRA-VIRGIN OLIVE OIL

SALT, TO TASTE

JUICE OF 1 LIME

1. Preheat the oven to 450ºF. Line a baking sheet with parchment paper, place the tomatoes, chiles, onion, and garlic on it, and place it in the oven.

2. Roast until the vegetables are charred all over, checking every 5 minutes or so and removing them as they become ready.

3. Peel the garlic cloves, remove the stem and seeds from the habanero, and place the roasted vegetables in a blender. Puree until smooth.

4. Place the olive oil in a medium saucepan and warm it over medium-high heat. Carefully pour the puree into the pan, reduce the heat, and simmer until it has reduced slightly and the flavor is to your liking, 15 to 20 minutes.

5. Season with salt, stir in the lime juice, and let the salsa cool. Taste, adjust the seasoning as necessary, and enjoy.

Salsa Verde

YIELD: 1½ CUPS | **ACTIVE TIME:** 20 MINUTES | **TOTAL TIME:** 30 MINUTES

1 LB. TOMATILLOS, HUSKED AND RINSED

5 GARLIC CLOVES, UNPEELED

1 SMALL WHITE ONION, QUARTERED

10 SERRANO CHILE PEPPERS

2 BUNCHES OF FRESH CILANTRO

SALT, TO TASTE

1. Warm a cast-iron skillet over high heat. Place the tomatillos, garlic, onion, and chiles in the pan and cook until charred all over, turning them occasionally.

2. Remove the vegetables from the pan and let them cool slightly.

3. Peel the garlic cloves and remove the stems and seeds from the chiles. Place the charred vegetables in a blender, add the cilantro, and puree until smooth.

4. Season the salsa with salt and enjoy.

Peanut Hoisin Dipping Sauce

YIELD: 1 CUP | **ACTIVE TIME:** 15 MINUTES | **TOTAL TIME:** 30 MINUTES

CANOLA OIL, AS NEEDED

¼ CUP PEANUTS

¼ CUP HOISIN SAUCE (SEE PAGE 282)

¼ CUP RICE VINEGAR

2 TABLESPOONS SUGAR

2 TABLESPOONS SOY SAUCE

2 TABLESPOONS SWEET CHILI DIPPING SAUCE (SEE PAGE 273)

1. Add canola oil to a small cast-iron skillet until it is about 1 inch deep and warm it to 350ºF.

2. Add the peanuts to the warm oil and fry until they are golden brown, 3 to 4 minutes. Transfer the fried peanuts to a paper towel–lined plate to drain and cool. When they are cool enough to handle, chop the peanuts and set them aside.

3. Place the remaining ingredients in a bowl and stir to combine. Top the sauce with the peanuts and use immediately or store in the refrigerator.

Chili Garlic Sauce

YIELD: 1 CUP | **ACTIVE TIME:** 15 MINUTES | **TOTAL TIME:** 30 MINUTES

1 CUP CHOPPED FRESNO CHILE PEPPERS

8 GARLIC CLOVES, CHOPPED

¼ CUP WHITE VINEGAR

2 TABLESPOONS SUGAR

1 TEASPOON KOSHER SALT, PLUS MORE TO TASTE

BLACK PEPPER, TO TASTE

1. Place the chiles, garlic, and vinegar in a small saucepan and bring to a simmer over medium heat, stirring occasionally. Cook for 10 minutes.

2. Transfer the mixture to a blender and puree until smooth.

3. Strain the puree through a fine sieve into a clean saucepan. Add the sugar and salt and bring the sauce to a simmer. Season the sauce with salt and pepper, remove the pan from heat, and let the sauce cool completely before using or storing.

Nuoc Cham

YIELD: 1 CUP | **ACTIVE TIME:** 10 MINUTES | **TOTAL TIME:** 10 MINUTES

¼ CUP FISH SAUCE

⅓ CUP WATER

2 TABLESPOONS SUGAR

¼ CUP FRESH LIME JUICE

1 GARLIC CLOVE, MINCED

2 BIRD'S EYE CHILIES, STEMS AND SEEDS REMOVED, SLICED THIN

1 TABLESPOON CHILI GARLIC SAUCE (SEE OPPOSITE PAGE)

1. Place all of the ingredients in a mixing bowl and stir until the sugar has dissolved and the mixture is well combined.

2. Taste, adjust the seasoning as necessary, and use as desired.

Cilantro Pesto

YIELD: 1½ CUPS | **ACTIVE TIME:** 5 MINUTES | **TOTAL TIME:** 5 MINUTES

1 CUP FRESH CILANTRO

1 GARLIC CLOVE

¼ CUP ROASTED AND SHELLED SUNFLOWER SEEDS

¼ CUP SHREDDED QUESO ENCHILADO

¼ CUP EXTRA-VIRGIN OLIVE OIL

1 TEASPOON FRESH LEMON JUICE

SALT AND PEPPER, TO TASTE

1. Place of the ingredients in a food processor and blitz until emulsified and smooth. Use immediately or store in the refrigerator.

Hoisin Sauce

YIELD: ½ CUP | **ACTIVE TIME:** 5 MINUTES | **TOTAL TIME:** 10 MINUTES

2 TABLESPOONS AVOCADO OIL

4 GARLIC CLOVES, MINCED

¼ CUP SOY SAUCE

3 TABLESPOONS HONEY

2 TABLESPOONS WHITE VINEGAR

2 TABLESPOONS TAHINI

2 TEASPOONS SRIRACHA

1. Place the avocado oil in a saucepan and warm it over medium heat. Add the garlic and cook, stirring frequently, for 1 minute.

2. Stir in the remaining ingredients and cook until the sauce is smooth, about 5 minutes. Remove the pan from heat and let the sauce cool before using or storing in the refrigerator.

Smoked Egg Aioli

YIELD: 1 CUP | **ACTIVE TIME:** 20 MINUTES | **TOTAL TIME:** 45 MINUTES

2 EGG YOLKS

½ CUP WOOD CHIPS

1 TABLESPOON WHITE VINEGAR

1 TEASPOON KOSHER SALT

1 CUP AVOCADO OIL

1. Place the yolks in a metal bowl and set the bowl in a roasting pan.

2. Place the wood chips in a cast-iron skillet and warm them over high heat. Remove the pan from heat, light the wood chips on fire, and place the skillet in the roasting pan beside the bowl. Cover the roasting pan with aluminum foil and allow the smoke to flavor the yolks for 20 minutes.

3. Place the yolks and vinegar in a bowl, gently break the yolks, and let the mixture sit for 5 minutes.

4. Add the salt to the egg yolk mixture. Slowly drizzle the oil into the mixture while beating it with an electric mixer or immersion blender until it is thick and creamy. Use immediately or store in the refrigerator.

Okonomiyaki Sauce

YIELD: ½ CUP | **ACTIVE TIME:** 5 MINUTES | **TOTAL TIME:** 5 MINUTES

3 TABLESPOONS WORCESTERSHIRE SAUCE

3½ TABLESPOONS KETCHUP

2 TABLESPOONS OYSTER SAUCE

1½ TABLESPOONS LIGHT BROWN SUGAR

1. Place all of the ingredients in a bowl and whisk until the brown sugar has dissolved and the mixture is well combined.

2. Use immediately or store in the refrigerator.

Harissa Sauce

YIELD: 1 CUP | **ACTIVE TIME:** 10 MINUTES | **TOTAL TIME:** 1 HOUR

3 OZ. GUAJILLO CHILE PEPPERS, STEMS AND SEEDS REMOVED, TORN

1 OZ. DRIED CHIPOTLE CHILE PEPPERS, STEMS AND SEEDS REMOVED, TORN

1 TABLESPOON NIGELLA SEEDS

1 TEASPOON CORIANDER SEEDS

2 GARLIC CLOVES

1 TABLESPOON CUMIN

1 TEASPOON KOSHER SALT

½ TEASPOON ALEPPO PEPPER

½ CUP EXTRA-VIRGIN OLIVE OIL

2 TABLESPOONS WHITE WINE VINEGAR

1. Place the guajillo and chipotle chiles in a large heatproof bowl and cover them with boiling water. Let the chiles soak until they have softened, 40 to 45 minutes.

2. Drain the chiles and set them aside.

3. Grind the nigella seeds and coriander seeds into a powder using a spice mill or a mortar and pestle. Transfer the powder to a food processor and add the garlic, cumin, salt, and Aleppo pepper. Pulse until the garlic is very finely chopped.

4. Add the chiles and pulse until they are chopped.

5. Add the oil and vinegar and pulse until the sauce is a chunky paste. Use immediately or store in the refrigerator until needed.

Pickled Applesauce

YIELD: 6 CUPS | **ACTIVE TIME:** 20 MINUTES | **TOTAL TIME:** 1 HOUR

3 LBS. GRANNY SMITH APPLES, PEELED AND SLICED

1 TEASPOON CINNAMON

PINCH OF GROUND CLOVES

½ CUP SUGAR

1½ CUPS WHITE VINEGAR

1. Place the ingredients in a large saucepan and bring to a boil over high heat.

2. Reduce the heat to medium-high and simmer until the liquid has reduced by one-third. Remove the pan from heat and let it cool to room temperature.

3. Place the mixture in a food processor and puree on high until smooth, about 2 minutes. Serve immediately or store in the refrigerator.

Okonomiyaki Sauce

SEE PAGE 284

Roasted Garlic Aioli

YIELD: ½ CUP | **ACTIVE TIME:** 10 MINUTES | **TOTAL TIME:** 40 MINUTES

1 HEAD OF GARLIC

½ CUP EXTRA-VIRGIN OLIVE OIL, PLUS MORE AS NEEDED

SALT AND PEPPER, TO TASTE

1 EGG YOLK

1 TEASPOON FRESH LEMON JUICE

1. Preheat the oven to 350°F. Cut off the top ½ inch of the head of garlic. Place the remainder in a piece of aluminum foil, drizzle olive oil over it, and season it with salt.

2. Place the garlic in the oven and roast until the garlic cloves have softened and are caramelized, about 30 minutes. Remove from the oven, remove the cloves from the head of garlic, and place them in a mixing bowl.

3. Add the egg yolk and lemon juice and whisk to combine. While whisking continually, add the olive oil in a slow stream. When all the oil has been emulsified, season the aioli with salt and pepper and serve.

Pesto

2 CUPS PACKED FRESH BASIL LEAVES

1 CUP PACKED FRESH BABY SPINACH

2 CUPS FRESHLY GRATED PARMESAN CHEESE

¼ CUP PINE NUTS

1 GARLIC CLOVE

2 TEASPOONS FRESH LEMON JUICE

SALT AND PEPPER, TO TASTE

½ CUP EXTRA-VIRGIN OLIVE OIL

1. Place all the ingredients, except for the olive oil, in a food processor and pulse until pureed.

2. Transfer the puree to a mixing bowl. While whisking, add the olive oil in a slow stream until it is emulsified. Use immediately or store in the refrigerator.

Mignonette Sauce

YIELD: ½ CUP | **ACTIVE TIME:** 5 MINUTES | **TOTAL TIME:** 1 HOUR AND 5 MINUTES

½ CUP RED WINE VINEGAR

1½ TABLESPOONS MINCED
SHALLOT

½ TEASPOON FRESHLY
CRACKED BLACK PEPPER

1. Place the ingredients in a bowl, stir to combine, and chill in the
   refrigerator for 1 hour before serving.

Romesco Sauce

YIELD: 1 CUP | **ACTIVE TIME:** 5 MINUTES | **TOTAL TIME:** 5 MINUTES

2 LARGE ROASTED RED BELL PEPPERS

1 GARLIC CLOVE, SMASHED

½ CUP SLIVERED ALMONDS, TOASTED

¼ CUP TOMATO PUREE

2 TABLESPOONS FINELY CHOPPED FLAT-LEAF PARSLEY

2 TABLESPOONS SHERRY VINEGAR

1 TEASPOON SMOKED PAPRIKA

SALT AND PEPPER, TO TASTE

½ CUP EXTRA-VIRGIN OLIVE OIL

1. Place all of the ingredients, except for the olive oil, in a blender or food processor and pulse until the mixture is smooth.

2. Add the olive oil in a steady stream and blitz until emulsified. Season with salt and pepper and use immediately.

Marinara Sauce

YIELD: 8 CUPS | **ACTIVE TIME:** 20 MINUTES | **TOTAL TIME:** 2 HOURS

4 LBS. TOMATOES, QUARTERED

1 LARGE YELLOW ONION, SLICED

15 GARLIC CLOVES, CRUSHED

2 TEASPOONS FINELY CHOPPED FRESH THYME

2 TEASPOONS FINELY CHOPPED FRESH OREGANO

2 TABLESPOONS EXTRA-VIRGIN OLIVE OIL

1½ TABLESPOONS KOSHER SALT

1 TEASPOON BLACK PEPPER

2 TABLESPOONS FINELY CHOPPED FRESH BASIL

1 TABLESPOON FINELY CHOPPED FRESH PARSLEY

1. Place all of the ingredients, except for the basil and parsley, in a Dutch oven and cook over medium heat, stirring constantly, until the tomatoes release their liquid and begin to collapse, about 10 minutes.

2. Reduce the heat to low and cook, stirring occasionally, for about 1½ hours, or until the flavor is to your liking.

3. Stir in the basil and parsley and season to taste. The sauce will be chunky. If you prefer a smoother texture, transfer the sauce to a blender and puree before serving.

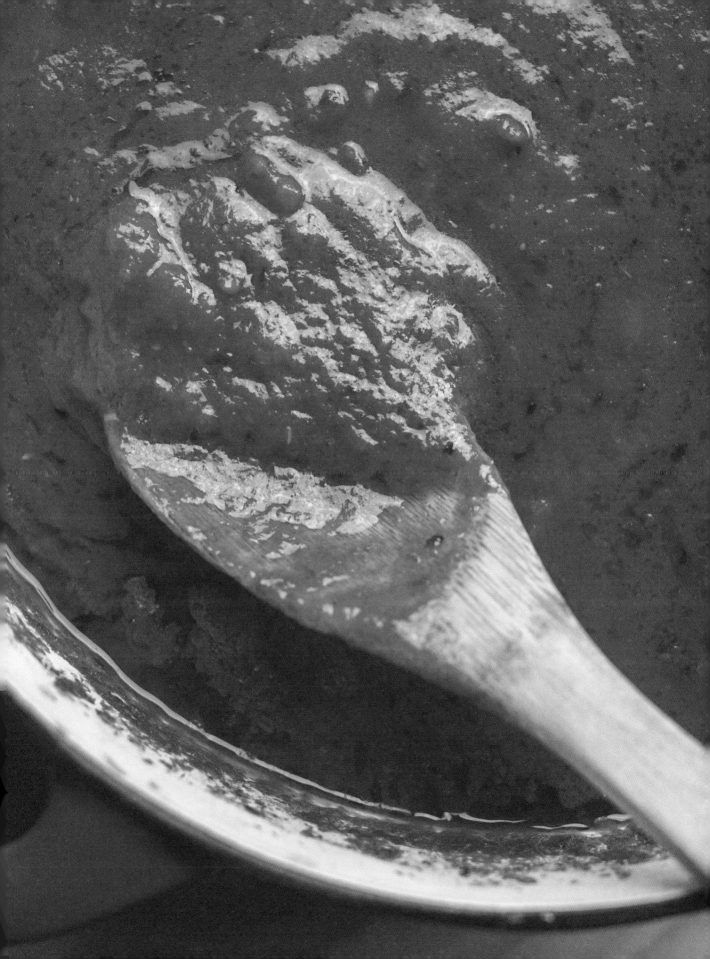

Aioli

YIELD: 1 CUP | **ACTIVE TIME:** 5 MINUTES | **TOTAL TIME:** 5 MINUTES

2 LARGE EGG YOLKS

2 TEASPOONS DIJON MUSTARD

2 TEASPOONS FRESH LEMON JUICE

1 GARLIC CLOVE, MASHED

¾ CUP CANOLA OIL

¼ CUP EXTRA-VIRGIN OLIVE OIL

SALT AND PEPPER, TO TASTE

1. Place the egg yolks, mustard, lemon juice, and garlic in a food processor and blitz until combined.

2. With the food processor running on low, slowly drizzle in the oils until they are emulsified. If the aioli becomes too thick for your liking, stir in water 1 teaspoon at a time until it has thinned out.

3. Season the aioli with salt and pepper and use as desired.

Charred Scallion Sauce

YIELD: 1 CUP | **ACTIVE TIME:** 10 MINUTES | **TOTAL TIME:** 10 MINUTES

3 SCALLIONS

2 GARLIC CLOVES, MINCED

2 BIRD'S EYE CHILI PEPPERS, STEMS AND SEEDS REMOVED, MINCED

¼ CUP CHOPPED FRESH CILANTRO

1 TABLESPOON GRATED FRESH GINGER

1 TABLESPOON SESAME OIL

½ CUP SOY SAUCE

1 TABLESPOON SAMBAL OELEK

2 TABLESPOONS FRESH LIME JUICE

1 TEASPOON SUGAR

1 TABLESPOON SESAME SEEDS

SALT AND PEPPER, TO TASTE

1. On a grill or over an open flame on a gas stove, char the scallions all over. Remove the charred scallions from heat and let them cool.

2. Slice the charred scallions, place them in a mixing bowl, and add the remaining ingredients. Stir to combine, taste the sauce, and adjust the seasoning as necessary. Use immediately or store in the refrigerator until needed.

Lemony Yogurt Sauce

YIELD: 2½ CUPS | **ACTIVE TIME:** 5 MINUTES | **TOTAL TIME:** 5 MINUTES

6 TABLESPOONS FRESH LEMON JUICE

1 GARLIC CLOVE, GRATED

1 TEASPOON KOSHER SALT

1 TEASPOON BLACK PEPPER

2 CUPS FULL-FAT GREEK YOGURT

1. Place all of the ingredients in a mixing bowl and stir until thoroughly combined. Use immediately or store in the refrigerator.

Cocktail Sauce

YIELD: ¾ CUP | **ACTIVE TIME:** 20 MINUTES | **TOTAL TIME:** 1 HOUR

½ CUP KETCHUP

2 TABLESPOONS HORSERADISH

2 TABLESPOONS WORCESTERSHIRE SAUCE

JUICE OF ½ LEMON

1 TEASPOON OLD BAY SEASONING

1. Place all of the ingredients in a bowl, stir to combine, and chill the cocktail sauce in the refrigerator for 1 hour before serving.

Cocktail Sauce
SEE PAGE 299

Crab & Mango Salsa

YIELD: 2 CUPS | **ACTIVE TIME:** 15 MINUTES | **TOTAL TIME:** 45 MINUTES

½ CUP FINELY DICED MANGO

½ CUP FINELY DICED RED BELL PEPPER

3 TABLESPOONS MINCED RED ONION

1 TEASPOON MINCED FRESH CHIVES

1 TEASPOON RICE VINEGAR

2 TABLESPOONS EXTRA-VIRGIN OLIVE OIL

SALT, TO TASTE

½ LB. PEEKYTOE CRABMEAT, PICKED OVER AND COOKED

1. Place the mango, bell pepper, red onion, chives, rice vinegar, and olive oil in a mixing bowl and stir gently until combined. Season the salsa with salt and chill it in the refrigerator for 30 minutes.

2. Top the salsa with the crab and use immediately or store in the refrigerator.

Salsa Brava

YIELD: 2½ CUPS | **ACTIVE TIME:** 45 MINUTES | **TOTAL TIME:** 1 HOUR AND 15 MINUTES

1 ONION, WITH SKIN AND ROOT, HALVED

3 TABLESPOONS EXTRA-VIRGIN OLIVE OIL

2 CUPS WOOD CHIPS

1 HEAD OF GARLIC, TOP ½ INCH REMOVED

1 (14 OZ.) CAN OF DICED TOMATOES, DRAINED

1 TABLESPOON SWEET PAPRIKA

1 TABLESPOON SHERRY VINEGAR

SALT, TO TASTE

1. Place the onion and 1 tablespoon of the olive oil in a mixing bowl and toss to coat.

2. Line a large cast-iron skillet with aluminum foil, making sure that the foil extends over the side of the pan. Add the wood chips and place the skillet over medium heat.

3. When the wood chips are smoking heavily, place a wire rack above the wood chips and place the onion and garlic on top. Cover the skillet, fold the foil over the lid to seal the pan as best you can, and smoke the vegetables for 20 minutes. After 20 minutes, remove the pan from heat and keep it covered for another 20 minutes.

4. Place the tomatoes, paprika, vinegar, and remaining olive oil in a food processor and blitz until smooth. Set the mixture aside.

5. Remove the garlic and onion from the smoker. Peel the vegetables and chop them. Add them to the mixture in the blender and puree until smooth. Season the salsa brava with salt and use immediately or store in the refrigerator.

Vegetable Stock

YIELD: 6 CUPS | **ACTIVE TIME:** 20 MINUTES | **TOTAL TIME:** 3 HOURS

2 TABLESPOONS EXTRA-VIRGIN OLIVE OIL

2 LARGE LEEKS, TRIMMED AND RINSED WELL

2 LARGE CARROTS, PEELED AND SLICED

2 CELERY STALKS, SLICED

2 LARGE YELLOW ONIONS, SLICED

3 GARLIC CLOVES, UNPEELED BUT SMASHED

2 SPRIGS OF FRESH PARSLEY

2 SPRIGS OF FRESH THYME

1 BAY LEAF

8 CUPS WATER

½ TEASPOON BLACK PEPPERCORNS

SALT, TO TASTE

1. Place the olive oil and the vegetables in a large stockpot and cook over low heat until the liquid they release has evaporated. This will allow the flavor of the vegetables to become concentrated.

2. Add the garlic, parsley, thyme, bay leaf, water, peppercorns, and salt. Raise the heat to high and bring to a boil. Reduce the heat so that the stock simmers and cook for 2 hours, while skimming to remove any impurities that float to the surface.

3. Strain through a fine sieve, let the stock cool slightly, and place in the refrigerator, uncovered, to chill. Remove the fat layer and cover the stock. The stock will keep in the refrigerator for 3 to 5 days, and in the freezer for up to 3 months.

Chicken Stock

YIELD: 8 CUPS | **ACTIVE TIME:** 20 MINUTES | **TOTAL TIME:** 6 HOURS

7 LBS. CHICKEN BONES, RINSED

4 CUPS CHOPPED YELLOW ONIONS

2 CUPS CHOPPED CARROTS

2 CUPS CHOPPED CELERY

3 GARLIC CLOVES, CRUSHED

3 SPRIGS OF FRESH THYME

1 TEASPOON BLACK PEPPERCORNS

1 BAY LEAF

1. Place the chicken bones in a stockpot and cover them with cold water. Bring the water to a simmer over medium-high heat and use a ladle to skim off any impurities that rise to the surface.

2. Add the vegetables, thyme, peppercorns, and bay leaf, reduce the heat to low, and simmer for 5 hours, skimming the stock occasionally to remove any impurities that rise to the surface.

3. Strain the stock, let it cool slightly, and transfer it to the refrigerator. Leave the stock uncovered and let it cool completely. Remove the layer of fat and cover. The stock will keep in the refrigerator for 3 to 5 days, and in the freezer for up to 3 months.

Cocktail Sauce, Baja Style

YIELD: 3 CUPS | **ACTIVE TIME:** 15 MINUTES | **TOTAL TIME:** 15 MINUTES

7 TABLESPOONS FRESH
LIME JUICE

1½ TABLESPOONS FRESH
LEMON JUICE

5 TABLESPOONS ORANGE
JUICE

1 TABLESPOON
HORSERADISH

14 TABLESPOONS KETCHUP

1¼ TABLESPOONS FISH
SAUCE

7 TABLESPOONS HOT
SAUCE

7 TABLESPOONS SPICY
CLAMATO

2 ⅔ TABLESPOONS
WORCESTERSHIRE SAUCE

1 SMALL RED ONION, SLICED
THIN

5 GARLIC CLOVES, GRATED

FLESH OF 1 AVOCADO,
DICED

2 JALAPEÑO CHILE
PEPPERS, STEMS AND SEEDS
REMOVED, DICED

2 TOMATOES, DICED

SALT, TO TASTE

1. Place the lime juice, lemon juice, orange juice, horseradish, ketchup, fish sauce, hot sauce, Clamato, and Worcestershire sauce in a mixing bowl and stir to combine.

2. Add the onion, garlic, avocado, jalapeños, and tomatoes to the mixture and fold to incorporate. Season the sauce with salt and use immediately or store in the refrigerator.

Beef Stock

YIELD: 8 CUPS | **ACTIVE TIME:** 20 MINUTES | **TOTAL TIME:** 6 HOURS

7 LBS. BEEF BONES, RINSED

4 CUPS CHOPPED YELLOW ONIONS

2 CUPS CHOPPED CARROTS

2 CUPS CHOPPED CELERY

3 GARLIC CLOVES, CRUSHED

3 SPRIGS OF FRESH THYME

1 TEASPOON BLACK PEPPERCORNS

1 BAY LEAF

1. Place the beef bones in a stockpot and cover them with cold water. Bring the water to a simmer over medium-high heat and use a ladle to skim off any impurities that rise to the surface.

2. Add the remaining ingredients, reduce the heat to low, and simmer for 5 hours, occasionally skimming the stock to remove any impurities that rise to the surface.

3. Strain the stock, let it cool slightly, and transfer it to the refrigerator. Leave the stock uncovered and let it cool completely. Remove the layer of fat and cover. The stock will keep in the refrigerator for 3 to 5 days, and in the freezer for up to 3 months.

Dashi Stock

YIELD: 6 CUPS | **ACTIVE TIME:** 10 MINUTES | **TOTAL TIME:** 40 MINUTES

8 CUPS COLD WATER

2 OZ. KOMBU

1 CUP BONITO FLAKES

1. Place the water and the kombu in a medium saucepan. Soak the kombu for 20 minutes, remove it, and score it gently with a knife.

2. Return the kombu to the saucepan and bring to a boil. Remove the kombu as soon as the water boils, so that the stock doesn't become bitter.

3. Add the bonito flakes to the water and return it to a boil. Turn off the heat and let the mixture stand.

4. Strain the stock through a fine sieve. Use immediately or let it cool before using or storing.

Tuk Trey

YIELD: 1 CUP | **ACTIVE TIME:** 5 MINUTES | **TOTAL TIME:** 5 MINUTES

2 TEASPOONS SUGAR

3 TABLESPOONS FISH SAUCE

JUICE OF 1 LIME

¼ CUP WATER

2 GARLIC CLOVES, MINCED

½ CUP ROASTED PEANUTS, CHOPPED

1 BIRD'S EYE CHILI PEPPER, STEM AND SEEDS REMOVED, MINCED

1. Place all of the ingredients in a bowl, stir to combine, and use immediately or store in the refrigerator.

Lime Aioli

YIELD: ½ CUP | **ACTIVE TIME:** 5 MINUTES | **TOTAL TIME:** 5 MINUTES

7 TABLESPOONS MAYONNAISE

2 GARLIC CLOVES, GRATED

2 TABLESPOONS FRESH LIME JUICE

1. Place all of the ingredients in a bowl, stir to combine, and use immediately or store in the refrigerator.

Dashi Stock
SEE PAGE 306

Agristada Sauce

YIELD: 2 CUPS | **ACTIVE TIME:** 10 MINUTES | **TOTAL TIME:** 20 MINUTES

4 EGGS

2 CUPS WARM WATER

2 TABLESPOONS ALL-PURPOSE FLOUR

¼ CUP AVOCADO OIL

⅓ CUP FRESH LEMON JUICE

½ TEASPOON KOSHER SALT

1. Place the eggs in a medium saucepan and whisk until scrambled. Set the eggs aside.

2. Place the warm water and the flour in a mixing bowl and vigorously whisk the mixture until there are no visible lumps in it. Strain the mixture into the saucepan.

3. Add the avocado oil, lemon juice, and salt and warm the mixture over medium-low heat, stirring constantly with a wooden spoon. Cook until the sauce has thickened, 10 to 12 minutes.

4. When the sauce is just about to boil, remove the pan from heat, stir for another minute, and then strain the sauce into a bowl.

5. Taste, adjust the seasoning as necessary, and place plastic wrap directly on the surface of the sauce to prevent a skin from forming. Let the sauce cool to room temperature before serving or storing in the refrigerator.

Grilled Corn & Jalapeño Salsa

YIELD: 2 CUPS | **ACTIVE TIME:** 25 MINUTES | **TOTAL TIME:** 1 HOUR AND 30 MINUTES

2 EARS OF CORN, HUSKED AND RINSED

1 TABLESPOON EXTRA-VIRGIN OLIVE OIL

SALT AND PEPPER, TO TASTE

1 SMALL JALAPEÑO CHILE PEPPER, STEM AND SEEDS REMOVED, DICED

¼ CUP DICED RED ONION

1 GARLIC CLOVE, MINCED

1½ TABLESPOONS FRESH LIME JUICE

¼ CUP CHOPPED FRESH CILANTRO

½ CUP DICED TOMATO

1. Prepare a gas or charcoal grill for medium heat (about 400°F). Place the corn on the grill and cook until they are charred all over and just tender, about 15 minutes, turning them as necessary. Remove the corn from the grill and let them cool briefly.

2. Cut the kernels off the cobs and place the kernels in a bowl. Add the remaining ingredients, stir to combine, and chill the salsa in the refrigerator for 1 hour before serving.

THE ENCYCLOPEDIA OF SEASONING

Mango Salsa

YIELD: 2 CUPS | **ACTIVE TIME:** 5 MINUTES | **TOTAL TIME:** 35 MINUTES

FLESH OF 2 MANGOES, DICED

½ CUP FINELY DICED RED BELL PEPPER

¼ CUP CHOPPED FRESH CILANTRO

½ CUP FINELY DICED RED ONION

3½ TABLESPOONS FRESH LIME JUICE

2 TABLESPOONS FRESH LEMON JUICE

SALT AND PEPPER, TO TASTE

1. Place the mangoes, bell pepper, cilantro, onion, lime juice, and lemon juice in a small bowl, season the mixture with salt and pepper, and gently toss to combine. Cover the bowl with plastic wrap and chill the salsa in the refrigerator for 30 minutes before serving.

Corn Salsa

YIELD: 4 CUPS | **ACTIVE TIME:** 5 MINUTES | **TOTAL TIME:** 1 HOUR AND 5 MINUTES

2 CUPS DICED TOMATOES

1 CUP CANNED CORN, DRAINED

1 SMALL RED BELL PEPPER, STEM AND SEEDS REMOVED, FINELY DICED

1 CUP CANNED BLACK BEANS, DRAINED AND RINSED

1 ONION, FINELY DICED

¼ CUP CHOPPED FRESH CILANTRO

1 SERRANO CHILE PEPPER, STEM AND SEEDS REMOVED, FINELY DICED

1 TEASPOON LIME ZEST

1 TABLESPOON FRESH LIME JUICE

¼ TEASPOON CUMIN

SALT AND PEPPER, TO TASTE

1. Place all of the ingredients in a large bowl and stir until well combined. Cover the salsa with plastic wrap and let it marinate in the refrigerator for 1 hour before serving.

Nakji Sauce

YIELD: 1 CUP | **ACTIVE TIME:** 5 MINUTES | **TOTAL TIME:** 5 MINUTES

¼ CUP GOCHUJANG

2 TABLESPOONS
GOCHUGARU

3 TABLESPOONS SOY SAUCE

2 TABLESPOONS SUGAR

1½ TABLESPOONS
SHAOXING WINE

2 GARLIC CLOVES, MINCED

2 TEASPOONS GRATED
FRESH GINGER

3 TABLESPOONS CHOPPED
SCALLIONS

1 TABLESPOON SESAME OIL

BLACK PEPPER, TO TASTE

1. Place all of the ingredients in a bowl, stir to combine, and use immediately or store in the refrigerator.

Cucumber & Dill Cream Sauce

YIELD: 2½ CUPS | **ACTIVE TIME:** 35 MINUTES | **TOTAL TIME:** 3 HOURS AND 45 MINUTES

1 ENGLISH CUCUMBER, TRIMMED, PEELED, AND FINELY DICED

1 CUP FULL-FAT GREEK YOGURT

1 CUP SOUR CREAM

3 GARLIC CLOVES, MINCED

1 TABLESPOON CHOPPED FRESH DILL

3½ TABLESPOONS EXTRA-VIRGIN OLIVE OIL

1 TABLESPOON RED WINE VINEGAR

SALT AND PEPPER, TO TASTE

1. Place the cucumber in a fine-mesh sieve and press down on it to remove as much liquid as possible. Transfer the cucumber to a paper towel and let it drain for 15 minutes.

2. Place the yogurt, sour cream, garlic, dill, olive oil, and red wine vinegar in a mixing bowl and stir until well combined. Add the cucumber, season the sauce with salt and pepper, and fold to combine. Cover the bowl with plastic wrap and chill the sauce in the refrigerator for 3 hours before serving.

Clam Sauce

YIELD: 4 CUPS | **ACTIVE TIME:** 20 MINUTES | **TOTAL TIME:** 40 MINUTES

¼ CUP EXTRA-VIRGIN OLIVE OIL

3 GARLIC CLOVES, SLICED THIN

32 LITTLENECK CLAMS, SCRUBBED AND RINSED WELL

1 CUP WHITE WINE

1 CUP CLAM JUICE

1 CUP CHOPPED PARSLEY

¼ CUP FRESHLY GRATED PARMESAN CHEESE

SALT AND PEPPER, TO TASTE

1. Place a Dutch oven over medium heat. Add the olive oil and the garlic and cook, stirring continually, until the garlic starts to brown, about 2 minutes. Add the clams and wine, cover the pot, and cook until the majority of the clams have opened, 5 to 7 minutes. Use a slotted spoon to transfer the clams to a colander and let them drain. Discard any clams that did not open.

2. Add the clam juice and parsley to the Dutch oven. Cook, stirring occasionally, until the sauce starts to thicken, about 10 minutes. Remove all the clams from their shells and mince one-quarter of them.

3. Add the Parmesan, season the sauce with salt and pepper, and stir until the cheese begins to melt. Use immediately, and top with the clams.

Béarnaise Sauce

YIELD: 1½ CUPS | **ACTIVE TIME:** 30 MINUTES | **TOTAL TIME:** 30 MINUTES

¼ CUP WHITE WINE VINEGAR

¼ CUP DRY WHITE WINE

1 LARGE SHALLOT, FINELY DICED

¼ CUP FRESH TARRAGON, CHOPPED

SALT AND PEPPER, TO TASTE

½ CUP UNSALTED BUTTER, CUBED

3 LARGE EGG YOLKS

1. Place the vinegar, white wine, shallot, and half of the tarragon in a medium saucepan, season the mixture generously with salt, and bring it to a boil over medium heat. Cook until ¼ cup liquid remains, strain the sauce into a heatproof bowl, and set it aside.

2. Place the butter in a large saucepan and cook it over medium-low heat until the white solids separate from the fat, 20 to 25 minutes. Carefully pour the clarified butter into a jar and discard the solids that remain the saucepan.

3. Fill a medium saucepan halfway with water and bring it to a simmer. Place the heatproof bowl containing the reduction over the simmering water, add the egg yolks, and whisk until the mixture is frothy and has thickened, 3 to 4 minutes.

4. While whisking continually, slowly add the clarified butter. Remove the bowl from heat if the sauce is separating, as it is too hot.

5. Stir the remaining tarragon into the sauce, season it with salt and pepper, and use immediately.

Strawberry & Cilantro Salsa

YIELD: 3 CUPS | **ACTIVE TIME:** 20 MINUTES | **TOTAL TIME:** 30 MINUTES

1 SHALLOT, FINELY DICED

½ SMALL JALAPEÑO CHILE PEPPER, FINELY DICED

2 CUPS STRAWBERRIES, HULLED AND DICED

ZEST AND JUICE OF ½ LIME

PINCH OF BROWN SUGAR

SALT AND PEPPER, TO TASTE

HANDFUL OF FRESH CILANTRO, CHOPPED

1 TABLESPOON CHOPPED FRESH MINT

1. Place all of the ingredients in a bowl, stir to combine, and use immediately or store in the refrigerator.

Spinach & Blue Cheese Sauce

YIELD: 4 CUPS | **ACTIVE TIME:** 45 MINUTES | **TOTAL TIME:** 45 MINUTES

4 TABLESPOONS UNSALTED BUTTER, CHOPPED

¼ CUP ALL-PURPOSE FLOUR

4 CUPS MILK

½ CUP HEAVY CREAM

1 CUP CRUMBLED BLUE CHEESE

1 CUP GRATED CHEDDAR CHEESE

SALT AND PEPPER, TO TASTE

6 CUPS BABY SPINACH

1. Bring 3 inches of water to a simmer in a medium saucepan. Place the butter in a large saucepan and melt it over medium heat. While stirring continually, add the flour to the butter and cook, continuing to stir, until the roux is golden, 2 to 3 minutes.

2. While whisking continually, add half of the milk in a slow, steady stream. Whisk in the remaining milk and then the cream. Bring the sauce to a simmer and cook until it has thickened, 8 to 10 minutes, stirring frequently.

3. Add the blue cheese and cheddar and stir until they have melted and the sauce is smooth. Season the sauce with salt and pepper and remove the pan from heat.

4. Place the spinach in a steaming basket and place the basket over the simmering water. Steam the spinach for 2 minutes, place it in a linen towel, and wring the towel to remove as much liquid from the spinach as possible.

5. Gently stir the spinach into the sauce. Use immediately or store in the refrigerator.

Béarnaise Sauce
SEE PAGE 318

Crab Stock

YIELD: 8 CUPS | **ACTIVE TIME:** 30 MINUTES | **TOTAL TIME:** 2 TO 4 HOURS

2 TABLESPOONS EXTRA-VIRGIN OLIVE OIL

1 ONION, CHOPPED

1 CARROT, PEELED AND CHOPPED

1 CELERY STALK, CHOPPED

SHELLS FROM 3 LBS. COOKED CRAB LEGS

½ CUP WHITE WINE

¼ CUP TOMATO PASTE

2 SPRIGS OF FRESH THYME

2 SPRIGS OF FRESH PARSLEY

3 SPRIGS OF FRESH TARRAGON

1 BAY LEAF

½ TEASPOON BLACK PEPPERCORNS

1 TEASPOON KOSHER SALT

8 CARDAMOM PODS

1. In a large stockpot, add the olive oil and warm it over low heat. Add the vegetables and cook until any moisture they release has evaporated. This will allow the flavor of the vegetables to become concentrated. Add the remaining ingredients and enough water to cover the crab shells by 1 inch.

2. Raise the heat to high and bring the stock to a boil. Reduce the heat so that the stock simmers and cook until the flavor has developed to your liking, a minimum of 2 hours. Skim the fat and impurities from the surface as the stock cooks.

3. When the flavor of the stock has developed to your liking, strain it through a fine-mesh sieve or a colander lined with cheesecloth. Place the stock in the refrigerator and chill until it is completely cool.

4. Remove the fat layer from the top of the cooled stock. The stock will keep in the refrigerator for 3 to 5 days, and in the freezer for up to 3 months.

Shrimp Stock

YIELD: 8 CUPS | **ACTIVE TIME:** 15 MINUTES | **TOTAL TIME:** 1 HOUR AND 45 MINUTES

SHELLS FROM 2 LBS. RAW SHRIMP

8 CUPS WATER

1 CUP DRY WHITE WINE

1 CARROT, PEELED AND CHOPPED

1 ONION, SLICED

1 CELERY STALK, SLICED

1 TABLESPOON BLACK PEPPERCORNS

3 SPRIGS OF FRESH PARSLEY

3 SPRIGS OF FRESH THYME

2 GARLIC CLOVES

1 BAY LEAF

1. Place all of the ingredients in a large stockpot and bring to a boil over high heat. Reduce the heat to low and simmer the stock for 1½ hours, skimming to remove any impurities that rise to the surface.

2. Strain the stock through a fine sieve, let it cool slightly, and place it in the refrigerator, uncovered, to chill. Remove the fat layer and cover. The stock will keep in the refrigerator for up to 5 days, and in the freezer for up to 3 months.

Lobster Stock

YIELD: 8 CUPS | **ACTIVE TIME:** 30 MINUTES | **TOTAL TIME:** 4 HOURS AND 30 MINUTES

5 LBS. LOBSTER SHELLS AND BODIES

2 TABLESPOONS EXTRA-VIRGIN OLIVE OIL

½ LB. CARROTS, PEELED AND CHOPPED

½ LB. ONIONS, CHOPPED

10 TOMATOES, CHOPPED

1 CUP V8

5 SPRIGS OF FRESH THYME

5 SPRIGS OF FRESH PARSLEY

5 SPRIGS OF FRESH TARRAGON

5 SPRIGS OF FRESH DILL

1 GARLIC CLOVE

2 CUPS WHITE WINE

1. Preheat the oven to 350°F. Arrange the lobster bodies and shells on two baking sheets, place them in the oven, and roast them for 30 to 45 minutes. Remove the roasted bodies and shells from the oven and set them aside.

2. While the lobster bodies and shells are in the oven, place the olive oil in a large stockpot and warm it over medium heat. Add the carrots and onions and cook, stirring occasionally, until the onions start to brown, about 10 minutes. Remove the pan from heat.

3. Add the lobster bodies and shells, tomatoes, V8, fresh herbs, garlic, and white wine to the stockpot. Add enough water to cover the mixture, raise the heat to high, and bring to a boil. Reduce the heat and simmer the stock for at least 2 hours, occasionally skimming to remove any impurities that rise to the surface.

4. When the flavor of the stock has developed to your liking, strain it through a fine-mesh sieve or a colander lined with cheesecloth. Place the stock in the refrigerator and chill until it is completely cool.

5. Remove the fat layer from the top of the cooled stock. The stock will keep in the refrigerator for 3 to 5 days, and in the freezer for up to 3 months.

Spicy Poke Sauce

YIELD: 1¼ CUPS | **ACTIVE TIME:** 5 MINUTES | **TOTAL TIME:** 5 MINUTES

1 CUP MAYONNAISE

1 TABLESPOON RICE VINEGAR

1 TABLESPOON SUGAR

1 TABLESPOON SRIRACHA

1 TABLESPOON MASAGO OR FLYING FISH ROE

1. Place all of the ingredients, except the masago, in a bowl and stir until thoroughly combined.

2. Add the masago and gently fold until incorporated.

3. Use immediately or store in the refrigerator for up to a week.

Tomato Sauce

YIELD: 4 CUPS | **ACTIVE TIME:** 15 MINUTES | **TOTAL TIME:** 45 MINUTES

2 TABLESPOONS AVOCADO OIL

1 LARGE GARLIC CLOVE, CHOPPED

1 TEASPOON GRATED FRESH GINGER

1 CINNAMON STICK

1 (28 OZ.) CAN OF CHOPPED SAN MARZANO TOMATOES, WITH THEIR LIQUID

½ TEASPOON CUMIN

¼ TEASPOON CORIANDER

⅛ TEASPOON CAYENNE PEPPER

1. Place the avocado oil in a large saucepan and warm it over medium heat. Add the garlic and ginger and cook, stirring frequently, until the mixture is fragrant, about 1 minute.

2. Add the cinnamon stick and cook, stirring continually, for 30 seconds. Add the remaining ingredients and bring the sauce to a boil.

3. Reduce the heat and simmer the sauce until the flavor has developed to your liking, about 30 minutes.

4. Remove the cinnamon stick from the sauce and use as desired or store in the refrigerator.

Remoulade Sauce

YIELD: 2 CUPS | **ACTIVE TIME:** 5 MINUTES | **TOTAL TIME:** 5 MINUTES

1½ CUPS MAYONNAISE

½ CUP CREOLE MUSTARD

JUICE OF 2 LEMONS

3 TABLESPOONS SRIRACHA

3 TABLESPOONS SWEET RELISH

¾ TEASPOON KOSHER SALT

½ TEASPOON BLACK PEPPER

1. Place all of the ingredients in a bowl and whisk until thoroughly combined. Use immediately or store in the refrigerator.

Creamy Balsamic & Mushroom Sauce

YIELD: 2 CUPS | **ACTIVE TIME:** 30 MINUTES | **TOTAL TIME:** 30 MINUTES

4 TABLESPOONS UNSALTED BUTTER

2 CUPS SLICED MUSHROOMS

2 ONIONS, DICED

2 TEASPOONS TOMATO PASTE

1 CUP VEGETABLE STOCK (SEE PAGE 303)

1 CUP HEAVY CREAM

SALT AND PEPPER, TO TASTE

2 TEASPOONS BALSAMIC VINEGAR

2 TEASPOONS DRIED THYME

¼ CUP CHOPPED FRESH PARSLEY

2 TABLESPOONS CORNSTARCH

1. Place 2 tablespoons of the butter in a large skillet and melt it over medium heat. Add the mushrooms and cook, stirring one or two times, until browned all over, about 10 minutes. Remove the mushrooms from the pan and set them aside.

2. Place the remaining butter in the pan, add the onions, and cook, stirring occasionally, until they have softened, about 5 minutes. Add the tomato paste and cook, stirring continually, for 2 minutes.

3. Deglaze the pan with the stock and heavy cream, scraping up any browned bits from the bottom of the pan. Cook until the liquid has been reduced by half.

4. Add the mushrooms back to the pan and season the sauce with salt and pepper. Stir in the vinegar, thyme, and parsley and let the mixture simmer.

5. Place the cornstarch in a small bowl and add a splash of water. Whisk to combine and then whisk the slurry into the sauce. Continue whisking until the sauce has thickened, about 2 minutes, and use as desired.

Chipotle Mayonnaise

YIELD: ½ CUP | **ACTIVE TIME:** 5 MINUTES | **TOTAL TIME:** 5 MINUTES

½ CUP MAYONNAISE

1¼ TEASPOONS MINCED CHIPOTLES IN ADOBO

1 TEASPOON FRESH LEMON JUICE

1. Place all of the ingredients in a mixing bowl and stir until well combined. Use as desired or store in the refrigerator.

Remoulade Sauce
SEE PAGE 326

Saffron Water

YIELD: 1 CUP | **ACTIVE TIME:** 5 MINUTES | **TOTAL TIME:** 25 MINUTES

1 TABLESPOON SAFFRON

1 CUP BOILING WATER

1. Preheat the oven to 425°F. Place the saffron on a small piece of aluminum foil and fold it over to ensure that the saffron is secure inside. Toast the saffron in the oven for no more than 1 minute.

2. Remove the saffron from the oven and use your fingers to crumble it into tiny pieces. Place the saffron in a small glass jar, pour in the boiling water, and shake until well blended. Let the mixture steep for 15 minutes and strain before using or storing.

Chermoula Sauce

YIELD: 5 CUPS | **ACTIVE TIME:** 5 MINUTES | **TOTAL TIME:** 10 MINUTES

1 TABLESPOON SAFFRON

4 CUPS MAYONNAISE

1 TABLESPOON RAS EL HANOUT (SEE PAGE 55)

1 TABLESPOON BERBERE SEASONING

2 TABLESPOONS ZA'ATAR (SEE PAGE 68)

1 TABLESPOON SUMAC

2 CUPS CHOPPED FRESH HERBS (TARRAGON, PARSLEY, CHIVES, AND CILANTRO RECOMMENDED)

1 TABLESPOON DRIED OREGANO

1 TABLESPOON KOSHER SALT

1 TABLESPOON BLACK PEPPER

1. Place the saffron in ¼ cup water and let it bloom. Remove the saffron from the water and reserve the liquid for another preparation (it's really good in a tomato sauce, for example)—using it in this sauce will make it too loose.

2. Place the saffron and the remaining ingredients in a large bowl and stir until thoroughly combined. Use immediately or transfer to an airtight container and store in the refrigerator.

Pizza Sauce

YIELD: 2 CUPS | **ACTIVE TIME:** 5 MINUTES | **TOTAL TIME:** 5 MINUTES

1 LB. PEELED, WHOLE SAN
MARZANO TOMATOES,
WITH THEIR LIQUID,
CRUSHED BY HAND

1½ TABLESPOONS EXTRA-
VIRGIN OLIVE OIL

SALT, TO TASTE

DRIED OREGANO, TO TASTE

1. Place the tomatoes and their juices in a bowl, add the olive oil, and stir until it has been thoroughly incorporated.

2. Season the sauce with salt and oregano and stir to incorporate. If using within 2 hours, leave the sauce at room temperature. If storing in the refrigerator, where the sauce will keep for up to 3 days, return to room temperature before using.

Tartar Sauce

YIELD: 1¼ CUPS | **ACTIVE TIME:** 5 MINUTES | **TOTAL TIME:** 5 MINUTES

1 CUP MAYONNAISE

½ GARLIC CLOVE, MINCED

2 TABLESPOONS CHOPPED
GHERKINS

1 TABLESPOON CHOPPED
FRESH DILL

1 TABLESPOON HOT WATER

1. Place all of the ingredients in a bowl and stir to combine. Use immediately or store in the refrigerator.

Buffalo Wing Sauce

YIELD: 1 CUP | **ACTIVE TIME:** 10 MINUTES | **TOTAL TIME:** 35 MINUTES

4 TABLESPOONS UNSALTED BUTTER

1 TABLESPOON WHITE VINEGAR

¾ CUP HOT SAUCE

1 TEASPOON CAYENNE PEPPER

SALT AND PEPPER, TO TASTE

1. Place the butter in a saucepan and melt it over medium heat.

2. Stir in the vinegar, hot sauce, and cayenne, making sure not to breathe in the spicy steam.

3. Transfer the sauce to a mixing bowl, season it with salt and pepper, and use immediately or store in the refrigerator.

Smoky Southern BBQ Sauce

YIELD: 1½ CUPS | **ACTIVE TIME:** 30 MINUTES | **TOTAL TIME:** 1 HOUR AND 30 MINUTES

1 CUP HICKORY WOOD CHIPS

2 GARLIC CLOVES, MINCED

1 WHITE ONION, MINCED

1 CUP CRUSHED TOMATOES, DRAINED

¼ CUP TOMATO PASTE

2 TABLESPOONS WHITE WINE VINEGAR

2 TABLESPOONS BALSAMIC VINEGAR

1 TABLESPOON DIJON MUSTARD

JUICE FROM 1 LIME

1-INCH PIECE OF FRESH GINGER, PEELED AND MINCED

1 TEASPOON SMOKED PAPRIKA

½ TEASPOON CINNAMON

2 DRIED CHIPOTLE PEPPERS, STEMS AND SEEDS REMOVED, MINCED

1 HABANERO PEPPER, STEMS AND SEEDS REMOVED, MINCED

SALT AND PEPPER, TO TASTE

1. Soak the wood chips in a bowl of water for 20 minutes.

2. Prepare a gas or charcoal grill for medium-high heat (about 450ºF).

3. Place the garlic, onion, tomatoes, and tomato paste in a food processor and blitz until combined. Add the remaining ingredients and blitz until incorporated. Pour the sauce into a saucepan.

4. When the grill is ready, drain the woodchips and spread them over the coals or pour them into a smoker box if using a gas grill. Place the saucepan on the grill and then bring the sauce to a boil with the grill covered. Let the sauce cook until it has reduced by about one-third, about 20 minutes.

5. Taste, adjust the seasoning if necessary, and use immediately or store in the refrigerator.

Maple BBQ Sauce

YIELD: 1½ CUPS | **ACTIVE TIME:** 15 MINUTES | **TOTAL TIME:** 35 MINUTES

2 TABLESPOONS EXTRA-VIRGIN OLIVE OIL

¼ WHITE ONION, MINCED

2 GARLIC CLOVES, MINCED

1 CUP KETCHUP

3 TABLESPOONS APPLE CIDER VINEGAR

1 TABLESPOON UNSALTED BUTTER

½ CUP REAL MAPLE SYRUP

2 TABLESPOONS MOLASSES

2 TEASPOONS DRY MUSTARD

SALT AND PEPPER, TO TASTE

1. Place the olive oil in a saucepan and warm it over medium-high heat. Add the onion and cook, stirring occasionally, until it is translucent, about 3 minutes.

2. Stir in the remaining ingredients and bring the sauce to a boil. Reduce the heat to medium and simmer until the sauce has reduced by one-third, about 20 minutes. Taste, adjust the seasoning if necessary, and use immediately, or let the sauce cool and store it in the refrigerator.

Apple & Mustard BBQ Sauce

YIELD: 1½ CUPS | **ACTIVE TIME:** 15 MINUTES | **TOTAL TIME:** 35 MINUTES

1 TABLESPOON EXTRA-VIRGIN OLIVE OIL

½ SHALLOT, MINCED

½ CUP APPLE CIDER

½ CUP WHITE WINE VINEGAR

1 TABLESPOON TEQUILA

2 TEASPOONS CHOPPED FRESH PARSLEY

2 TABLESPOONS FISH SAUCE

1 TABLESPOON HONEY

1 TABLESPOON DIJON MUSTARD

2 TEASPOONS SPICY MUSTARD

SALT AND PEPPER, TO TASTE

1. Place the olive oil in a saucepan and warm it over medium-high heat. Add the shallot and cook, stirring occasionally, until it is translucent, about 3 minutes.

2. Stir in the remaining ingredients and bring the sauce to a boil. Reduce the heat to medium and simmer until the sauce has reduced by one-third, about 20 minutes. Taste, adjust the seasoning if necessary, and use immediately, or let the sauce cool and store it in the refrigerator.

Kansas City BBQ Sauce

YIELD: 1½ CUPS | **ACTIVE TIME:** 10 MINUTES | **TOTAL TIME:** 25 MINUTES

1 TABLESPOON EXTRA-VIRGIN OLIVE OIL

4 GARLIC CLOVES, MINCED

1 CUP KETCHUP

¼ CUP WATER

2 TABLESPOONS MOLASSES

2 TABLESPOONS DARK BROWN SUGAR

1 TABLESPOON APPLE CIDER VINEGAR

1 TABLESPOON WORCESTERSHIRE SAUCE

1 BAY LEAF

1 TEASPOON DRY MUSTARD

1 TEASPOON CHILI POWDER

1 TEASPOON ONION POWDER

1 TEASPOON LIQUID SMOKE

1 TEASPOON BLACK PEPPER

1 TEASPOON KOSHER SALT

1. Place the olive oil in a saucepan and warm it over medium-high heat. Add the garlic and cook, stirring continually, for 1 minute.

2. Stir in the remaining ingredients and bring the sauce to a boil. Reduce the heat to medium and simmer until the sauce has reduced by one-third, about 20 minutes.

3. Remove the bay leaf and discard it. Taste, adjust the seasoning if necessary, and use immediately, or let the sauce cool and store it in the refrigerator.

South Carolina BBQ Sauce

YIELD: 2 CUPS | **ACTIVE TIME:** 5 MINUTES | **TOTAL TIME:** 30 MINUTES

1 CUP YELLOW MUSTARD

½ CUP HONEY

½ CUP APPLE CIDER VINEGAR

2 TABLESPOONS KETCHUP

1 TABLESPOON LIGHT BROWN SUGAR

2 TEASPOONS WORCESTERSHIRE SAUCE

3 GARLIC CLOVES, MINCED

1 TEASPOON GROUND BLACK PEPPER

SALT, TO TASTE

1. Place all of the ingredients in a saucepan, stir to combine, and bring to a boil over medium-high heat. Reduce the heat to medium and cook until the sauce has reduced by one-third, about 20 minutes.

2. Taste, adjust the seasoning if necessary, and use immediately, or let the sauce cool and store it in the refrigerator.

Maple BBQ Sauce
SEE PAGE 336

Charred Peach BBQ Sauce

YIELD: 2 CUPS | **ACTIVE TIME:** 20 MINUTES | **TOTAL TIME:** 40 MINUTES

4 PEACHES, HALVED, PITS REMOVED

2 TABLESPOONS EXTRA-VIRGIN OLIVE OIL

1 SMALL ONION, MINCED

4 GARLIC CLOVES, MINCED

1 CUP PUREED TOMATOES

½ CUP KETCHUP

¼ CUP LIGHT BROWN SUGAR

¼ CUP MOLASSES

2 TABLESPOONS HONEY

1 TABLESPOON WORCESTERSHIRE SAUCE

2 TABLESPOONS PEACH PRESERVES

JUICE FROM ½ LEMON

1 TEASPOON BLACK PEPPER

1 TEASPOON KOSHER SALT

1. Prepare a gas or charcoal grill for medium-high heat (about 450ºF). Place the peaches on the grill, cut side down, and cook until they are charred and starting to caramelize, about 6 minutes. Remove the peaches from the grill and let them cool slightly.

2. Place the peaches in a food processor, blitz until pureed, and set the puree aside.

3. Place the olive oil in a saucepan and warm it over medium-high heat. Add the onion and cook, stirring occasionally, until it is translucent, about 3 minutes.

4. Stir in the peach puree and the remaining ingredients and bring the sauce to a boil. Reduce the heat to medium and simmer until the sauce has reduced by one-third, about 20 minutes. Taste, adjust the seasoning if necessary, and use immediately, or let the sauce cool and store it in the refrigerator.

St. Louis BBQ Sauce

YIELD: 2 CUPS | **ACTIVE TIME:** 15 MINUTES | **TOTAL TIME:** 1 HOUR AND 30 MINUTES

2 CUPS PUREED TOMATOES

2 TABLESPOONS DIJON MUSTARD

¼ CUP APPLE CIDER VINEGAR

¼ CUP MOLASSES

1 CUP DARK BROWN SUGAR

1 TEASPOON WORCESTERSHIRE SAUCE

2 GARLIC CLOVES, MINCED

1 TEASPOON BLACK PEPPER

1 TEASPOON KOSHER SALT

1. Place all of the ingredients in a saucepan, stir to combine, and bring the sauce to a boil over medium-high heat. Reduce the heat to medium-low and gently simmer the sauce for 1 hour, stirring occasionally.

2. Taste, adjust the seasoning if necessary, and use immediately, or let the sauce cool and store it in the refrigerator.

Basic au Jus

YIELD: 1½ CUPS | **ACTIVE TIME:** 10 MINUTES | **TOTAL TIME:** 10 MINUTES

1 CUP DRY RED WINE

2 CUPS BEEF STOCK (SEE PAGE 306)

1 TABLESPOON UNSALTED BUTTER

SALT AND PEPPER, TO TASTE

1. After removing the beef roast from the oven, pour the juices from the roasting pan into a fat separator; discard the fat and return the juices to the original roasting pan. Note that there is still flavor blanketing the roasting pan, so be sure to use the same pan.

2. Add the wine and stock and bring the mixture to a boil over medium-high heat, stirring and scraping up any browned bits from the bottom of the pan. Cook until the mixture has reduced by half.

3. Stir in the butter, season the au jus with salt and pepper, and use immediately or store in the refrigerator.

Poultry au Jus

YIELD: 1½ CUPS | **ACTIVE TIME:** 10 MINUTES | **TOTAL TIME:** 10 MINUTES

1 CUP DRY WHITE WINE

2 CUPS CHICKEN STOCK (SEE PAGE 303)

2 TEASPOONS CHOPPED FRESH PARSLEY

1 TABLESPOON UNSALTED BUTTER

SALT AND PEPPER, TO TASTE

1. After removing the chicken from the oven, pour the juices from the roasting pan into a fat separator; discard the fat and return the juices to the original roasting pan. Note that there is still flavor blanketing the roasting pan, so be sure to use the same pan.

2. Add the wine and stock and bring the mixture to a boil over medium-high heat, stirring and scraping up any browned bits from the bottom of the pan. Cook until the mixture has reduced by half.

3. Stir in the parsley and butter, season the au jus with salt and pepper, and use immediately or store in the refrigerator.

Au Jus with Herbs

YIELD: 1½ CUPS | **ACTIVE TIME:** 10 MINUTES | **TOTAL TIME:** 10 MINUTES

1 CUP DRY RED WINE

2 CUPS BEEF STOCK (SEE PAGE 306)

1 TEASPOON CHOPPED FRESH ROSEMARY

1 TEASPOON FRESH THYME

1 TEASPOON CHOPPED FRESH PARSLEY

1 TEASPOON WORCESTERSHIRE SAUCE

SALT AND PEPPER, TO TASTE

1. After removing the beef roast from the oven, pour the juices from the roasting pan into a fat separator; discard the fat and return the juices to the original roasting pan. Note that there is still flavor blanketing the roasting pan, so be sure to use the same pan.

2. Add the wine and stock and bring the mixture to a boil over medium-high heat, stirring and scraping up any browned bits from the bottom of the pan. Cook until the mixture has reduced by half.

3. Stir in the herbs and Worcestershire sauce, season the au jus with salt and pepper, and use immediately or store in the refrigerator.

Miso BBQ Sauce

YIELD: 1½ CUPS | **ACTIVE TIME:** 10 MINUTES | **TOTAL TIME:** 30 MINUTES

6 TABLESPOONS RED MISO

¼ CUP WATER

4 GARLIC CLOVES, MINCED

6 TABLESPOONS DARK BROWN SUGAR

6 TABLESPOONS WHITE VINEGAR

¼ CUP KETCHUP

2 TEASPOONS BLACK PEPPER

2 TEASPOONS KOSHER SALT

1. Place all of the ingredients in a saucepan, stir to combine, and bring the sauce to a boil over medium-high heat. Reduce the heat to medium and cook the sauce until it has reduced by one-third, about 20 minutes.

2. Taste, adjust the seasoning if necessary, and use immediately, or let the sauce cool and store it in the refrigerator.

Honey & Bourbon BBQ Sauce

YIELD: 1½ CUPS | **ACTIVE TIME:** 10 MINUTES | **TOTAL TIME:** 35 MINUTES

2 TABLESPOONS EXTRA-VIRGIN OLIVE OIL

4 GARLIC CLOVES, MINCED

1 CUP KETCHUP

½ CUP BOURBON

3 TABLESPOONS HONEY

2 TABLESPOONS BROWN SUGAR

1 TABLESPOON SOY SAUCE

1 TABLESPOON WORCESTERSHIRE SAUCE

1 TABLESPOON DIJON MUSTARD

1 TEASPOON LIQUID SMOKE

1 TEASPOON BLACK PEPPER

1 TEASPOON KOSHER SALT

1. Place the olive oil in a saucepan and warm it over medium-high heat. Add the garlic and cook, stirring continually, for 1 minute.

2. Stir in the remaining ingredients and bring the sauce to a boil. Reduce the heat to medium and simmer until the sauce has reduced by one-third, about 20 minutes.

3. Taste, adjust the seasoning if necessary, and use immediately, or let the sauce cool and store it in the refrigerator.

Coffee & Bourbon BBQ Sauce

YIELD: 2 CUPS | **ACTIVE TIME:** 5 MINUTES | **TOTAL TIME:** 30 MINUTES

2 CUPS BREWED COFFEE

¼ CUP DARK BROWN SUGAR

¾ CUP BOURBON

3 TABLESPOONS MOLASSES

¼ CUP APPLE CIDER VINEGAR

2 TABLESPOONS WORCESTERSHIRE SAUCE

¼ CUP KETCHUP

1 TABLESPOON GRANULATED GARLIC

½ TABLESPOON BLACK PEPPER

1 TABLESPOON CORNSTARCH

1. Place all of the ingredients in a saucepan, stir to combine, and bring the sauce to a boil over medium-high heat. Reduce the heat to medium and simmer the sauce until it has reduced by one-third, about 20 minutes.

2. Taste, adjust the seasoning as necessary, and use immediately, or let the sauce cool and store it in the refrigerator.

Smoky Stout BBQ Sauce

YIELD: 2 CUPS | **ACTIVE TIME:** 5 MINUTES | **TOTAL TIME:** 30 MINUTES

1 CUP GUINNESS OR
PREFERRED STOUT

1 CUP KETCHUP

½ CUP APPLE CIDER
VINEGAR

½ CUP GENTLY PACKED
DARK BROWN SUGAR

2 TABLESPOONS HONEY

2 TABLESPOONS
WORCESTERSHIRE SAUCE

1 TEASPOON LIQUID SMOKE

1 TEASPOON BLACK PEPPER

1 TEASPOON KOSHER SALT

1. Place all of the ingredients in a saucepan, stir to combine, and bring the sauce to a boil over medium-high heat. Reduce the heat to medium and cook the sauce until it has reduced by one-third, about 20 minutes.

2. Taste, adjust the seasoning if necessary, and use immediately, or let the sauce cool and store it in the refrigerator.

Universal BBQ Sauce

YIELD: 2 CUPS | **ACTIVE TIME:** 10 MINUTES | **TOTAL TIME:** 30 MINUTES

1¼ CUPS KETCHUP

1 CUP DARK BROWN SUGAR

¼ CUP MOLASSES

¼ CUP APPLE CIDER VINEGAR

¼ CUP WATER

1 TABLESPOON WORCESTERSHIRE SAUCE

2 TEASPOONS DRY MUSTARD

2 TEASPOONS GARLIC POWDER

2 TEASPOONS SMOKED PAPRIKA

¼ TEASPOON CAYENNE PEPPER

SALT AND PEPPER, TO TASTE

1 TABLESPOON ALL-PURPOSE FLOUR

1. Place all of the ingredients, except for the flour, in a saucepan, stir to combine, and bring the sauce to a boil over medium-high heat. Reduce the heat to medium and cook the sauce until it has reduced by one-third, about 20 minutes.

2. Gradually add the flour to the sauce, stirring continually to prevent lumps from forming.

3. Simmer the sauce for 5 another minutes, taste, adjust the seasoning as necessary, and use immediately, or let the sauce cool and store it in the refrigerator until it is ready to use.

Korean BBQ Sauce

YIELD: 1 CUP | **ACTIVE TIME:** 10 MINUTES | **TOTAL TIME:** 30 MINUTES

½ CUP SOY SAUCE

¼ CUP KETCHUP

¼ CUP RICE WINE VINEGAR

3 TABLESPOONS LIGHT BROWN SUGAR

1 TABLESPOON GOCHUJANG

2 GARLIC CLOVES, MINCED

1 TEASPOON SESAME OIL

½-INCH PIECE OF FRESH GINGER, PEELED AND GRATED

4 SCALLIONS, TRIMMED AND CHOPPED

1 TEASPOON BLACK PEPPER

1. Place all of the ingredients in a saucepan, stir to combine, and bring the sauce to a boil over medium-high heat. Reduce the heat to medium and cook the sauce until it has reduced by one-third, about 20 minutes.

2. Taste, adjust the seasoning if necessary, and use immediately, or let the sauce cool and store it in the refrigerator.

Quick BBQ Sauce

YIELD: 1 CUP | **ACTIVE TIME:** 5 MINUTES | **TOTAL TIME:** 5 MINUTES

⅔ CUP KETCHUP

¼ CUP APPLE CIDER VINEGAR

¼ CUP BOURBON

¼ CUP LIGHT BROWN SUGAR

2 TEASPOONS PAPRIKA

1½ TEASPOONS CUMIN

SALT AND PEPPER, TO TASTE

1. Place all of the ingredients in a saucepan, stir to combine, and bring the sauce to a boil over medium-high heat. Cook the sauce until it thickens and the alcohol has been cooked off, about 5 minutes.

2. Taste, adjust the seasoning if necessary, and use immediately, or let the sauce cool and store it in the refrigerator.

Smoky Maple BBQ Sauce

YIELD: 2½ CUPS | **ACTIVE TIME:** 10 MINUTES | **TOTAL TIME:** 30 MINUTES

2 CUPS TOMATO SAUCE (SEE PAGE 326)

¼ CUP TOMATO PASTE

⅓ CUP APPLE CIDER VINEGAR

2 TABLESPOONS SPICY MUSTARD

¼ CUP MOLASSES

¼ CUP MAPLE SYRUP

2 TABLESPOONS BOURBON

2 TABLESPOONS WORCESTERSHIRE SAUCE

2 TEASPOONS PAPRIKA

1 TEASPOON LIQUID SMOKE

½ TEASPOON CUMIN

¼ TEASPOON CAYENNE PEPPER

½ TEASPOON KOSHER SALT

½ TEASPOON BLACK PEPPER

1. Place all of the ingredients in a saucepan, stir to combine, and bring the sauce to a boil over medium-high heat. Reduce the heat to medium and cook the sauce until it has reduced by one-third, about 20 minutes.

2. Taste, adjust the seasoning if necessary, and use immediately, or let the sauce cool and store it in the refrigerator.

Port Reduction

YIELD: 1 CUP | **ACTIVE TIME:** 10 MINUTES | **TOTAL TIME:** 40 MINUTES

2 TABLESPOONS EXTRA-VIRGIN OLIVE OIL

½ SHALLOT, MINCED

3 GARLIC CLOVES, MINCED

1 TEASPOON CHOPPED FRESH OREGANO

1 CUP PORT WINE

1 CUP DRY WHITE WINE

3 TABLESPOONS BALSAMIC VINEGAR

¼ CUP FRESH PARSLEY, CHOPPED

SALT AND PEPPER, TO TASTE

1. Place the olive oil in a saucepan and warm it over medium-high heat. Add the shallot and cook, stirring occasionally, until it is translucent, about 3 minutes.

2. Stir in the remaining ingredients and bring the mixture to a boil. Reduce the heat to medium and simmer until the mixture has reduced by three-quarters, about 30 minutes.

3. Use immediately, or let the reduction cool and store it in the refrigerator.

Blueberry BBQ Sauce

YIELD: 2 CUPS | **ACTIVE TIME:** 10 MINUTES | **TOTAL TIME:** 30 MINUTES

2 TABLESPOONS CLARIFIED BUTTER (SEE PAGE 318)

3 TABLESPOONS EXTRA-VIRGIN OLIVE OIL

¾ CUP RED WINE

SALT AND PEPPER, TO TASTE

2¾ CUPS BLUEBERRIES

½ CUP HONEY

1. Place all of the ingredients in a food processor and blitz until smooth.

2. Place the puree in a saucepan and bring it to a boil over medium-high heat. Reduce the heat to medium and simmer until the sauce has reduced by one-third, about 20 minutes. Use immediately, or let the sauce cool and store it in the refrigerator.

Parsley & Mint Sauce

YIELD: 2 CUPS | **ACTIVE TIME:** 5 MINUTES | **TOTAL TIME:** 5 MINUTES

1 GARLIC CLOVE, MINCED

1 CUP FRESH PARSLEY, CHOPPED

¼ CUP FRESH MINT, CHOPPED

2 ANCHOVIES IN OLIVE OIL, DRAINED AND MINCED

JUICE OF ½ LEMON

½ CUP EXTRA-VIRGIN OLIVE OIL

SALT AND PEPPER, TO TASTE

1. Place the garlic, parsley, mint, anchovies, and lemon juice in a bowl and whisk to combine.

2. While whisking continually, add the olive oil in a slow stream until it has emulsified. Season the sauce with salt and pepper and use immediately or store it in the refrigerator.

Tare Sauce

YIELD: 2½ CUPS | **ACTIVE TIME:** 5 MINUTES | **TOTAL TIME:** 30 MINUTES

½ CUP CHICKEN STOCK (SEE PAGE 303)

½ CUP SOY SAUCE

½ CUP MIRIN

¼ CUP SAKE

½ CUP BROWN SUGAR

2 GARLIC CLOVES, SMASHED

1-INCH PIECE OF FRESH GINGER, PEELED AND GRATED

1½ SCALLIONS, SLICED

1. Place the ingredients in a small saucepan, stir to combine, and bring the sauce to a simmer over low heat. Simmer for 10 minutes, stirring once or twice.

2. Remove the pan from heat, let the sauce cool, and strain before using or storing in the refrigerator.

Basil & Cilantro Puree

YIELD: 1½ CUPS | **ACTIVE TIME:** 5 MINUTES | **TOTAL TIME:** 5 MINUTES

½ CUP FRESH CILANTRO

½ CUP FRESH BASIL

2 TABLESPOONS CHOPPED FRESH PARSLEY

2 GARLIC CLOVES, MINCED

1 JALAPEÑO CHILE PEPPER, STEM AND SEEDS REMOVED, MINCED

JUICE OF ½ SMALL LIME

¼ CUP EXTRA-VIRGIN OLIVE OIL

SALT AND PEPPER, TO TASTE

1. Place the cilantro, basil, parsley, garlic, jalepeño, and lime juice in a food processor and blitz until smooth.

2. With the food processor running, add the olive oil in a slow stream until it has emulsified. Season the puree with salt and pepper and use immediately or store in the refrigerator.

Dill Aioli

YIELD: 1¼ CUPS | **ACTIVE TIME:** 5 MINUTES | **TOTAL TIME:** 5 MINUTES

¼ CUP FRESH DILL, CHOPPED

¼ CUP FRESH PARSLEY, CHOPPED

JUICE OF ½ LEMON

1 GARLIC CLOVE, MINCED

¾ CUP EXTRA-VIRGIN OLIVE OIL

SALT, TO TASTE

1. Place the dill, parsley, lemon juice, and garlic in a food processor and blitz until smooth.

2. With the food processor running, add the olive oil in a slow stream until it has emulsified. Season the aioli with salt and use immediately or store in the refrigerator.

Tare Sauce
SEE PAGE 358

Blackstrap BBQ Sauce

YIELD: 1 CUP | **ACTIVE TIME:** 15 MINUTES | **TOTAL TIME:** 30 MINUTES

½ CUP KETCHUP

¼ CUP DARK BROWN SUGAR

2 TABLESPOONS SUGAR

2 TABLESPOONS DIJON MUSTARD

3 TABLESPOONS APPLE CIDER VINEGAR

2 GARLIC CLOVES, MINCED

¼ CUP BLACKSTRAP MOLASSES

¼ TEASPOON GROUND CLOVES

½ TEASPOON HOT SAUCE

¼ CUP HONEY

1. Place all of the ingredients in a saucepan, stir to combine, and bring the sauce to a boil over medium-high heat. Reduce the heat to medium and cook the sauce until it has reduced by one-third, about 20 minutes.

2. Taste, adjust the seasoning if necessary, and use immediately, or let the sauce cool and store it in the refrigerator.

Radish Leaf Chimichurri

YIELD: 1½ CUPS | **ACTIVE TIME:** 5 MINUTES | **TOTAL TIME:** 5 MINUTES

1 SMALL SHALLOT, MINCED

2 GARLIC CLOVES, MINCED

¼ TEASPOON RED PEPPER FLAKES

¼ CUP RED WINE VINEGAR

⅔ CUP CHOPPED RADISH LEAVES

1 TABLESPOON CHOPPED FRESH OREGANO

½ CUP EXTRA-VIRGIN OLIVE OIL

2 TEASPOONS KOSHER SALT

1. Place all of the ingredients in a bowl, stir to combine, and use immediately or store in the refrigerator.

Overripe Peach Hot Sauce

YIELD: 3 CUPS | **ACTIVE TIME:** 15 MINUTES | **TOTAL TIME:** 30 MINUTES

8 OVERLY RIPE PEACHES, PITS REMOVED, QUARTERED

2 CUPS APPLE CIDER VINEGAR

¾ CUP SUGAR

3 GARLIC CLOVES, CHOPPED

6 JALAPEÑO CHILE PEPPERS, STEMS AND SEEDS REMOVED, DICED

4 CHILES DE ÀRBOL, STEMS AND SEEDS REMOVED, DICED

1. Preheat the oven to 400°F. Place the peaches on a baking sheet, cut sides facing up, and place the peaches in the oven. Roast until they begin to darken, about 10 minutes. You can also grill the peaches if you're after a slightly smokier hot sauce.

2. Remove the peaches from the oven and place them in a medium saucepan. Add the remaining ingredients and bring the mixture to a simmer over medium-low heat. Simmer the sauce for 10 minutes, stirring occasionally.

3. Transfer the mixture to a blender, puree until smooth, and use immediately or store in the refrigerator.

Tomatillo Sauce

YIELD: 3 CUPS | **ACTIVE TIME:** 5 MINUTES | **TOTAL TIME:** 5 MINUTES

1 LB. TOMATILLOS, HUSKED, RINSED, AND QUARTERED

½ WHITE ONION, CHOPPED

1 SERRANO CHILE PEPPER, STEM AND SEEDS REMOVED

1 GARLIC CLOVE, CRUSHED

1 BUNCH OF FRESH CILANTRO, CHOPPED

2 TABLESPOONS EXTRA-VIRGIN OLIVE OIL

2 TABLESPOONS FRESH LIME JUICE

1. Place a dry skillet over high heat and add the tomatillos, onion, and serrano pepper. Cook until the vegetables are charred slightly, about 5 minutes, turning them as necessary.

2. Transfer the vegetables to a food processor, add the remaining ingredients, and blitz until smooth. Use immediately or store in the refrigerator.

Salsa Chipotle de Adobo

YIELD: 1½ CUPS | **ACTIVE TIME:** 10 MINUTES | **TOTAL TIME:** 10 MINUTES

1 TABLESPOON LARD

½ WHITE ONION, DICED

2 GARLIC CLOVES, DICED

1 TABLESPOON GARLIC POWDER

1 TABLESPOON CHILI POWDER

1 TABLESPOON CUMIN

SALT AND PEPPER, TO TASTE

2 TABLESPOONS CHOPPED CHIPOTLES EN ADOBO

½ CUP CHICKEN STOCK (SEE PAGE 303)

2 TABLESPOONS CHOPPED FRESH CILANTRO

1. Place the lard in a saucepan and warm it over medium heat. Add the onion and cook, stirring occasionally, until it is translucent, about 3 minutes.

2. Stir in the remaining ingredients and simmer the salsa until the flavor has developed to your liking. Remove the pan from heat and let the salsa cool before using or storing in the refrigerator.

Salsa Roja

YIELD: 1 CUP | **ACTIVE TIME:** 20 MINUTES | **TOTAL TIME:** 30 MINUTES

5 LARGE TOMATOES

4 JALAPEÑO CHILE PEPPERS

½ WHITE ONION

3 GARLIC CLOVES, UNPEELED

1 TABLESPOON EXTRA-VIRGIN OLIVE OIL

SALT, TO TASTE

1. Warm a dry skillet over medium heat. Add the tomatoes, jalapeños, onion, and garlic and cook until charred, turning the vegetables as needed. Peel the garlic cloves, transfer the vegetables to a food processor, and blitz until smooth.

2. Place the olive oil in a large skillet and warm it over high heat. Add the salsa, season it with salt, and cook for 3 minutes. Remove the pan from heat and let the salsa cool before using or storing in the refrigerator.

Chile Rojo

YIELD: 1 CUP | **ACTIVE TIME:** 15 MINUTES | **TOTAL TIME:** 40 MINUTES

4 GUAJILLO CHILE PEPPERS, STEMS AND SEEDS REMOVED

2 PASILLA CHILE PEPPERS, STEMS AND SEEDS REMOVED

4 CHIPOTLE MORITA CHILE PEPPERS, STEMS AND SEEDS REMOVED

2 TABLESPOONS CUMIN SEEDS

1 TABLESPOON DRIED THYME

SALT, TO TASTE

1. Place the chile peppers in a dry skillet and toast them over medium heat until they darken and become fragrant and pliable, about 30 seconds. Transfer the chiles to a bowl, cover them with hot water, and let them soak for 20 minutes.

2. Place the cumin seeds in the skillet and toast them until they are fragrant, about 1 minute, shaking the pan frequently. Transfer the toasted cumin seeds to a small dish.

3. Drain the chiles and reserve the soaking liquid. Place the chiles, thyme, and toasted cumin seeds in a food processor and blitz until smooth, adding the reserved liquid as needed to get the desired texture.

4. Season the sauce with salt and use immediately or store in the refrigerator.

Salpicon de Rabano y Chile Habanero

YIELD: 1½ CUPS | **ACTIVE TIME:** 20 MINUTES | **TOTAL TIME:** 1 HOUR AND 30 MINUTES

2 HABANERO CHILE PEPPERS

4 RADISHES, TRIMMED AND JULIENNED

1 BAY LEAF

⅛ TEASPOON DRIED MEXICAN OREGANO

½ CUP FRESH LIME JUICE

½ CUP ORANGE JUICE

1 TABLESPOON EXTRA-VIRGIN OLIVE OIL

SALT, TO TASTE

1. Roast the habaneros over an open flame, in the oven, or on the grill until they are charred all over. Let them cool briefly, remove the stems and seeds, and mince the remaining flesh.

2. Place the habaneros in a bowl, add the remaining ingredients, and stir to combine. Refrigerate the salsa for at least 1 hour before serving.

Barbacoa Adobo

YIELD: 1½ CUPS | **ACTIVE TIME:** 20 MINUTES | **TOTAL TIME:** 45 MINUTES

1 TABLESPOON CORIANDER SEEDS

1½ TEASPOONS WHOLE CLOVES

1½ TEASPOONS ALLSPICE BERRIES

1 TABLESPOON CUMIN SEEDS

1½ TABLESPOONS BLACK PEPPERCORNS

1 ANCHO CHILE PEPPER, STEMS AND SEEDS REMOVED

1 GUAJILLO CHILE PEPPER, STEMS AND SEEDS REMOVED

1 CHIPOTLE CHILE PEPPER, STEMS AND SEEDS REMOVED

1 PASILLA CHILE PEPPER, STEMS AND SEEDS REMOVED

14 TABLESPOONS ORANGE JUICE

14 TABLESPOONS FRESH LIME JUICE

2 SMALL ONIONS, SLICED

5 GARLIC CLOVES

2 AVOCADO LEAVES (OPTIONAL)

SALT, TO TASTE

1. Place the coriander seeds, cloves, allspice berries, cumin seeds, and peppercorns in a dry skillet and toast them until they are fragrant, shaking the pan frequently to keep them from burning. Using a mortar and pestle, grind the mixture into a fine powder.

2. Place the chiles in the pan and toast them until they are fragrant and pliable, about 30 seconds. Place the toasted chiles in a bowl, cover them with hot water, and soak them for 20 minutes.

3. Drain the chiles and reserve the soaking liquid. Place the chiles in a food processor, add the toasted spice powder, juices, onions, garlic, and avocado leaves (if using), and puree until smooth, adding the reserved liquid as needed to get the desired texture.

4. Season the adobo with salt and use immediately or store in the refrigerator.

X'nipek

YIELD: 1 CUP | **ACTIVE TIME:** 10 MINUTES | **TOTAL TIME:** 20 MINUTES

4 ROMA TOMATOES, SEEDS REMOVED, DICED

2 HABANERO CHILE PEPPERS, STEMS AND SEEDS REMOVED, MINCED

1½ SMALL RED ONIONS, JULIENNED

1¼ CUPS FRESH CILANTRO, CHOPPED

1¾ OZ. FRESH LIME JUICE

10 TABLESPOONS ORANGE JUICE

1½ TEASPOONS DRIED MEXICAN OREGANO

SALT, TO TASTE

1. Place all of the ingredients, except for the salt, in a bowl and stir until combined. Let the mixture macerate for 10 minutes.

2. Season the salsa with salt and use immediately or store in the refrigerator.

Salsa de Arbol

YIELD: ½ CUP | **ACTIVE TIME:** 10 MINUTES | **TOTAL TIME:** 30 MINUTES

¼ CUP LARD

3½ OZ. DRIED CHILES DE ÀRBOL, STEMS AND SEEDS REMOVED

1 OZ. GUAJILLO CHILE PEPPERS, STEMS AND SEEDS REMOVED

10 GARLIC CLOVES

SALT, TO TASTE

1. Place the lard in a cast-iron skillet and warm it over medium heat. Add the chiles and fry until they are fragrant and pliable, about 30 seconds. Place the chiles in a bowl, cover them with hot water, and let them soak for 20 minutes.

2. Place the garlic in the skillet and fry, stirring continually, until fragrant, about 1 minute. Place them in a food processor.

3. Drain the chiles and reserve the soaking liquid. Add the chiles to the food processor and blitz until the mixture is smooth, adding the reserved liquid as needed to get the desired texture.

4. Season the salsa with salt and use immediately or store in the refrigerator.

Fermented Chile Adobo

YIELD: 2 CUPS | **ACTIVE TIME:** 10 MINUTES | **TOTAL TIME:** 3 TO 5 DAYS

13¼ CUPS WATER

⅓ CUP KOSHER SALT

2¼ LBS. CHIPOTLE MORITA CHILE PEPPERS, STEMS AND SEEDS REMOVED

2 BAY LEAVES

10 GARLIC CLOVES, SMASHED

1 CINNAMON STICK

⅛ TEASPOON WHOLE CLOVES

½ CUP APPLE CIDER VINEGAR

1 TEASPOON DRIED OREGANO

1. Place the water and salt in a saucepan and bring it to a simmer, stirring to dissolve the salt. Turn off the heat and let the brine cool slightly.

2. Place the chiles, bay leaves, and garlic in a fermentation crock or large, food-grade storage container. Cover the mixture with the brine and place some plastic wrap directly on the surface. Let the mixture sit at room temperature for 3 to 5 days.

3. Place the cinnamon stick and cloves in a dry skillet and toast the mixture until fragrant, 1 to 2 minutes, shaking the pan to prevent them from burning. Use a mortar and pestle to grind the mixture into a fine powder.

4. Strain the liquid from the fermented mixture and reserve it.

5. Place the chiles and garlic in a food processor, add the toasted spice powder, vinegar, and oregano, and blitz until the mixture is smooth, adding the reserved liquid as needed to get the desired texture. Use immediately or store in the refrigerator.

Morita Salsa

YIELD: 2 CUPS | **ACTIVE TIME:** 15 MINUTES | **TOTAL TIME:** 45 MINUTES

3½ OZ. CHIPOTLE MORITA CHILE PEPPERS, STEMS AND SEEDS REMOVED

5 ROMA TOMATOES, HALVED

1 SMALL WHITE ONION, QUARTERED

5 GARLIC CLOVES

SALT, TO TASTE

1. Place the chiles in a dry skillet and gently toast them until they are fragrant and pliable, about 30 seconds. Place the chiles in a bowl, cover them with hot water, and let them soak for 30 minutes.

2. Drain the chiles, place them in a food processor, and add the tomatoes, onion, and garlic. Blitz until smooth, season the salsa with salt, and use immediately or store in the refrigerator.

Strawberry Hot Sauce

YIELD: 4 CUPS | **ACTIVE TIME:** 30 MINUTES | **TOTAL TIME:** 2 HOURS

1 LB. STRAWBERRIES, RINSED AND HULLED

2 TEASPOONS KOSHER SALT, PLUS MORE TO TASTE

3½ OZ. CHILES DE ÀRBOL

4 CUPS WATER

1½ TEASPOONS CUMIN

1 TABLESPOON CORIANDER

1¼ CUPS PLUS 1 TABLESPOON APPLE CIDER VINEGAR

1¾ CUPS DISTILLED WHITE VINEGAR

1. Place the strawberries and salt in a food processor and blitz until smooth. Let the mixture sit at room temperature for 1 hour.

2. Place the chiles, strawberry puree, and water in a saucepan and bring the mixture to a boil, making sure to stir and scrape the bottom of the pan frequently to keep a skin from forming.

3. Add the cumin and coriander and cook another 20 minutes, stirring the sauce and scraping the bottom of the pan frequently.

4. Working in batches, transfer the sauce to the blender and puree for about 3 minutes. The strawberry seeds should break down, as they have been cooking for a while.

5. Strain the mixture through a fine-mesh sieve into a clean saucepan. Add the vinegars and cook over medium-high heat until the sauce has reduced by half.

6. Season the sauce generously with salt and use immediately, or let it cool and store it in the refrigerator.

Pipian Rojo

YIELD: 2 CUPS | **ACTIVE TIME:** 30 MINUTES | **TOTAL TIME:** 45 MINUTES

4 GUAJILLO CHILE PEPPERS, STEMS AND SEEDS REMOVED

1 ANCHO CHILE PEPPER, STEMS AND SEEDS REMOVED

2 DRIED CHILES DE ÀRBOL, STEMS AND SEEDS REMOVED

3½ OZ. PUMPKIN SEEDS, HULLED

⅔ CUP SESAME SEEDS

2½ ROMA TOMATOES

¾ SMALL WHITE ONION

4 GARLIC CLOVES

2 ALLSPICE BERRIES

1 WHOLE CLOVE

4 CINNAMON STICKS

2 CORN TORTILLAS, TOASTED

4 CUPS CHICKEN STOCK (SEE PAGE 303)

3 LARGE CHAYOTES, PITS REMOVED

2 TABLESPOONS LARD

SALT, TO TASTE

1. Warm a dry cast-iron skillet over medium heat. Place the chiles in the pan and toast them until they are fragrant and pliable, about 30 seconds. Place the toasted chiles in a bowl, cover them with hot water, and soak them for 20 minutes.

2. Drain the chiles and reserve the soaking liquid. Place the chiles in a food processor, add all of the remaining ingredients except for the lard and salt, and blitz until smooth.

3. Place the lard in a medium saucepan and warm it over medium-high heat. Carefully add the puree and cook, stirring continually, for 1 minute. Reduce the heat and simmer the sauce until it is the desired texture.

4. Season the sauce with salt and use immediately or store it in the refrigerator.

Salsa de Aguacate

YIELD: 2 CUPS | **ACTIVE TIME:** 10 MINUTES | **TOTAL TIME:** 10 MINUTES

½ LB. TOMATILLOS, HUSKED AND RINSED

½ WHITE ONION

4 GARLIC CLOVES

⅔ CUP DICED AVOCADO

4 CUPS FRESH CILANTRO

FRESH LIME JUICE, TO TASTE

SALT, TO TASTE

1. Place the tomatillos, onion, garlic, and avocado in a food processor and blitz until smooth.

2. Add the cilantro and pulse to incorporate. Season the salsa with lime juice and salt and use immediately or store in the refrigerator.

Dzikil P'aak

YIELD: 1½ CUPS | **ACTIVE TIME:** 30 MINUTES | **TOTAL TIME:** 30 MINUTES

3 ROMA TOMATOES

4 OZ. TOMATILLOS, HUSKED AND RINSED

¾ SMALL WHITE ONION

4 GARLIC CLOVES, UNPEELED

2 HABANERO CHILE PEPPERS

7 OZ. PUMPKIN SEEDS, HULLED AND ROASTED

7 TABLESPOONS FRESH LIME JUICE

7 TABLESPOONS ORANGE JUICE

1½ CUPS FRESH CILANTRO

1 TEASPOON MAGGI SEASONING SAUCE

SALT, TO TASTE

1. Warm a dry cast-iron skillet over medium-high heat. Add the tomatoes, tomatillos, onion, garlic, and habanero and toast until charred all over, turning them as needed.

2. Remove the vegetables from the pan and let them cool. When cool enough to handle, peel the garlic cloves, remove the stems and seeds from the habaneros, and place the mixture in a food processor.

3. Place the pumpkin seeds in the food processor and pulse until the mixture is a thick paste. Add the juices, cilantro, and Maggi sauce and pulse until the mixture has a hummus-like consistency.

4. Season the salsa with salt and use immediately or store in the refrigerator.

Salsa Macha

YIELD: ½ CUP | **ACTIVE TIME:** 15 MINUTES | **TOTAL TIME:** 25 MINUTES

1 OZ. WHITE SESAME SEEDS

¼ CUP LARD

¼ CUP UNSALTED ALMONDS

10 DRIED CHILES DE ÀRBOL, STEMS AND SEEDS REMOVED

1 ANCHO CHILE PEPPER, STEMS AND SEEDS REMOVED

2 GARLIC CLOVES, SLICED THIN

2 TABLESPOONS WHITE VINEGAR

1 TEASPOON SUGAR

1. Place the sesame seeds in a dry skillet and toast them over low heat until browned, shaking the pan as needed to keep them from burning. Remove them from the pan and set them aside.

2. Place the lard in the skillet and warm it over medium heat. Add the almonds and fry until golden brown, shaking the pan to prevent them from burning. Remove the almonds from the pan and set them aside.

3. Reduce the heat to low, add the chiles to the pan, and fry them until fragrant and lightly toasted, about 30 seconds. Remove the chiles from the pan and set them aside.

4. Using a mortar and pestle, grind the sesame seeds, almonds, chiles, and the remaining ingredients until it is a slightly chunky puree. Use immediately or store in the refrigerator.

Chocolate Mole

YIELD: 12 CUPS | **ACTIVE TIME:** 30 MINUTES | **TOTAL TIME:** 1 HOUR

6 CUPS WATER

1 LB. UNSALTED BUTTER

1½ LBS. SUGAR

1⅔ LBS. BROWN SUGAR

8¼ CUPS HEAVY CREAM

½ TEASPOON FINE SEA SALT

2.2 LBS. COCOA POWDER

1 CUP SESAME SEEDS, TOASTED

¼ CUP PEANUT BUTTER

1 TABLESPOON MEXICAN VANILLA EXTRACT

2 TEASPOONS CAYENNE PEPPER

1 TEASPOON CINNAMON

1 TEASPOON ORANGE ZEST

1. Prepare an ice bath. Place the water, butter, and sugars in a large saucepan and bring the mixture to a boil.

2. Add the cream, salt, and cocoa powder and whisk until the mixture is smooth.

3. Strain the mixture into a heatproof bowl. Add the remaining ingredients and stir until well combined. Place the bowl in the ice bath and stir until it has completely cooled.

4. Place the mixture in a food processor and blitz until smooth. Strain and use immediately or store in the refrigerator.

Toum

YIELD: 1½ CUPS | **ACTIVE TIME:** 10 MINUTES | **TOTAL TIME:** 40 MINUTES

1 CUP AVOCADO OIL

⅓ CUP GARLIC CLOVES

2 TABLESPOONS FRESH LEMON JUICE

2 TABLESPOONS ICE WATER

SALT, TO TASTE

1. Place the avocado oil in the freezer for 30 minutes. This will help the sauce emulsify.

2. Place the garlic, lemon juice, ¼ cup of the chilled avocado oil, and 1 tablespoon of the ice water in a food processor and pulse until the mixture is smooth. With the food processor running, slowly drizzle in another ½ cup of the avocado oil.

3. Scrape down the work bowl and slowly drizzle in the remaining avocado oil with the food processor running, until the mixture has emulsified and comes together as a thick sauce—it should cling to a spoon.

4. Add the remaining ice water, season the toum with salt, and pulse to incorporate. This whole process will take 8 to 10 minutes, so remain patient. Use immediately or store in the refrigerator.

Pomegranate Sauce

YIELD: 4 CUPS | **ACTIVE TIME:** 30 MINUTES | **TOTAL TIME:** 30 MINUTES

2 TABLESPOONS AVOCADO OIL

1 LARGE ONION, SLICED

6 GARLIC CLOVES, SMASHED

1 TEASPOON CINNAMON

1 TEASPOON CORIANDER

½ TEASPOON GROUND GINGER

1 TEASPOON CUMIN

24 JUNIPER BERRIES

2 TABLESPOONS TOMATO PASTE

1 CUP SWEET RED WINE

2 CUPS BEEF STOCK (SEE PAGE 306)

1 CUP POMEGRANATE JUICE

SALT AND PEPPER, TO TASTE

1. Place the avocado oil in a saucepan and warm it over medium-high heat. Add the onion and garlic, reduce the heat to medium, and cook, stirring frequently, until the onion has softened slightly, about 5 minutes.

2. Add the spices, tomato paste, wine, and stock and cook, stirring continuously, for 5 minutes.

3. Stir in the pomegranate juice and cook until the sauce has thickened, about 20 minutes. Season it with salt and pepper and use immediately or store in the refrigerator.

Walnut Sauce

YIELD: 6 CUPS | **ACTIVE TIME:** 20 MINUTES | **TOTAL TIME:** 40 MINUTES

2 TABLESPOONS EXTRA-VIRGIN OLIVE OIL

1 ONION, CHOPPED

3 GARLIC CLOVES, MINCED

½ CUP WHITE WINE

4 CUPS CHICKEN STOCK (SEE PAGE 303)

1 TABLESPOON PAPRIKA

¼ TEASPOON CAYENNE PEPPER

1 CUP DAY-OLD BREAD PIECES

2 CUPS WALNUTS, TOASTED

SALT AND PEPPER, TO TASTE

1. Place the olive oil in a Dutch oven and warm it over medium heat. Add the onion and cook, stirring occasionally, until it has softened, about 5 minutes. Add the garlic and cook, stirring continually, for 1 minute.

2. Add the white wine and cook until the alcohol has been cooked off, about 3 minutes, scraping up any browned bits from the bottom of the pan.

3. Add the stock, paprika, and cayenne and bring the mixture to a boil.

4. Remove the pan from heat and strain the liquid into a bowl. Place the liquid, bread, and walnuts in a food processor and blitz until the sauce is smooth and thick. Season the sauce with salt and pepper and use immediately or store in the refrigerator.

Toum
SEE PAGE 382

Tahini Sauce

YIELD: ¾ CUP | **ACTIVE TIME:** 10 MINUTES | **TOTAL TIME:** 10 MINUTES

5 OZ. TAHINI PASTE

½ CUP WATER

3 GARLIC CLOVES

1 TEASPOON KOSHER SALT

JUICE OF 1 LEMON

PINCH OF CUMIN

1. Place the tahini and water in a food processor and pulse to combine. Let the mixture sit for 30 seconds.

2. Add the garlic, salt, lemon juice, and cumin. Blitz on high for 2 to 3 minutes, until the sauce is creamy and smooth. Use immediately or store in the refrigerator.

Shrimp & Pistou Sauce

YIELD: 5 CUPS | **ACTIVE TIME:** 35 MINUTES | **TOTAL TIME:** 1 HOUR

1½ LBS. SHRIMP, PEELED AND DEVEINED

4 GARLIC CLOVES

5 TABLESPOONS TOMATO PASTE

SALT AND PEPPER, TO TASTE

½ CUP FRESHLY GRATED PARMESAN CHEESE

2 HANDFULS OF FRESH BASIL LEAVES, TORN

6½ TABLESPOONS EXTRA-VIRGIN OLIVE OIL

3 CUPS MARINARA SAUCE (SEE PAGE 296)

½ CUP WATER

1. Place the shrimp on a paper towel–lined plate and let them come to room temperature.

2. Place the garlic, tomato paste, and a generous pinch of salt in a food processor and pulse until thoroughly combined.

3. Add the Parmesan and pulse to incorporate. Add the basil and pulse once. Transfer the mixture to a small bowl and whisk in ¼ cup of the olive oil. Set the pistou aside.

4. Place the remaining olive oil in a large skillet and warm it over medium heat. Pat the shrimp dry with paper towels. Add the shrimp to the pan, working in batches to ensure the pan isn't crowded. Cook the shrimp until they are cooked through, 3 to 5 minutes, and transfer the cooked shrimp to a plate.

5. Place the Marinara Sauce and water in the skillet and bring the mixture to a simmer over medium-high heat. Stir in the pistou and shrimp, season the sauce with salt and pepper, and use immediately or store in the refrigerator.

Hot Sauce, Yemeni Style

YIELD: 8 CUPS | **ACTIVE TIME:** 45 MINUTES | **TOTAL TIME:** 2 HOURS

8 CUPS WHITE VINEGAR

4 FRESNO CHILE PEPPERS, STEMS REMOVED

1 BUNCH OF FRESH CILANTRO, CHOPPED

½ WHITE ONION, CHOPPED

4 GARLIC CLOVES

1 TEASPOON CUMIN

2 TEASPOONS KOSHER SALT

2 TABLESPOONS CHICKEN FAT

1. Place the vinegar, chiles, cilantro, onion, garlic, cumin, and salt in a saucepan and bring the mixture to a boil over high heat. Reduce the heat to medium and simmer the mixture, stirring occasionally, for 45 minutes to 1 hour.

2. Remove the pan from heat and let the mixture cool.

3. Place the mixture in a food processor or blender and pulse until the solids are finely chopped and it is well combined.

4. Strain the liquid into a bowl or mason jar and discard the solids.

5. Place the chicken fat in a small saucepan and warm it over low heat.

6. Add the chicken fat to the sauce and stir until it has a velvety texture. Use immediately or store in the refrigerator.

Lemon & Caper Sauce

YIELD: ½ CUP | **ACTIVE TIME:** 5 MINUTES | **TOTAL TIME:** 5 MINUTES

6 TABLESPOONS EXTRA-VIRGIN OLIVE OIL

SALT AND PEPPER, TO TASTE

2 TABLESPOONS CHOPPED FRESH PARSLEY

1 TABLESPOON CAPERS, DRAINED AND CHOPPED

ZEST AND JUICE OF 1 LEMON

1. Place the ingredients in a bowl, whisk to combine, and use immediately or store in the refrigerator.

Oxtail Ragout

YIELD: 6 CUPS | **ACTIVE TIME:** 30 MINUTES | **TOTAL TIME:** 3 TO 4 HOURS

1 TABLESPOON EXTRA-VIRGIN OLIVE OIL

1½ LBS. OXTAILS

SALT AND PEPPER, TO TASTE

1 ONION, CHOPPED

4 GARLIC CLOVES, MINCED

1 TEASPOON FRESH THYME

2 CINNAMON STICKS

½ TEASPOON GROUND CLOVES

⅓ CUP RED WINE

4 CUPS BEEF STOCK (SEE PAGE 306)

1 (28 OZ.) CAN OF DICED TOMATOES, WITH THEIR LIQUID

1. Preheat the oven to 300°F. Place the olive oil in a Dutch oven and warm it over medium heat. Season the oxtails with salt and pepper, place them in the pot, and sear until golden brown all over, about 6 minutes, turning them as necessary. Remove the oxtails from the pot and set them aside.

2. Add the onion and cook, stirring occasionally, until it has softened, about 5 minutes. Add the garlic, thyme, cinnamon sticks, and cloves and cook, stirring continually, for 1 minute.

3. Add the red wine and cook until the alcohol has cooked off, about 4 minutes. Add the stock and tomatoes and bring the mixture to a boil. Return the seared oxtails to the pot, cover the pot, and place it in the oven.

4. Braise until the oxtails are falling off the bone, 3 to 4 hours.

5. Remove the ragout from the oven, remove the oxtails from the sauce, and place them on a cutting board. Let them cool slightly and then use two forks to shred the meat.

6. Remove the cinnamon sticks from the sauce and stir in the shredded oxtails. Use immediately or store in the refrigerator.

Eggplant & Pine Nut Ragout

YIELD: 2 CUPS | **ACTIVE TIME:** 20 MINUTES | **TOTAL TIME:** 40 MINUTES

1 TABLESPOON EXTRA-VIRGIN OLIVE OIL

1 EGGPLANT, TRIMMED AND CHOPPED (¾-INCH CUBES)

½ TEASPOON RAS EL HANOUT (SEE PAGE 55)

1 TABLESPOON RAISINS

2 TABLESPOONS PINE NUTS, TOASTED

1 TEASPOON LEMON ZEST

SALT AND PEPPER, TO TASTE

1. Place the olive oil in a large saucepan and warm it over medium heat. Add the eggplant, cover the pan, and cook the eggplant, stirring occasionally, for 5 minutes. Remove the cover and cook, stirring occasionally, until the eggplant is browned, about 10 minutes.

2. Stir in the remaining ingredients and cook, stirring occasionally, until the eggplant has collapsed and the flavor has developed to your liking, 10 to 15 minutes. Use immediately or store in the refrigerator.

Spiced Yogurt Sauce

YIELD: 1¼ CUPS | **ACTIVE TIME:** 5 MINUTES | **TOTAL TIME:** 5 MINUTES

1 CUP FULL-FAT GREEK YOGURT

¼ CUP GREEN ZHUG (SEE PAGE 557)

1 TEASPOON FRESH LEMON JUICE

2 GARLIC CLOVES, MINCED

SALT AND PEPPER, TO TASTE

1. Place all of the ingredients in a mixing bowl and whisk until combined. Use immediately or store in the refrigerator.

Garlic Cream Sauce

YIELD: 3 CUPS | **ACTIVE TIME:** 20 MINUTES | **TOTAL TIME:** 35 MINUTES

3 GARLIC CLOVES, MINCED

2 CUPS HEAVY CREAM

3 TABLESPOONS UNSALTED BUTTER

1 CUP DICED PANCETTA

SALT AND PEPPER, TO TASTE

1. Place the garlic, cream, and butter in a medium saucepan and bring the mixture to a simmer over medium heat.

2. Place the pancetta in a skillet and cook it over medium-high heat, stirring occasionally, until it just starts to turn golden brown, about 4 minutes. Stir the pancetta into the sauce, taste the sauce, and season it with salt and pepper. Use immediately or store in the refrigerator.

Pistachio & Raisin Sauce

YIELD: 1 CUP | **ACTIVE TIME:** 5 MINUTES | **TOTAL TIME:** 5 MINUTES

2 SHALLOTS, CHOPPED

⅓ CUP CHOPPED FRESH PARSLEY

½ CUP ORANGE JUICE

⅓ CUP RAISINS

¼ CUP PISTACHIOS, SHELLS REMOVED, TOASTED

½ TEASPOON CINNAMON

1 TABLESPOON WHITE WINE VINEGAR

2 TABLESPOONS EXTRA-VIRGIN OLIVE OIL

SALT AND PEPPER, TO TASTE

1. Place the shallots, parsley, orange juice, raisins, pistachios, cinnamon, and vinegar in a food processor and blitz until the mixture is a thick paste.

2. With the food processor running, add the olive oil in a slow stream and blitz until it has emulsified. Season the sauce with salt and pepper and use immediately or store in the refrigerator.

Spiced Yogurt Sauce
SEE PAGE 390

Mole Verde

YIELD: 2 CUPS | **ACTIVE TIME:** 20 MINUTES | **TOTAL TIME:** 40 MINUTES

¼ TEASPOON WHOLE CLOVES

¼ TEASPOON ALLSPICE BERRIES

¼ TEASPOON CUMIN SEEDS

½ TEASPOON CORIANDER SEEDS

⅓ CUP SESAME SEEDS

3 TABLESPOONS PUMPKIN SEEDS

SALT, TO TASTE

1½ CUPS FRESH EPAZOTE LEAVES

½ CUP FRESH MINT LEAVES

½ CUP FRESH PARSLEY LEAVES

1 CUP FRESH HOJA SANTA LEAVES

2 CUPS FRESH CILANTRO LEAVES

2 OZ. KALE, STEMS AND RIBS REMOVED

½ LB. TOMATILLOS, HUSKED AND RINSED

3 SERRANO CHILE PEPPERS

10 GARLIC CLOVES

1 SMALL WHITE ONION, QUARTERED

1. Preheat the oven to 325°F. Place the cloves, allspice, cumin, and coriander in a dry skillet and toast until fragrant, shaking the pan to keep them from burning. Use a mortar and pestle or a spice grinder to grind the mixture into a fine powder.

2. Place the sesame and pumpkin seeds on a parchment-lined baking sheet, place it in the oven, and toast until just golden brown, about 7 minutes. Remove from the oven and let the seeds cool.

3. Prepare an ice bath and bring generously salted water to a simmer in a large saucepan. Add the fresh herbs and the kale and cook for 30 to 45 seconds. Drain and shock them in the ice bath. Place the mixture in a linen towel and wring it to extract as much water as possible. Transfer the mixture to a blender.

4. Place the tomatillos, serrano peppers, garlic, and onion in a saucepan and cover by 1 inch with water. Season the water with salt and bring to a simmer. Cook until the vegetables are tender, about 15 minutes. Drain and add them to the blender.

5. Add the toasted seeds and the fine spice powder to the blender and puree until smooth. Season the mole with salt and gently warm it before serving.

Lamb Ragù

YIELD: 8 CUPS | **ACTIVE TIME:** 40 MINUTES | **TOTAL TIME:** 3 HOURS

2 TABLESPOONS EXTRA-VIRGIN OLIVE OIL

2 SMALL ONIONS, MINCED

2 CELERY STALKS, PEELED AND MINCED

SALT AND PEPPER, TO TASTE

2 LBS. GROUND LAMB

1 CUP DRY RED WINE

2 TEASPOONS FRESH THYME

2 TEASPOONS FRESH MARJORAM

1 TEASPOON RED PEPPER FLAKES

2 (28 OZ.) CANS OF PEELED WHOLE SAN MARZANO TOMATOES, WITH THEIR LIQUID, CRUSHED BY HAND

1. Place the olive oil in a Dutch oven and warm it over medium heat. Add the onions and celery, season the mixture with salt, and cook for 3 minutes, stirring occasionally. Reduce the heat to low, cover the pot, and cook, stirring occasionally, until the vegetables are very tender and golden brown, about 30 minutes.

2. Add the ground lamb to the pot and cook, breaking it up with a wooden spoon, until it is no longer pink. Raise the heat to medium-high, add the wine, and cook until it has reduced by half, about 5 minutes.

3. Stir in the thyme, marjoram, and red pepper flakes and cook for 2 minutes. Add the tomatoes, season the sauce with salt and pepper, stir, and bring the sauce to a boil. Reduce the heat to medium-low and simmer, stirring occasionally, until the sauce has visibly thickened and the fat has separated and is bubbling on the surface, about 2 hours.

4. Use immediately or store in the refrigerator.

Arrabbiata Sauce

YIELD: 3 CUPS | **ACTIVE TIME:** 10 MINUTES | **TOTAL TIME:** 25 MINUTES

2 TABLESPOONS EXTRA-VIRGIN OLIVE OIL

3 GARLIC CLOVES, CRUSHED

2 DRIED CHILE PEPPERS, STEMS AND SEEDS REMOVED, CHOPPED

1 (28 OZ.) CAN OF PEELED WHOLE SAN MARZANO TOMATOES, WITH THEIR LIQUID

1 HANDFUL OF FRESH PARSLEY, CHOPPED

SALT AND PEPPER, TO TASTE

1. Warm a large skillet over low heat for 1 to 2 minutes. Add the olive oil, garlic, and chiles, raise the heat to medium-low, and cook until the garlic begins to brown, about 1 minute.

2. Remove the garlic and as much of the chiles as possible and add the tomatoes, breaking them up with your hands as you add them to the pan. Add the liquid from the can, raise the heat to medium-high, and bring the sauce to a boil. Reduce the heat to medium-low and cook, stirring occasionally, until the sauce has thickened and the oil has risen to the surface, about 20 minutes.

3. Stir in the parsley, season the sauce with salt and pepper, and use immediately or store in the refrigerator.

Calamari Fra Diavolo

YIELD: 6 CUPS | **ACTIVE TIME:** 40 MINUTES | **TOTAL TIME:** 1 HOUR

1 CUP DRY RED WINE

2 LBS. SQUID, BODIES CUT INTO RINGS, TENTACLES HALVED LENGTHWISE

3½ TABLESPOONS EXTRA-VIRGIN OLIVE OIL

4 GARLIC CLOVES, MINCED

1 TEASPOON RED PEPPER FLAKES

SALT, TO TASTE

3 ANCHOVIES IN OLIVE OIL, DRAINED

2 HANDFULS OF FRESH PARSLEY, CHOPPED

1 (28 OZ.) CAN OF PUREED SAN MARZANO TOMATOES

½ CUP CLAM JUICE

1. Place the wine in a small saucepan, bring it to a boil, and cook until it has reduced by half, about 5 minutes. Remove the pan from heat and set it aside.

2. Thoroughly rinse the squid and transfer it to a paper towel–lined plate. Pat the squid dry with paper towels.

3. Place the olive oil in a large skillet and warm it over medium heat. Add the garlic, half of the red pepper flakes, and a pinch of salt and cook, stirring continually, until the garlic starts to brown, about 1 minute.

4. Raise the heat to medium-high and add the squid, anchovies, and half of the parsley. Cook, stirring occasionally, until the anchovies have dissolved and the calamari is golden brown, about 5 minutes.

5. Add the reduced wine and continue to cook until the liquid in the mixture has reduced by one-third, about 5 minutes.

6. Stir in the tomatoes, the clam juice, and remaining red pepper flakes, season the sauce with salt, and bring it to a boil. Reduce the heat to medium-low and simmer the sauce until it has thickened slightly, about 20 minutes.

7. Use immediately or store in the refrigerator.

Aromatic Walnut Sauce

YIELD: 2 CUPS | **ACTIVE TIME:** 20 MINUTES | **TOTAL TIME:** 50 MINUTES

1 CUP DAY-OLD BREAD PIECES

1 CUP WALNUTS

1 GARLIC CLOVE, SLICED THIN

¼ CUP BREAD CRUMBS

HANDFUL OF FRESH PARSLEY, CHOPPED

2 TABLESPOONS CHOPPED FRESH MARJORAM

3 TABLESPOONS WALNUT OIL

3 TABLESPOONS HEAVY CREAM

5 TABLESPOONS UNSALTED BUTTER, AT ROOM TEMPERATURE

SALT, TO TASTE

1. Place the bread in a small bowl, cover it with warm water, and let it soak for 30 minutes. Drain, squeeze the bread to remove as much water from it as possible, and set it aside.

2. Bring water to a boil in a small saucepan, add the walnuts, and cook for 2 minutes. Drain and let the walnuts cool briefly. When cool enough to handle, rub the walnuts to remove their skins and place them on paper towels to dry.

3. When the walnuts are dry, chop them and transfer them to a small bowl.

4. Place the bread, walnuts, garlic, bread crumbs, parsley, and half of the marjoram in a food processor and pulse until the mixture is a smooth paste. Transfer the mixture to a bowl, add the walnut oil, and whisk until it has been thoroughly incorporated.

5. Stir in the cream and butter, season the sauce with salt, and use immediately or store in the refrigerator.

Puttanesca Sauce

YIELD: 3 CUPS | **ACTIVE TIME:** 15 MINUTES | **TOTAL TIME:** 30 MINUTES

½ CUP EXTRA-VIRGIN OLIVE OIL

3 GARLIC CLOVES, MINCED

1 (28 OZ.) CAN OF PEELED WHOLE SAN MARZANO TOMATOES, WITH THEIR LIQUID, CRUSHED BY HAND

½ LB. BLACK OLIVES, PITTED

¼ CUP CAPERS

5 ANCHOVIES IN OLIVE OIL, DRAINED

1 TEASPOON RED PEPPER FLAKES

SALT AND PEPPER, TO TASTE

1. Place the olive oil in a large skillet and warm it over medium heat. Add the garlic and cook, stirring continually, until fragrant, about 1 minute.

2. Add the tomatoes, olives, capers, and anchovies and stir, pressing down on the anchovies to break them up. Cook until the anchovies have dissolved.

3. Stir in the red pepper flakes, season the sauce with salt and pepper, and raise the heat to medium. Simmer the sauce, stirring occasionally, until it thickens slightly, about 10 minutes. Taste the sauce, adjust the seasoning as necessary, and use immediately or store in the refrigerator.

Bolognese Sauce

YIELD: 8 CUPS | **ACTIVE TIME:** 45 MINUTES | **TOTAL TIME:** 2 HOURS

2 TABLESPOONS EXTRA-VIRGIN OLIVE OIL

½ LB. BACON

1½ LBS. GROUND BEEF

SALT AND PEPPER, TO TASTE

1 CARROT, PEELED AND MINCED

3 CELERY STALKS, PEELED AND CHOPPED

1 ONION, CHOPPED

2 GARLIC CLOVES, MINCED

1 TEASPOON FRESH THYME

2 CUPS SHERRY

8 CUPS MARINARA SAUCE (SEE PAGE 296)

1 CUP WATER

1 CUP HEAVY CREAM

2 TABLESPOONS CHOPPED FRESH SAGE

1 CUP FRESHLY GRATED PARMESAN CHEESE

1. Place the olive oil in a Dutch oven and warm it over medium heat. Add the bacon and cook until it is crispy, about 6 minutes. Add the ground beef, season it with salt and pepper, and cook, breaking up the meat with a wooden spoon as it browns, until it is cooked through, about 8 minutes. Remove the bacon and the ground beef from the pot and set them aside.

2. Add the carrots, celery, onion, and garlic to the Dutch oven, season the mixture with salt, and cook, stirring frequently, until the carrots are tender, about 8 minutes.

3. Return the bacon and ground beef to the pot, add the thyme and sherry, and cook until the sherry has nearly evaporated. Stir in the Marinara Sauce and water, reduce the heat to low, and cook the sauce until it has thickened noticeably, about 45 minutes.

4. Stir the cream and sage into the sauce and cook it for an additional 15 minutes.

5. Add the Parmesan and stir until it has melted. Taste, adjust the seasoning as necessary, and use immediately or store in the refrigerator.

Salsa Cruda Verde

YIELD: 1 CUP | **ACTIVE TIME:** 5 MINUTES | **TOTAL TIME:** 15 MINUTES

4 TOMATILLOS, HUSKED, RINSED, AND QUARTERED

5 SERRANO CHILE PEPPERS, STEMS AND SEEDS REMOVED

1 GARLIC CLOVE

FLESH OF ½ AVOCADO

SALT, TO TASTE

1. Place the tomatillos, serrano peppers, and garlic in a food processor and blitz until combined but still chunky.

2. Add the avocado and pulse until incorporated.

3. Season the salsa with salt and use immediately or store in the refrigerator.

Puttanesca Sauce
SEE PAGE 402

Roasted Tomato & Garlic Sauce

YIELD: 6 CUPS | **ACTIVE TIME:** 15 MINUTES | **TOTAL TIME:** 2 HOURS

3 LBS. TOMATOES, HALVED

¼ CUP EXTRA-VIRGIN OLIVE OIL

5 LARGE GARLIC CLOVES, UNPEELED

SALT AND PEPPER, TO TASTE

1 HANDFUL OF FRESH BASIL LEAVES

1. Preheat the oven to 350°F. Place the tomatoes on a parchment-lined baking sheet and drizzle the olive oil over them. Stir to ensure the tomatoes are coated evenly, place them in the oven, and lower the oven's temperature to 325°F. Roast the tomatoes for 1 hour.

2. Remove the baking sheet from the oven, place the garlic on the baking sheet with the tomatoes, return it to the oven, and roast for 30 minutes.

3. Remove the baking sheet from the oven and let the tomatoes and garlic cool slightly.

4. When the garlic is cool enough to handle, peel it and place it in a bowl. Add the tomatoes, season the mixture with salt and pepper, and let it cool completely.

5. Place the roasted tomatoes, roasted garlic, and basil leaves in a food processor and blitz until smooth. Place the puree in a medium saucepan and bring to a simmer over medium heat, stirring occasionally. Taste, adjust the seasoning as necessary, and use immediately or store in the refrigerator.

Tomato & Eggplant Sauce alla Norma

YIELD: 6 CUPS | **ACTIVE TIME:** 40 MINUTES | **TOTAL TIME:** 1 HOUR AND 30 MINUTES

2 MEDIUM EGGPLANTS, CHOPPED

2 TABLESPOONS KOSHER SALT, PLUS MORE TO TASTE

3 TABLESPOONS EXTRA-VIRGIN OLIVE OIL

5 CUPS MARINARA SAUCE (SEE PAGE 296)

1 CUP RICOTTA CHEESE

BLACK PEPPER, TO TASTE

1. Place the eggplants in a colander and sprinkle the salt over them. Let the eggplants rest for 30 minutes.

2. Rinse the eggplants and pat them dry with paper towels.

3. Preheat the oven to 400°F. Place the eggplants in a large mixing bowl, drizzle the olive oil over them, and stir to make sure the pieces are evenly coated. Place the eggplants on a parchment-lined baking sheet, place it in the oven, and roast the eggplants, stirring occasionally, until they are tender and golden brown, about 25 minutes.

4. Remove the eggplants from the oven and let them cool.

5. Place the eggplants, sauce, ricotta cheese, and pepper in a large saucepan, stir to combine, and bring the sauce to a simmer over medium heat. Taste, adjust the seasoning as necessary, and use immediately or store in the refrigerator.

Sofia's Spiced Pork Sauce

YIELD: 4 CUPS | **ACTIVE TIME:** 20 MINUTES | **TOTAL TIME:** 1 HOUR AND 30 MINUTES

6 TABLESPOONS UNSALTED BUTTER

1 YELLOW ONION, GRATED

2 CELERY STALKS, PEELED AND GRATED

SALT, TO TASTE

1½ LBS. GROUND PORK

1 CUP MILK

½ TEASPOON GROUND CLOVES

1 CUP CHICKEN STOCK (SEE PAGE 303)

2 TABLESPOONS TOMATO PASTE

2 BAY LEAVES

6 FRESH SAGE LEAVES

1. Place half of the butter in a large saucepan and melt it over medium-high heat. Add the onion, celery, and a few pinches of salt and cook, stirring occasionally, until the onion is translucent, about 3 minutes. Reduce the heat to low, cover the pan, and cook, stirring occasionally, until the vegetables are very tender, about 30 minutes.

2. Add the ground pork to the pan and raise the heat to medium-high. Season the pork with salt and cook, using a wooden spoon to break it up as it browns. When the pork is browned all over, stir in the milk and cook until the milk has completely evaporated, about 10 minutes.

3. Stir in the cloves, cook for 2 minutes, and then add the stock, tomato paste, and bay leaves. Bring the sauce to a boil, reduce the heat to low, and let the sauce simmer, stirring occasionally, until the flavor has developed to your liking, about 45 minutes.

4. Place the remaining butter in a small skillet and melt it over medium-low heat. Add the sage leaves and cook until the leaves are slightly crispy. Remove the sage leaves and discard them. Stir the seasoned butter into the sauce, taste, and adjust the seasoning as necessary. Use immediately or store in the refrigerator.

DRESSINGS & INFUSED OILS

Balsamic Ranch Dressing

YIELD: 2 CUPS | **ACTIVE TIME:** 5 MINUTES | **TOTAL TIME:** 5 MINUTES

½ CUP MAYONNAISE

½ CUP SOUR CREAM

½ CUP BUTTERMILK

3 TABLESPOONS BALSAMIC VINEGAR

¼ TEASPOON ONION POWDER

½ TEASPOON GARLIC POWDER

2 TEASPOONS CHOPPED FRESH PARSLEY

1. Place all the ingredients in a mixing bowl and whisk until the mixture is thoroughly combined.

2. Taste, adjust the seasoning as necessary, and use immediately or store in the refrigerator.

Red Plum–Infused Vinegar

YIELD: 2 CUPS | **ACTIVE TIME:** 15 MINUTES | **TOTAL TIME:** 2 HOURS AND 30 MINUTES

3 CUPS BLACK VINEGAR

8 DRIED RED PLUMS

1. Place the ingredients in a small saucepan and cook the mixture over the lowest possible heat until the liquid has reduced by one-third, about 30 minutes.

2. Remove the pan from heat and let the mixture cool completely.

3. Strain the vinegar into a mason jar and use immediately or store in the refrigerator.

Chili & Curry Dressing

YIELD: 1½ CUPS | **ACTIVE TIME:** 5 MINUTES | **TOTAL TIME:** 5 MINUTES

2 BIRD'S EYE CHILI PEPPERS, STEMS AND SEEDS REMOVED

½ CUP SOY SAUCE

½ CUP SAMBAL OELEK

JUICE OF 3 LIMES

¼ CUP BROWN SUGAR

1 TABLESPOON MINCED FRESH GINGER

2 TABLESPOONS CURRY POWDER

1. Place all of the ingredients in a food processor, blitz until smooth, and use immediately or store in the refrigerator.

Oregano Vinaigrette

YIELD: 1 CUP | **ACTIVE TIME:** 5 MINUTES | **TOTAL TIME:** 5 MINUTES

¼ CUP CHAMPAGNE VINEGAR

½ SHALLOT, CHOPPED

1 TEASPOON DIJON MUSTARD

2 TABLESPOONS HONEY

1 TEASPOON KOSHER SALT

¼ TEASPOON BLACK PEPPER

1 TABLESPOON CHOPPED FRESH OREGANO

¾ CUP EXTRA-VIRGIN OLIVE OIL

1. Place all of the ingredients, except for the olive oil, in a food processor and blitz until smooth.

2. With the food processor running, add the olive oil in a slow, steady stream until it has emulsified. Use immediately or store in an airtight container.

Spicy Garlic Oil

YIELD: ½ CUP | **ACTIVE TIME:** 10 MINUTES | **TOTAL TIME:** 1 HOUR

½ CUP EXTRA-VIRGIN OLIVE OIL

6 GARLIC CLOVES, MINCED

2 TEASPOONS RED PEPPER FLAKES

SOY SAUCE, TO TASTE

1. Place the olive oil in a saucepan and warm it over low heat for 2 minutes.

2. Add the garlic and red pepper flakes and cook for 2 minutes.

3. Remove the pan from heat and let the mixture cool.

4. Season the infused oil with soy sauce, stir to combine, and use immediately or store in an airtight container.

Avocado & Lime Yogurt Dressing

YIELD: 1½ CUPS | **ACTIVE TIME:** 5 MINUTES | **TOTAL TIME:** 5 MINUTES

FLESH OF ½ RIPE AVOCADO

1 CUP FULL-FAT GREEK YOGURT

ZEST AND JUICE OF 1 LIME

PINCH OF CAYENNE PEPPER

1 TABLESPOON FRESH CILANTRO

1. Place all of the ingredients in a food processor, blitz until smooth, and use immediately or store in the refrigerator.

White Wine Vinaigrette

YIELD: 1 CUP | **ACTIVE TIME:** 5 MINUTES | **TOTAL TIME:** 5 MINUTES

¼ CUP WHITE WINE VINEGAR

4 TEASPOONS WHOLE-GRAIN MUSTARD

2 TABLESPOONS HONEY

2 TABLESPOONS CHOPPED FRESH CHIVES

4 TEASPOONS FRESH THYME

4 TEASPOONS KOSHER SALT

½ CUP EXTRA-VIRGIN OLIVE OIL

1. Place all of the ingredients, except for the olive oil, in a food processor and blitz until smooth.

2. With the food processor running, add the olive oil in a slow, steady stream until it has emulsified. Use immediately or store in an airtight container.

Parsley & Lemon Oil

YIELD: 1¼ CUPS | **ACTIVE TIME:** 15 MINUTES | **TOTAL TIME:** 1 HOUR AND 15 MINUTES

1 CUP EXTRA-VIRGIN OLIVE OIL

1 SHALLOT, MINCED

ZEST AND JUICE OF 1 LEMON

2 TABLESPOONS CHOPPED FRESH PARSLEY

1. Place the olive oil in a saucepan and warm it over medium heat.

2. Add the shallot and cook until it has softened, about 5 minutes.

3. Remove the pan from heat, stir in the lemon zest, and let the mixture steep for 1 hour.

4. Stir in the lemon juice and parsley and use immediately or store in the refrigerator.

Horseradish Oil

YIELD: 1 CUP | **ACTIVE TIME:** 10 MINUTES | **TOTAL TIME:** 1 HOUR AND 15 MINUTES

½ CUP FRESH HORSERADISH, PEELED AND GRATED

ZEST OF ½ LEMON

1 CUP EXTRA-VIRGIN OLIVE OIL

1. Place the ingredients in a saucepan and warm the mixture over medium heat for 5 minutes.

2. Remove the pan from heat and let the mixture steep for 1 hour.

3. Strain the oil through a fine-mesh sieve and use immediately or store in an airtight container.

Avocado & Lime Yogurt Dressing
SEE PAGE 418

Green Goddess Dressing

YIELD: 1½ CUPS | **ACTIVE TIME:** 5 MINUTES | **TOTAL TIME:** 5 MINUTES

½ CUP MAYONNAISE

⅔ CUP BUTTERMILK

1 TABLESPOON FRESH LEMON JUICE

2 TABLESPOONS CHOPPED CELERY LEAVES

2 TABLESPOONS CHOPPED FRESH PARSLEY

2 TABLESPOONS CHOPPED FRESH TARRAGON

2 TABLESPOONS SLICED FRESH CHIVES

2 TEASPOONS KOSHER SALT

1 TEASPOON BLACK PEPPER

1. Place all of the ingredients in a food processor, blitz until smooth, and use immediately or store in the refrigerator.

Preserved Lemon Vinaigrette

YIELD: 1¼ CUPS | **ACTIVE TIME:** 5 MINUTES | **TOTAL TIME:** 5 MINUTES

2 TABLESPOONS MINCED PRESERVED LEMON

¾ CUP EXTRA-VIRGIN OLIVE OIL

¼ CUP FRESH LEMON JUICE

½ TEASPOON RED PEPPER FLAKES

2 TEASPOONS FRESH THYME

PINCH OF KOSHER SALT

1. Place all of the ingredients in a bowl, whisk to combine, and use immediately or store in the refrigerator.

Leek Oil

YIELD: 1 CUP | **ACTIVE TIME:** 15 MINUTES | **TOTAL TIME:** 1 HOUR AND 15 MINUTES

1 CUP CHOPPED LEEKS, GREEN PARTS ONLY

1 CUP SPINACH

1 CUP EXTRA-VIRGIN OLIVE OIL

1. Bring water to a boil in a small saucepan. Prepare an ice bath.

2. Add the leeks and spinach to the pan and cook for 1 minute. Drain the mixture and plunge it into the ice water. Drain the mixture again.

3. Place the mixture in a food processor, add the olive oil, and blitz until smooth, about 3 minutes.

4. Strain the oil and use immediately or store in an airtight container.

Chorizo Oil

YIELD: ¼ CUP | **ACTIVE TIME:** 10 MINUTES | **TOTAL TIME:** 1 HOUR

¼ CUP EXTRA-VIRGIN OLIVE OIL

2 TABLESPOONS CHOPPED CHORIZO

1 GARLIC CLOVE, CHOPPED

1. Place the olive oil in a saucepan and warm it over medium heat.

2. Add the chorizo and garlic and cook, stirring continually, for 2 minutes.

3. Remove the pan from heat and let the mixture cool completely.

4. Strain the oil and use immediately or store in an airtight container.

Epazote Oil

YIELD: 1 CUP | **ACTIVE TIME:** 5 MINUTES | **TOTAL TIME:** 5 MINUTES

3½ OZ. FRESH EPAZOTE LEAVES

14 TABLESPOONS EXTRA-VIRGIN OLIVE OIL

1. Place the ingredients in a food processor and blitz until combined, making sure it takes no longer than 40 seconds.

2. Strain the oil through a coffee filter and use immediately or store in an airtight container.

Preserved Lemon Vinaigrette
SEE PAGE 424

Sichuan Peppercorn & Chili Oil

YIELD: 1¾ CUPS | **ACTIVE TIME:** 5 MINUTES | **TOTAL TIME:** 1 HOUR

1½ CUPS CANOLA OIL

5 STAR ANISE PODS

1 CINNAMON STICK

2 BAY LEAVES

3 TABLESPOONS SICHUAN PEPPERCORNS

⅓ CUP RED PEPPER FLAKES

1 TEASPOON KOSHER SALT

1. Place the canola oil in a saucepan and warm it over low heat for 2 minutes.

2. Add the star anise, cinnamon stick, bay leaves, and peppercorns and reduce the heat to the lowest possible setting. Cook for 20 minutes, stirring occasionally.

3. Place the red pepper flakes in a small bowl and strain the warm oil over the flakes. Let the oil cool completely.

4. Stir in the salt and use immediately or store in an airtight container.

Basil Oil

YIELD: 1 CUP | **ACTIVE TIME:** 15 MINUTES | **TOTAL TIME:** 20 MINUTES

1 CUP BASIL LEAVES

1 CUP BABY SPINACH

1 CUP EXTRA-VIRGIN OLIVE OIL

1. Bring water to a boil in a small saucepan. Prepare an ice bath.

2. Add the basil and spinach to the pan and cook for 1 minute. Drain the mixture and plunge it into the ice water.

3. Place the mixture in a linen towel and wring the towel to remove as much water from it as possible.

4. Place the mixture in a food processor, add the olive oil, and blitz until smooth, about 3 minutes.

5. Strain the oil and use immediately or store in an airtight container.

Harissa Vinaigrette

YIELD: 1½ CUPS | **ACTIVE TIME:** 5 MINUTES | **TOTAL TIME:** 5 MINUTES

3 TABLESPOONS HARISSA PASTE

1 TEASPOON RAS EL HANOUT (SEE PAGE 55)

⅓ CUP RICE WINE VINEGAR

1 TABLESPOON FRESH LEMON JUICE

3 TABLESPOONS HONEY

2 GARLIC CLOVES

2 TEASPOONS GRATED FRESH GINGER

SALT, TO TASTE

1 CUP EXTRA-VIRGIN OLIVE OIL

1. Place all of the ingredients, except for the olive oil, in a food processor and blitz until smooth.

2. With the food processor running, add the olive oil in a slow stream until it has emulsified. Use immediately or store in the refrigerator.

Paprika Oil

YIELD: 2 CUPS | **ACTIVE TIME:** 5 MINUTES | **TOTAL TIME:** 5 MINUTES

½ CUP SWEET PAPRIKA

2 CUPS AVOCADO OIL

1. Place the paprika and avocado oil in a mason jar and shake until thoroughly combined.

2. Store the oil in a dark, dry place and always shake before using.

Thai Chili Dressing

YIELD: 1½ CUPS | **ACTIVE TIME:** 5 MINUTES | **TOTAL TIME:** 5 MINUTES

2 RED BIRD'S EYE CHILI PEPPERS

½ CUP SOY SAUCE

½ CUP SAMBAL OELEK

JUICE OF 3 LIMES

¼ CUP BROWN SUGAR

1 TABLESPOON MINCED FRESH GINGER

2 TABLESPOONS CURRY POWDER

1. Place all of the ingredients in a food processor, blitz until smooth, and use immediately or store in the refrigerator.

Basil Oil

SEE PAGE 430

Red Wine & Chile Dressing

YIELD: 1 CUP | **ACTIVE TIME:** 5 MINUTES | **TOTAL TIME:** 5 MINUTES

1 TEASPOON CHIPOTLE CHILE POWDER

½ TEASPOON BLACK PEPPER

½ TEASPOON ONION POWDER

½ TEASPOON GARLIC POWDER

½ TEASPOON PAPRIKA

1 TABLESPOON KOSHER SALT

2 SCALLIONS, SLICED THIN

2 FRESNO CHILE PEPPERS, STEMS AND SEEDS REMOVED, SLICED

3 TABLESPOONS SUGAR

¼ CUP RED WINE VINEGAR

¾ CUP EXTRA-VIRGIN OLIVE OIL

1. Place all of the ingredients, except for the olive oil, in a food processor and blitz until smooth.

2. With the food processor running, add the olive oil in a slow stream until it has emulsified. Use immediately or store in the refrigerator.

Red Wine & Maple Vinaigrette

YIELD: 1 CUP | **ACTIVE TIME:** 5 MINUTES | **TOTAL TIME:** 5 MINUTES

¼ CUP RED WINE VINEGAR

2 TEASPOONS DIJON MUSTARD

2 TEASPOONS MAPLE SYRUP

SALT AND PEPPER, TO TASTE

½ CUP EXTRA-VIRGIN OLIVE OIL

1. Place all of the ingredients, except for the olive oil, in a food processor and blitz until smooth.

2. With the food processor running, add the olive oil in a slow stream until it has emulsified. Use immediately or store in the refrigerator.

Benihana's Ginger Dressing

YIELD: ¾ CUP | **ACTIVE TIME:** 5 MINUTES | **TOTAL TIME:** 5 MINUTES

¼ CUP CHOPPED WHITE ONION

¼ CUP PEANUT OIL

1 TABLESPOON RICE VINEGAR

1 TABLESPOON MINCED FRESH GINGER

1 TABLESPOON MINCED CELERY

1 TABLESPOON SOY SAUCE

1 TEASPOON TOMATO PASTE

1½ TEASPOONS SUGAR

1 TEASPOON FRESH LEMON JUICE

½ TEASPOON KOSHER SALT

BLACK PEPPER, TO TASTE

1. Place all of the ingredients in a food processor, blitz until smooth, and use immediately or store in the refrigerator.

Chive & Shallot Oil

YIELD: ⅔ CUP | **ACTIVE TIME:** 5 MINUTES | **TOTAL TIME:** 15 MINUTES

½ CUP EXTRA-VIRGIN OLIVE OIL

1 SHALLOT, MINCED

1 TABLESPOON CHOPPED FRESH CHIVES

1. Place the olive oil in a saucepan and warm it over medium heat.

2. Add the shallot and cook, stirring occasionally, until it has softened, about 5 minutes.

3. Remove the pan from heat, stir in the chives, and use immediately or store in an airtight container.

Honey Mustard Vinaigrette

YIELD: 1 CUP | **ACTIVE TIME:** 5 MINUTES | **TOTAL TIME:** 5 MINUTES

¼ CUP HONEY

2 TABLESPOONS WHOLE
GRAIN MUSTARD

3 TABLESPOONS APPLE
CIDER VINEGAR

1 TEASPOON KOSHER SALT

½ TEASPOON BLACK PEPPER

⅓ CUP EXTRA-VIRGIN OLIVE
OIL

1. Place all of the ingredients, except for the olive oil, in a small mixing bowl and whisk to combine.

2. While whisking continually, add the oil in a slow stream until it has emulsified. Use immediately or store in the refrigerator.

Ginger & Tahini Dressing

YIELD: 1 CUP | **ACTIVE TIME:** 5 MINUTES | **TOTAL TIME:** 5 MINUTES

3 TABLESPOONS FRESH
LEMON JUICE

2 TABLESPOONS SOY SAUCE

2 TABLESPOONS TAHINI
PASTE

1 TEASPOON MAPLE SYRUP

1 TEASPOON GRATED FRESH
GINGER

1 TEASPOON RICE VINEGAR

1 TEASPOON TOASTED
SESAME OIL

½ CUP EXTRA-VIRGIN OLIVE
OIL

1. Place all of the ingredients in a bowl, whisk vigorously to
   combine, and use immediately or store in the refrigerator.

Ginger & Lemon Dressing

YIELD: 1 CUP | **ACTIVE TIME:** 5 MINUTES | **TOTAL TIME:** 5 MINUTES

ZEST AND JUICE OF 1 LEMON

2-INCH PIECE OF FRESH GINGER, PEELED AND GRATED

¼ CUP SOY SAUCE

¼ CUP RICE VINEGAR

1½ TABLESPOONS HONEY

½ TEASPOON THAI SEASONING BLEND

3 TABLESPOONS EXTRA-VIRGIN OLIVE OIL

2 TEASPOONS TOASTED SESAME OIL

1. Place all of the ingredients, except for the oils, in a food processor and blitz to combine.

2. With the food processor running, add the oils in a slow stream until it has emulsified. Use immediately or store in the refrigerator.

Blood Orange Vinaigrette

YIELD: 1½ CUPS | **ACTIVE TIME:** 5 MINUTES | **TOTAL TIME:** 5 MINUTES

½ CUP FRESH BLOOD ORANGE JUICE (ABOUT 2 BLOOD ORANGES)

½ TEASPOON KOSHER SALT

¼ TEASPOON BLACK PEPPER

1½ TABLESPOONS APPLE CIDER VINEGAR

1 TABLESPOON HONEY

1 ICE CUBE

1 CUP EXTRA-VIRGIN OLIVE OIL

1. Place all of the ingredients, except for the olive oil, in a food processor and blitz until smooth.

2. With the food processor running, add the olive oil in a slow stream until it has emulsified. Use immediately or store in the refrigerator.

Gooseberry Vinaigrette

YIELD: 1½ CUPS | **ACTIVE TIME:** 5 MINUTES | **TOTAL TIME:** 5 MINUTES

3½ OZ. GOOSEBERRIES, WASHED

¼ CUP RED WINE VINEGAR

¼ CUP HONEY

1 TABLESPOON KOSHER SALT

½ CUP EXTRA-VIRGIN OLIVE OIL

1. Place all of the ingredients, except for the olive oil, in a food processor and blitz until smooth.

2. With the food processor running, add the olive oil in a slow stream until it has emulsified. Use immediately or store in the refrigerator.

Maple & Mustard Vinaigrette

YIELD: 1 CUP | **ACTIVE TIME:** 5 MINUTES | **TOTAL TIME:** 5 MINUTES

2 TABLESPOONS DIJON MUSTARD

2 TABLESPOONS MAPLE SYRUP

¼ CUP APPLE CIDER VINEGAR

SALT AND PEPPER, TO TASTE

½ CUP EXTRA-VIRGIN OLIVE OIL

1. Place all of the ingredients, except for the olive oil, in a food processor and blitz to combine.

2. With the food processor running, add the olive oil in a slow stream until it has emulsified. Use immediately or store in the refrigerator.

Blood Orange Vinaigrette
SEE PAGE 440

Tahini Dressing

YIELD: ¾ CUP | **ACTIVE TIME:** 5 MINUTES | **TOTAL TIME:** 5 MINUTES

½ CUP TAHINI PASTE

2 GARLIC CLOVES, CRUSHED

¼ CUP EXTRA-VIRGIN OLIVE OIL

2 TEASPOONS HONEY

JUICE OF 2 LEMONS

SALT AND PEPPER, TO TASTE

ICE WATER, AS NEEDED

1. Place all of the ingredients, except for the water, in a bowl and whisk to combine.

2. Incorporate water 1 tablespoon at a time until the dressing has the desired texture. Use immediately or store in the refrigerator.

Miso Dressing

YIELD: 1½ CUPS | **ACTIVE TIME:** 5 MINUTES | **TOTAL TIME:** 5 MINUTES

¼ CUP WHITE MISO

¼ CUP RICE VINEGAR

4 TEASPOONS SESAME OIL

4 TEASPOONS MINCED
FRESH GINGER

4 TEASPOONS SOY SAUCE

¾ CUP PEANUT OIL

¼ CUP SESAME SEEDS

4 TEASPOONS REAL MAPLE
SYRUP

1. Place all of the ingredients in a bowl, whisk to combine, and use immediately or store in the refrigerator.

Cilantro Oil

YIELD: 1 CUP | **ACTIVE TIME:** 5 MINUTES | **TOTAL TIME:** 5 MINUTES

2 BUNCHES OF FRESH
CILANTRO

2 GARLIC CLOVES, MINCED

JUICE OF 1 LIME

½ CUP EXTRA-VIRGIN OLIVE
OIL

1. Place all of the ingredients, except for the olive oil, in a food processor and blitz to combine.

2. With the food processor running, add the olive oil in a slow stream until it has emulsified. Use immediately or store in the refrigerator.

White Balsamic Vinaigrette

YIELD: 1½ CUPS | **ACTIVE TIME:** 5 MINUTES | **TOTAL TIME:** 5 MINUTES

½ CUP WHITE BALSAMIC VINEGAR

2 TABLESPOONS MINCED SHALLOT

¼ CUP SLICED SCALLIONS

2 TABLESPOONS CHOPPED FRESH PARSLEY

2 TEASPOONS KOSHER SALT

1 TEASPOON BLACK PEPPER

¼ CUP EXTRA-VIRGIN OLIVE OIL

1. Place all of the ingredients, except for the olive oil, in a food processor and blitz to combine.

2. With the food processor running, add the olive oil in a slow stream until it has emulsified. Use immediately or store in the refrigerator.

Chile & Coriander Oil

YIELD: ¾ CUP | **ACTIVE TIME:** 5 MINUTES | **TOTAL TIME:** 15 MINUTES

2 DRIED CHILE PEPPERS, STEMS AND SEEDS REMOVED

¾ CUP EXTRA-VIRGIN OLIVE OIL

1 GARLIC CLOVE, CRUSHED

1 TEASPOON CORIANDER

1. Place the chile peppers in a small saucepan and toast them over medium-high heat until lightly charred, about 3 minutes. Remove the chiles from the pan and set them aside.

2. Add the olive oil to the saucepan and warm it over medium heat. Stir in the garlic and coriander and cook for 4 minutes.

3. Return the chiles to the pan and cook for another 4 minutes. Remove the pan from heat and let the oil cool.

4. Strain before using or storing in an airtight container.

Morita Oil

YIELD: 2 CUPS | **ACTIVE TIME:** 5 MINUTES | **TOTAL TIME:** 24 HOURS

3½ OZ. CHIPOTLE MORITA CHILE PEPPERS, STEMS AND SEEDS REMOVED

2 CUPS EXTRA-VIRGIN OLIVE OIL

1. Place the chiles and olive oil in a food processor and blitz for 7 minutes. Let the mixture sit at room temperature for 24 hours.

2. Strain the oil before using or storing in an airtight container.

Cumin & Cilantro Vinaigrette

YIELD: 2 CUPS | **ACTIVE TIME:** 5 MINUTES | **TOTAL TIME:** 5 MINUTES

¼ CUP CUMIN SEEDS

¼ CUP BROWN SUGAR

3 EGG YOLKS

⅓ CUP RED WINE VINEGAR

½ CUP WATER

2 CUPS FRESH CILANTRO, CHOPPED

SALT AND PEPPER, TO TASTE

1½ CUPS EXTRA-VIRGIN OLIVE OIL

1. Place the cumin seeds in a dry skillet and toast them over medium heat until they are fragrant, 1 to 2 minutes, shaking the pan frequently.

2. Place the toasted cumin seeds and all of the remaining ingredients, except for the olive oil, in a food processor and blitz to combine.

3. With the food processor running, add the olive oil in a slow stream until it has emulsified. Use immediately or store in the refrigerator.

Shallot, Honey & Herb Vinaigrette

YIELD: 1½ CUPS | **ACTIVE TIME:** 5 MINUTES | **TOTAL TIME:** 5 MINUTES

2 TABLESPOONS SLICED FRESH CHIVES

2 TEASPOONS FRESH THYME

2 TEASPOONS CHOPPED FRESH OREGANO

2 TABLESPOONS CHOPPED FRESH PARSLEY

6 TABLESPOONS APPLE CIDER VINEGAR

2 TABLESPOONS HONEY

4 TEASPOONS DICED SHALLOT

2 TEASPOONS KOSHER SALT

½ TEASPOON BLACK PEPPER

½ CUP EXTRA-VIRGIN OLIVE OIL

1. Place all of the ingredients, except for the olive oil, in a food processor and blitz to combine.

2. With the food processor running, add the olive oil in a slow stream until it has emulsified. Use immediately or store in the refrigerator.

Morita Oil
SEE PAGE 452

Bay Leaf Oil

YIELD: ½ CUP | **ACTIVE TIME:** 20 MINUTES | **TOTAL TIME:** 24 HOURS

1 OZ. BAY LEAVES

10 TABLESPOONS EXTRA-VIRGIN OLIVE OIL

SALT, TO TASTE

1. Place the bay leaves and olive oil in a food processor and blitz until smooth, about 5 minutes.

2. Strain the oil into a bowl through a coffee filter and season it with salt.

3. Prepare an ice bath and place the bowl containing the oil in it. Transfer the oil to the refrigerator and let it sit overnight.

4. Pour the mixture through a cheesecloth-lined sieve and let it sit until the oil is free of any debris. Use immediately or store in the refrigerator.

Garlic & Mustard Vinaigrette

YIELD: 1¾ CUPS | **ACTIVE TIME:** 5 MINUTES | **TOTAL TIME:** 5 MINUTES

¾ CUP RED WINE VINEGAR

½ CUP DIJON MUSTARD

4 GARLIC CLOVES, GRATED

SALT AND PEPPER, TO TASTE

½ CUP EXTRA-VIRGIN OLIVE OIL

1. Place all of the ingredients, except for the olive oil, in a food processor and blitz to combine.

2. With the food processor running, add the olive oil in a slow stream until it has emulsified. Use immediately or store in the refrigerator.

Coconut Dressing

YIELD: 3 CUPS | **ACTIVE TIME:** 15 MINUTES | **TOTAL TIME:** 45 MINUTES

1 (14 OZ.) CAN OF COCONUT MILK

3½ OZ. GRATED FRESH GINGER

14 TABLESPOONS FRESH LEMON JUICE

1½ TEASPOONS KOSHER SALT

5 TEASPOONS CASTER (SUPERFINE) SUGAR

1½ CUPS CHOPPED FRESH CILANTRO

1½ TABLESPOONS CRACKED CORIANDER SEEDS

1. Place all of the ingredients in a mixing bowl, stir to combine, and chill in the refrigerator for 30 minutes.

2. Place the mixture in a blender and puree until emulsified, making sure the mixture does not get hot at all.

3. Strain the dressing through a fine-mesh sieve and use immediately or store in an airtight container.

Yuzu Vinaigrette

YIELD: 1½ CUPS | **ACTIVE TIME:** 5 MINUTES | **TOTAL TIME:** 5 MINUTES

4 GARLIC CLOVES, MINCED

2 TABLESPOONS YUZU KOSHO

¼ CUP FRESH YUZU JUICE

SALT AND PEPPER, TO TASTE

¾ CUP EXTRA-VIRGIN OLIVE OIL

1. Place all of the ingredients, except for the olive oil, in a food processor and blitz to combine.

2. With the food processor running, add the olive oil in a slow stream until it has emulsified. Use immediately or store in the refrigerator.

Champagne & Herb Vinaigrette

YIELD: 2 CUPS | **ACTIVE TIME:** 5 MINUTES | **TOTAL TIME:** 5 MINUTES

2 SHALLOTS, MINCED

½ CUP HONEY

¼ CUP CHAMPAGNE VINEGAR

1 TABLESPOON DIJON MUSTARD

¼ CUP CHOPPED FRESH CHIVES

2 TABLESPOONS FRESH THYME

¾ CUP EXTRA-VIRGIN OLIVE OIL

1. Place all of the ingredients, except for the olive oil, in a food processor and blitz to combine.

2. With the food processor running, add the olive oil in a slow stream until it has emulsified. Use immediately or store in the refrigerator.

Garlic & Mustard Vinaigrette

SEE PAGE 458

Pomegranate & Mint Vinaigrette

YIELD: 1½ CUPS | **ACTIVE TIME:** 5 MINUTES | **TOTAL TIME:** 5 MINUTES

2 TABLESPOONS POMEGRANATE MOLASSES

1 CUP CHOPPED FRESH MINT LEAVES

1 TEASPOON RAS EL HANOUT (SEE PAGE 55)

SALT AND PEPPER, TO TASTE

⅓ CUP EXTRA-VIRGIN OLIVE OIL

1. Place all of the ingredients, except for the olive oil, in a food processor and blitz to combine.

2. With the food processor running, add the olive oil in a slow stream until it has emulsified. Use immediately or store in the refrigerator.

Harissa & Dijon Vinaigrette

YIELD: 1½ CUPS | **ACTIVE TIME:** 5 MINUTES | **TOTAL TIME:** 5 MINUTES

6 TABLESPOONS RED WINE VINEGAR

¼ CUP HARISSA SAUCE (SEE PAGE 285)

1 TABLESPOON DIJON MUSTARD

SALT AND PEPPER, TO TASTE

⅔ CUP EXTRA-VIRGIN OLIVE OIL

1. Place all of the ingredients, except for the olive oil, in a food processor and blitz to combine.

2. With the food processor running, add the olive oil in a slow stream until it has emulsified. Use immediately or store in the refrigerator.

Orange Vinaigrette

YIELD: 1½ CUPS | **ACTIVE TIME:** 5 MINUTES | **TOTAL TIME:** 5 MINUTES

¼ CUP FRESH ORANGE JUICE

2 SHALLOTS, FINELY DICED

2 TABLESPOONS CHAMPAGNE VINEGAR

SALT AND PEPPER, TO TASTE

PAPRIKA, TO TASTE

¾ CUP EXTRA-VIRGIN OLIVE OIL

1 TEASPOON POPPY SEEDS

1. Place all of the ingredients, except for the olive oil and poppy seeds, in a food processor and blitz to combine.

2. With the food processor running, add the olive oil in a slow stream until it has emulsified. Stir in the poppy seeds and use immediately or store in the refrigerator.

Spicy Honey Vinaigrette

YIELD: 1 CUP | **ACTIVE TIME:** 5 MINUTES | **TOTAL TIME:** 5 MINUTES

1 TEASPOON CHOPPED FRESH DILL

1 TEASPOON CHOPPED FRESH MINT

1 TABLESPOON CHOPPED FRESH PARSLEY

1 TABLESPOON HONEY

3 TABLESPOONS WHITE VINEGAR

1 TABLESPOON FRESH GRAPEFRUIT JUICE

1 JALAPEÑO CHILE PEPPER, STEM AND SEEDS REMOVED, SLICED THIN

SALT AND PEPPER, TO TASTE

½ CUP EXTRA-VIRGIN OLIVE OIL

1. Place all of the ingredients, except for the olive oil, in a food processor and blitz to combine.

2. With the food processor running, add the olive oil in a slow stream until it has emulsified. Use immediately or store in the refrigerator.

Olive & Whole Lemon Vinaigrette

YIELD: 1 CUP | **ACTIVE TIME:** 5 MINUTES | **TOTAL TIME:** 20 MINUTES

2 CUPS GREEN OLIVES

1 LEMON

2 SHALLOTS, MINCED

1 TABLESPOON FRESH LEMON JUICE

SALT AND PEPPER, TO TASTE

½ CUP EXTRA-VIRGIN OLIVE OIL

1. Crush the olives to break them up into large, craggy pieces. Discard the pits and place the olives in a large bowl.

2. Halve the lemon, remove the seeds, and finely dice the entire lemon, peel and all. Add the lemon, shallots, and lemon juice to the olives, toss to combine, and season with salt and pepper. Let the dressing stand for 5 minutes to allow the flavors to meld.

3. Place the olive oil in a small saucepan and warm it over medium heat. Add the dressing and cook, swirling the pan occasionally, until the dressing is warmed through and the shallots have softened slightly, about 4 minutes. Use immediately or store in the refrigerator.

Soy & Sesame Dressing

YIELD: ½ CUP | **ACTIVE TIME:** 5 MINUTES | **TOTAL TIME:** 5 MINUTES

½ CUP SOY SAUCE

2 TABLESPOONS SESAME OIL

1 TEASPOON WASABI

1. Place all of the ingredients in a bowl and whisk until thoroughly combined. Use immediately or store in the refrigerator.

Fig Vinaigrette

YIELD: 1½ CUPS | **ACTIVE TIME:** 5 MINUTES | **TOTAL TIME:** 5 MINUTES

3 TABLESPOONS BALSAMIC VINEGAR

1 TABLESPOON WATER

1 TABLESPOON FIG JAM

1 TABLESPOON DIJON MUSTARD

1 SHALLOT, MINCED

½ CUP EXTRA-VIRGIN OLIVE OIL

½ CUP DICED FIGS

2 TABLESPOONS CHOPPED FRESH CHIVES

SALT AND PEPPER, TO TASTE

1. Place the vinegar, water, jam, mustard, and shallot in a mixing bowl and whisk to combine.

2. While whisking continually, add the olive oil in a slow, steady stream until it has emulsified.

3. Add the figs and chives, whisk to incorporate, and season the vinaigrette with salt and pepper. Use immediately or store in the refrigerator until needed.

Pomegranate Vinaigrette

YIELD: 4 CUPS | **ACTIVE TIME:** 30 MINUTES | **TOTAL TIME:** 30 MINUTES

2 CUPS POMEGRANATE JUICE

½ CUP RED WINE VINEGAR

2 TABLESPOONS DIJON MUSTARD

2 TABLESPOONS HONEY

1 TABLESPOON ZA'ATAR (SEE PAGE 68)

2 TEASPOONS SUMAC

2 TABLESPOONS KOSHER SALT

1 TABLESPOON BLACK PEPPER

1 TABLESPOON CHOPPED FRESH OREGANO

1 TABLESPOON CHOPPED FRESH BASIL

1 TABLESPOON CHOPPED FRESH PARSLEY

1 TABLESPOON CHOPPED FRESH MINT

3 CUPS EXTRA-VIRGIN OLIVE OIL

1. Place the pomegranate juice in a small saucepan and bring it to a boil over medium-high heat. Boil until it has reduced to ¼ cup. Remove the pan from heat and let the reduction cool.

2. Place the pomegranate reduction and the remaining ingredients, except for the olive oil, in a food processor and blitz until smooth.

3. With the food processor running, add the olive oil in a slow stream until it has emulsified. Use immediately or store in the refrigerator.

Soy & Sesame Dressing
SEE PAGE 464

Dijon Dressing

YIELD: 1 CUP | **ACTIVE TIME:** 5 MINUTES | **TOTAL TIME:** 5 MINUTES

JUICE OF 2 LEMONS

1 TABLESPOON MINCED SHALLOT

1 TABLESPOON CHOPPED FRESH BASIL

2 TEASPOONS FRESH THYME

2 TEASPOONS CHOPPED FRESH OREGANO

2 TEASPOONS DIJON MUSTARD

2 ANCHOVIES IN OLIVE OIL, DRAINED AND FINELY CHOPPED

2 TEASPOONS CAPERS, DRAINED AND CHOPPED

SALT AND PEPPER, TO TASTE

¾ CUP EXTRA-VIRGIN OLIVE OIL

1. Place all of the ingredients, except for the olive oil, in a food processor and blitz to combine.

2. With the food processor running, add the olive oil in a slow stream until it has emulsified. Use immediately or store in the refrigerator.

Champagne Vinaigrette

YIELD: 2½ CUPS | **ACTIVE TIME:** 5 MINUTES | **TOTAL TIME:** 5 MINUTES

⅔ CUP CHAMPAGNE VINEGAR

¼ CUP WATER

2 TABLESPOONS DIJON MUSTARD

½ TEASPOON KOSHER SALT

½ TEASPOON BLACK PEPPER

1 TEASPOON FRESH THYME

2 TABLESPOONS HONEY

1½ CUPS EXTRA-VIRGIN OLIVE OIL

1. Place all of the ingredients, except for the olive oil, in a bowl and whisk to combine.

2. While whisking continually, add the olive oil in a slow stream until it has emulsified. Use immediately or store in the refrigerator.

Classic Caesar Dressing

YIELD: 1 CUP | **ACTIVE TIME:** 15 MINUTES | **TOTAL TIME:** 25 MINUTES

1 GARLIC CLOVE, HALVED

2 EGGS

2 TABLESPOONS FRESH LEMON JUICE

½ CUP EXTRA-VIRGIN OLIVE OIL

3 TABLESPOONS MINCED ANCHOVIES

DASH OF WORCESTERSHIRE SAUCE

SALT AND PEPPER, TO TASTE

1. Bring water to a boil in a small saucepan.

2. Rub the inside of a salad bowl with the garlic and then discard the garlic.

3. Using a needle, pierce a tiny hole in the wide end of each egg. Place them in the water and boil until the insides just begin to firm up, about 1 minute. Remove the eggs from the water, crack them into the salad bowl, making sure to scoop out any of the whites that cling to the shells.

4. While whisking continually, add the lemon juice and then the olive oil in a slow stream. Stir in the anchovies and Worcestershire sauce, season the dressing with salt and pepper, and use immediately.

THE ENCYCLOPEDIA OF SEASONING

Ranch Dressing

YIELD: 2 CUPS | **ACTIVE TIME:** 5 MINUTES | **TOTAL TIME:** 5 MINUTES

1 CUP MAYONNAISE

1 CUP BUTTERMILK

SALT AND PEPPER, TO TASTE

¼ CUP CHOPPED FRESH CHIVES

1. Place all of the ingredients in a bowl, whisk to combine, and use immediately or store in the refrigerator.

Honey Mustard & Tarragon Dressing

YIELD: 1 CUP | **ACTIVE TIME:** 5 MINUTES | **TOTAL TIME:** 5 MINUTES

2 TABLESPOONS WHITE WINE VINEGAR

1 TABLESPOON FRESH LEMON JUICE

1 TABLESPOON WHOLE-GRAIN MUSTARD

1 TEASPOON HONEY

½ CUP EXTRA-VIRGIN OLIVE OIL

1 SHALLOT, MINCED

2 TEASPOONS CHOPPED FRESH TARRAGON

SALT AND PEPPER, TO TASTE

1. Place the vinegar, lemon juice, mustard, and honey in a food processor and blitz until smooth.

2. With the food processor running, add the olive oil in a slow stream until it has emulsified.

3. Stir in the shallot and tarragon, season the dressing with salt and pepper, and use immediately or store in an airtight container.

Champagne Vinaigrette
SEE PAGE 470

Buttermilk Caesar Dressing

YIELD: 1 CUP | **ACTIVE TIME:** 5 MINUTES | **TOTAL TIME:** 5 MINUTES

1 LARGE GARLIC CLOVE, MINCED

1 TEASPOON WHITE MISO

⅔ CUP MAYONNAISE

¼ CUP BUTTERMILK

¼ CUP FRESHLY GRATED PARMESAN CHEESE

ZEST OF 1 LEMON

1 TEASPOON WORCESTERSHIRE SAUCE

1 TEASPOON KOSHER SALT, PLUS MORE TO TASTE

½ TEASPOON BLACK PEPPER, PLUS MORE TO TASTE

1. Place all of the ingredients in a food processor and blitz until smooth.

2. Taste, adjust the seasoning as necessary, and use immediately or store in the refrigerator.

Thousand Island Dressing

YIELD: 1½ CUPS | **ACTIVE TIME:** 5 MINUTES | **TOTAL TIME:** 5 MINUTES

1 HARD-BOILED EGG, CHOPPED

1 CUP MAYONNAISE

¼ CUP KETCHUP

2 TABLESPOONS FINELY DICED PIMENTO-STUFFED GREEN OLIVES

2 TABLESPOONS FINELY DICED SWEET PICKLES

1 TABLESPOON CHOPPED ONION

2 TEASPOONS CHOPPED FRESH PARSLEY

1 TEASPOON FRESH LEMON JUICE

1 TEASPOON SMOKED PAPRIKA

SALT AND PEPPER, TO TASTE

1. Place all of the ingredients in a bowl, stir to combine, and use immediately or store in the refrigerator.

Classic Panzanella Dressing

YIELD: 1½ CUPS | **ACTIVE TIME:** 5 MINUTES | **TOTAL TIME:** 5 MINUTES

¼ CUP RED WINE VINEGAR

½ CUP EXTRA-VIRGIN OLIVE OIL

2 TABLESPOONS CHOPPED FRESH BASIL

2 TABLESPOONS CHOPPED FRESH OREGANO

SALT AND PEPPER, TO TASTE

1. Place the vinegar in a bowl. While whisking continually, slowly drizzle in the olive oil. As this is a split vinaigrette, the oil will not emulsify. Add the herbs, season the dressing with salt and pepper, and stir to combine. Use immediately or store in an airtight container.

Basil & Cilantro Vinaigrette

YIELD: 1½ CUPS | **ACTIVE TIME:** 5 MINUTES | **TOTAL TIME:** 5 MINUTES

½ CUP CHOPPED FRESH CILANTRO

½ CUP CHOPPED FRESH BASIL

2 TABLESPOONS CHOPPED FRESH PARSLEY

1 GARLIC CLOVE, MINCED

2 TABLESPOONS MINCED JALAPEÑO PEPPER

2 TABLESPOONS FRESH LIME JUICE

1 TEASPOON BLACK PEPPER

1 TEASPOON KOSHER SALT

⅓ CUP EXTRA-VIRGIN OLIVE OIL

1. Place all of the ingredients, except for the olive oil, in a food processor and blitz until smooth.

2. With the food processor running, add the olive oil in a slow stream until it has emulsified. Use immediately or store in the refrigerator.

CONDIMENTS, SPREADS & BUTTERS

Lemon-Pepper Mayonnaise

YIELD: 1½ CUPS | **ACTIVE TIME:** 5 MINUTES | **TOTAL TIME:** 5 MINUTES

1 CUP MAYONNAISE

3 TABLESPOONS GRATED PARMESAN CHEESE

1 TABLESPOON LEMON ZEST

3 TABLESPOONS FRESH LEMON JUICE

1½ TEASPOONS BLACK PEPPER

2 TEASPOONS KOSHER SALT

1. Place all of the ingredients in a bowl, stir to combine, and use immediately or store in the refrigerator.

Maple Butter

YIELD: 1 CUP | **ACTIVE TIME:** 5 MINUTES | **TOTAL TIME:** 5 MINUTES

½ CUP REAL MAPLE SYRUP

½ CUP UNSALTED BUTTER, SOFTENED

SALT, TO TASTE

1. Place the ingredients in the work bowl of a stand mixer fitted with the whisk attachment and whip until combined. Use immediately or store in the refrigerator.

Apple Butter

YIELD: 3 CUPS | **ACTIVE TIME:** 25 MINUTES | **TOTAL TIME:** 2 HOURS

3 CUPS BRANDY

5 LBS. APPLES, RINSED WELL

½ CUP REAL MAPLE SYRUP

¼ CUP BROWN SUGAR

1 TEASPOON FINE SEA SALT

½ TEASPOON CINNAMON

¼ TEASPOON CORIANDER

¼ TEASPOON GROUND CLOVES

¼ TEASPOON NUTMEG

1. Place the brandy in a saucepan, bring it to a boil over medium-high heat, and cook until it has reduced by half, about 15 minutes. Remove the pan from heat and set it aside.

2. Cut the apples into quarters, place them in a stockpot, and cover them with cold water. Bring it to a boil over medium-high heat and then reduce the heat so that the apples simmer. Cook until tender, about 15 minutes, and then drain.

3. Preheat the oven to 225°F. Run the apples through a food mill and catch the pulp in a mixing bowl. Add the reduced brandy and the remaining ingredients, stir to combine, and transfer the mixture to a shallow baking dish.

4. Place the baking dish in the oven and bake the apple mixture, stirring every 10 minutes or so, until all of the excess water has evaporated, 1 to 1½ hours.

5. Remove the baking dish from the oven, transfer the mixture to a food processor, and blitz until smooth. Use immediately or store in the refrigerator.

Strawberry & Yuzu Emulsion

YIELD: 3 CUPS | **ACTIVE TIME:** 15 MINUTES | **TOTAL TIME:** 40 MINUTES

1½ CUPS QUARTERED STRAWBERRIES

3 OZ. YUZU JUICE

1 TEASPOON GRATED FRESH GINGER

3 TABLESPOONS HONEY

½ CUP RICE VINEGAR

SALT, TO TASTE

1 CUP EXTRA-VIRGIN OLIVE OIL

1 TEASPOON XANTHAN GUM

1. Place the strawberries, yuzu juice, ginger, honey, vinegar, and salt in a small saucepan and warm the mixture over low heat until the strawberries have softened, about 10 minutes.

2. Remove the pan from heat and let the mixture cool to room temperature.

3. Place the mixture in a food processor. With the food processor running at medium speed, add the olive oil in a slow stream until it has emulsified. Raise the speed to high, add the xanthan gum, and blitz until the emulsion has thickened slightly. Use immediately or store in the refrigerator.

Cabbage & Caraway Emulsion

YIELD: 2 CUPS | **ACTIVE TIME:** 10 MINUTES | **TOTAL TIME:** 30 MINUTES

2 CUPS CHOPPED SAVOY CABBAGE

1 CUP EXTRA-VIRGIN OLIVE OIL

1 TABLESPOON CARAWAY SEEDS

SALT AND PEPPER, TO TASTE

1. Bring water to a boil in a small saucepan and prepare an ice bath. Add salt and the cabbage to the pan and boil the cabbage for 3 minutes. Drain the cabbage, plunge it into the ice bath until it is cool, and drain it again.

2. Remove the cabbage from the ice water and squeeze to remove as much water from it as possible.

3. Transfer the cabbage to a food processor. Add the oil and caraway seeds and blitz until the mixture has emulsified. Season the emulsion with salt and pepper and use immediately or store in the refrigerator.

Charred Pepper Emulsion

YIELD: 3 CUPS | **ACTIVE TIME:** 15 MINUTES | **TOTAL TIME:** 1 HOUR AND 45 MINUTES

1 HEAD OF GARLIC

EXTRA-VIRGIN OLIVE OIL, TO TASTE

2 TABLESPOONS KOSHER SALT, PLUS MORE TO TASTE

1¼ LBS. POBLANO CHILE PEPPERS

1 CUP ALMONDS, TOASTED

1 TEASPOON CAPERS

½ CUP SHERRY VINEGAR

2 TABLESPOONS PAPRIKA

3 TABLESPOONS FRESH LEMON JUICE

1¼ CUPS GARLIC-INFUSED OLIVE OIL

1. Preheat the oven to 400°F. Cut off the top of the head of garlic, drizzle some olive oil over the cloves, and sprinkle salt on top. Place the top back on the garlic, place the entire head in a piece of aluminum foil, and seal it closed. Place the garlic in the oven and roast it until it is extremely tender, about 40 minutes. Remove the garlic from the oven and let it cool.

2. Preheat a gas or charcoal grill to medium-high heat (about 450°F). Place the poblanos and some olive oil in a mixing bowl and toss until the peppers are coated.

3. Place the peppers on the grill and cook until charred all over, turning them as needed. Place the peppers in a heatproof bowl, cover it with plastic wrap, and let them steam for 15 minutes.

4. Remove most of the charred skin from the peppers, leaving about one-quarter of it on. Remove the stems and seeds from the peppers, place the remaining flesh in a food processor, and squeeze the roasted garlic cloves into the blender.

5. Add the remaining ingredients, except for the infused oil, and blitz until smooth. With the food processor running, add the oil in a slow stream until it has been emulsified. Use immediately or store in the refrigerator.

Cranberry Jam

YIELD: 1½ CUPS | **ACTIVE TIME:** 5 MINUTES | **TOTAL TIME:** 1 HOUR

½ LB. FRESH CRANBERRIES

½ CUP SUGAR

½ CUP APPLE CIDER

½ TEASPOON GRATED FRESH GINGER

1 TEASPOON ORANGE ZEST

½ TEASPOON KOSHER SALT

1. Place all of the ingredients in a small saucepan and bring the mixture to a boil. Reduce the heat so that the mixture simmers and cook it until the cranberries have broken down and the mixture has thickened, 20 to 25 minutes.

2. Transfer the jam to a mason jar and let it cool completely before using or storing in the refrigerator. To can this jam, see page 486.

Canning 101

Bring a pot of water to a boil. Place your mason jars in the water for 15 to 20 minutes to sterilize them. Do not boil the mason jar lids, as this can prevent them from creating a proper seal when the time comes.

Bring water to a boil in the large canning pot. Fill the sterilized mason jars with whatever you are canning. Place the lids on the jars and secure the bands tightly. Place the jars in the boiling water for 40 minutes. Use a pair of canning tongs to remove the jars from the boiling water and let them cool. As they are cooling, you should hear the classic "ping and pop" sound of the lids creating a seal.

After 6 hours, check the lids. There should be no give in them and they should be suctioned onto the jars. Discard any lids and food that did not seal properly.

Cranberry Jam
SEE PAGE 485

Truffled Madeira Cream

YIELD: ½ CUP | **ACTIVE TIME:** 5 MINUTES | **TOTAL TIME:** 5 MINUTES

1 CUP MADEIRA

½ CUP HEAVY CREAM

1 TEASPOON CHOPPED FRESH PARSLEY

1 TABLESPOON TRUFFLE PASTE

SALT AND PEPPER, TO TASTE

1. Place the Madeira in a saucepan and bring it to a simmer. Cook the Madeira until it has reduced to a syrup. Remove the pan from heat and let the Madeira cool.

2. Place the heavy cream in the work bowl of a stand mixer fitted with the whisk attachment and whip until the cream holds soft peaks.

3. Add the Madeira reduction and whip until the mixture holds medium peaks.

4. Stir in the parsley and truffle paste, season the cream with salt and pepper, and use immediately or store in the refrigerator.

Red Pepper Jam

YIELD: 2 CUPS | **ACTIVE TIME:** 15 MINUTES | **TOTAL TIME:** 2 HOURS

¼ CUP PECTIN

1½ CUPS SUGAR, DIVIDED

3 RED PEPPERS, STEMS AND SEEDS REMOVED, DICED

⅓ CUP APPLE CIDER VINEGAR

1 TEASPOON RED PEPPER FLAKES

1 TEASPOON SALT

1. In a small bowl, whisk together the pectin and ¼ cup of sugar and set the mixture aside.

2. Place the peppers in a food processor and pulse until pureed.

3. Place the pepper puree in a saucepan, add the vinegar, red pepper flakes, salt, and the remaining sugar and bring the mixture to a boil. Cook for 4 minutes.

4. Stir in the pectin mixture and return the mixture to a boil. Cook, stirring occasionally, until the mixture starts to thicken. Remove the pan from heat and let the jam cool to room temperature before using or storing in the refrigerator. To can this jam, see page 486.

Kimchi Mayonnaise

YIELD: ½ CUP | **ACTIVE TIME:** 15 MINUTES | **TOTAL TIME:** 45 MINUTES

1 TABLESPOON CANOLA OIL

2 TABLESPOONS FINELY DICED KIMCHI (SEE PAGE 503)

1 TABLESPOON SUGAR

1 TABLESPOON RED PEPPER FLAKES

2 TABLESPOONS KIMCHI JUICE

JUICE OF 1 LIME

¼ CUP MAYONNAISE

1. Place the canola oil in a small skillet and warm it over medium-high heat. Add the kimchi and cook, stirring occasionally, until it caramelizes, about 8 minutes. Stir in the sugar, pepper flakes, and kimchi juice, remove the pan from heat, and let the mixture cool.

2. Place the kimchi mixture, lime juice, and mayonnaise in a bowl, stir to combine, and use immediately or store in the refrigerator.

Mixed Berry Jam

YIELD: 4 CUPS | **ACTIVE TIME:** 5 MINUTES | **TOTAL TIME:** 1 HOUR

6 CUPS STRAWBERRIES, HULLED AND QUARTERED

2 CUPS BLUEBERRIES

2 CUPS RASPBERRIES

½ CUP SUGAR

1¼ TABLESPOONS PECTIN

1. Place the berries and sugar in a large saucepan and cook over medium-high heat, stirring continually, until the sugar has dissolved and the berries start breaking down and releasing their liquid.

2. Reduce the heat to medium and cook, stirring every 10 minutes, until the berries are very soft and the mixture has thickened, 30 to 40 minutes.

3. While stirring continually, sprinkle the pectin onto the mixture and cook for another minute.

4. Transfer the jam to a mason jar and let it cool before using or storing in the refrigerator. To can this jam, see page 486.

Roasted Artichoke & Garlic Spread

YIELD: 1 CUP | **ACTIVE TIME:** 5 MINUTES | **TOTAL TIME:** 10 TO 20 MINUTES

¾ LB. FROZEN ARTICHOKE HEARTS, THAWED AND HALVED

4 GARLIC CLOVES, UNPEELED

2 TABLESPOONS APPLE CIDER VINEGAR

¼ TEASPOON KOSHER SALT

¼ CUP EXTRA-VIRGIN OLIVE OIL

PINCH OF ONION POWDER

BLACK PEPPER, TO TASTE

1. Turn the oven's broiler to low. Spread the artichoke hearts and garlic on a cookie sheet and broil, turning occasionally, until browned all over, 15 minutes

2. Peel the garlic and place it in a food processor with the artichoke hearts. Add the remaining ingredients and blitz until smooth. Use immediately or store in the refrigerator.

Fennel & Lemon Gremolata

YIELD: 1½ CUPS | **ACTIVE TIME:** 10 MINUTES | **TOTAL TIME:** 10 MINUTES

¼ CUP CHOPPED FENNEL FRONDS

¼ CUP CHOPPED FRESH PARSLEY

1 TEASPOON LEMON ZEST

1 TABLESPOON EXTRA-VIRGIN OLIVE OIL

SALT, TO TASTE

1. Place all of the ingredients in a food processor, pulse until combined, and use immediately or store in the refrigerator.

Lemon Mayonnaise

YIELD: ½ CUP | **ACTIVE TIME:** 5 MINUTES | **TOTAL TIME:** 5 MINUTES

½ CUP MAYONNAISE

1 TABLESPOON FRESH LEMON JUICE

1. Place the ingredients in a bowl, stir to combine, and use immediately or store in the refrigerator.

Cilantro Mayonnaise

YIELD: ½ CUP | **ACTIVE TIME:** 5 MINUTES | **TOTAL TIME:** 5 MINUTES

½ BUNCH OF FRESH CILANTRO

½ CUP MAYONNAISE

1 TABLESPOON FRESH LIME JUICE

PINCH OF SALT

1. Place all of the ingredients in a food processor, blitz until smooth, and use immediately or store in the refrigerator.

Pasilla Yogurt

YIELD: 2 CUPS | **ACTIVE TIME:** 5 MINUTES | **TOTAL TIME:** 5 MINUTES

4 PASILLA CHILE PEPPERS, STEMS AND SEEDS REMOVED

2 CUPS YOGURT

JUICE OF 1 LIME

SALT, TO TASTE

1. Place the chiles in a dry skillet and toast them over medium heat until fragrant and pliable. Remove the chiles from the pan and let them cool. Using a mortar and pestle, grind the chiles into a fine powder.

2. Add the pasilla powder to the yogurt and fold to combine. Stir in the lime juice and season the mixture with salt. Use immediately or store in the refrigerator.

Cilantro Mayonnaise
SEE PAGE 493

Green Tomato Chutney

YIELD: 4 CUPS | **ACTIVE TIME:** 35 MINUTES | **TOTAL TIME:** 5 TO 7 HOURS

1 LB. GREEN TOMATOES, DICED

¼ LARGE ONION, DICED

2 TEASPOONS MINCED FRESH GINGER

1 GARLIC CLOVE, CHOPPED

½ TEASPOON MUSTARD SEEDS

½ TEASPOON CUMIN

½ TEASPOON CORIANDER

½ TEASPOON KOSHER SALT

3 TABLESPOONS HONEY

⅓ CUP APPLE CIDER VINEGAR

⅓ CUP RAISINS

1. Place all of the ingredients in a large saucepan and bring the mixture to a boil. Reduce the heat so that the mixture simmers and cook, stirring occasionally, until the onions and tomatoes are tender and the mixture has thickened, 20 to 30 minutes.

2. Remove the pan from heat and let the chutney cool before serving or storing in the refrigerator.

Rosemary Butter

YIELD: ½ CUP | **ACTIVE TIME:** 5 MINUTES | **TOTAL TIME:** 5 MINUTES

½ CUP UNSALTED BUTTER, AT ROOM TEMPERATURE

SALT, TO TASTE

¼ CUP CHOPPED FRESH ROSEMARY

1. Place the butter, salt, and rosemary in the work bowl of a stand mixer fitted with the paddle attachment and beat until the butter is light and fluffy. Use immediately or store in the refrigerator.

Caramelized Onion Crème Fraîche

YIELD: 1½ CUPS | **ACTIVE TIME:** 30 MINUTES | **TOTAL TIME:** 1 HOUR

1 TABLESPOON EXTRA-VIRGIN OLIVE OIL

1 ONION, CHOPPED

SALT AND PEPPER, TO TASTE

1 CUP CRÈME FRAÎCHE

1. Place the olive oil in a skillet and warm it over low heat. Add the onion and cook, stirring occasionally, until it is caramelized, about 30 minutes.

2. Season the onion with salt and pepper, remove the pan from heat, and let the caramelized onion cool.

3. Place the caramelized onion and crème fraîche in a bowl, stir to combine, and use immediately or store in the refrigerator.

Rum Cream

YIELD: ½ CUP | **ACTIVE TIME:** 5 MINUTES | **TOTAL TIME:** 5 MINUTES

½ CUP HEAVY CREAM

¼ TEASPOON FRESH LEMON JUICE

⅛ TEASPOON LEMON ZEST

2 TABLESPOONS RUM

PINCH OF SUGAR

1. Place the heavy cream in the work bowl of a stand mixer fitted with the whisk attachment and whip until the cream holds medium peaks.

2. Stir in the lemon juice, lemon zest, rum, and sugar and use immediately or store in the refrigerator until ready to use.

Homemade Ketchup

YIELD: 5 CUPS | **ACTIVE TIME:** 10 MINUTES | **TOTAL TIME:** 15 MINUTES

3 CUPS PUREED TOMATOES

JUICE OF ½ LEMON

2 TABLESPOONS EXTRA-VIRGIN OLIVE OIL

½ MEDIUM WHITE ONION, FINELY DICED

2 GARLIC CLOVES, MINCED

¼ CUP DARK BROWN SUGAR

½ CUP APPLE CIDER VINEGAR

½ CUP WATER

SALT AND PEPPER, TO TASTE

1. Place the tomatoes, lemon juice, olive oil, onion, garlic, and brown sugar in a bowl and stir to combine. Let the mixture rest for 15 minutes.

2. While whisking continually, add the apple cider vinegar and then the water in a slow stream. Season the ketchup with salt and pepper and store in the refrigerator overnight before using.

Chicken Skin Butter

YIELD: ½ CUP | **ACTIVE TIME:** 10 MINUTES | **TOTAL TIME:** 20 MINUTES

SKIN FROM 2 LARGE CHICKEN THIGHS

SALT, TO TASTE

½ CUP UNSALTED BUTTER, SOFTENED

½ TEASPOON CHOPPED FRESH CHIVES

1. Preheat the oven to 400°F. Line a baking sheet with parchment paper. Place the chicken skins on a cutting board and use a paring knife to scrape off any excess fat and meat.

2. Stretch the skins out on the baking sheet and season them with salt. Lay a second sheet of parchment paper over the skins and then place another baking sheet on top. Place the trays in the oven and roast the chicken skins until they are golden brown and crispy, about 10 minutes. Remove the chicken skins from the oven and let them cool.

3. Finely dice the chicken skins and place them in a bowl. Add the butter and chives, stir until combined, and use immediately or store in the refrigerator.

Pernod Cream

YIELD: ⅔ CUP | **ACTIVE TIME:** 10 MINUTES | **TOTAL TIME:** 10 MINUTES

½ CUP HEAVY CREAM

1 TABLESPOON PERNOD

2 TEASPOONS CHOPPED FENNEL FRONDS

1 TEASPOON TOASTED FENNEL SEEDS

SALT AND PEPPER, TO TASTE

1. Place the heavy cream in the work bowl of a stand mixer fitted with the whisk attachment and whip until the cream holds soft peaks.

2. Add the Pernod and whip until the cream holds medium peaks.

3. Add the fennel fronds and toasted fennel seeds, season the cream with salt and pepper, and use immediately or store in the refrigerator.

Roasted Beet Spread

YIELD: 2 CUPS | **ACTIVE TIME:** 20 MINUTES | **TOTAL TIME:** 1 HOUR AND 30 MINUTES

4 BEETS, PEELED AND CUBED

¼ CUP EXTRA-VIRGIN OLIVE OIL

½ TEASPOON KOSHER SALT

¾ TEASPOON CUMIN SEEDS

¾ TEASPOON CORIANDER SEEDS

2 GARLIC CLOVES, MINCED

2 TEASPOONS MINCED GREEN CHILE PEPPER

2 TEASPOONS FRESH LEMON JUICE

⅓ CUP CHOPPED FRESH CILANTRO

1. Preheat the oven to 400°F. Line a baking sheet with parchment paper. Place the beets in a bowl with 2 tablespoons of the olive oil and ¼ teaspoon of the salt and toss to coat.

2. Arrange the beets on the baking sheet in a single layer, place them in the oven, and roast for about 1 hour, stirring occasionally, until they are tender. Remove the beets from the oven and let them cool.

3. Place the cumin and coriander seeds in a dry skillet and toast them over medium-high heat until fragrant, about 2 minutes, shaking the pan frequently. Using a mortar and pestle, grind the seeds into a fine powder.

4. Place the beets in a food processor with the garlic, chile, lemon juice, cilantro, remaining olive oil and salt, and the toasted seed powder. Blitz until smooth, taste, and adjust the seasoning as necessary. Use immediately or store in the refrigerator.

Roasted Beet Spread

SEE PAGE 499

Garlic Custard

YIELD: 2 CUPS | **TOTAL TIME:** 1 HOUR | **ACTIVE TIME:** 2 HOURS

1 TABLESPOON UNSALTED BUTTER

3 GARLIC CLOVES, MINCED

1 CUP HEAVY CREAM

½ TEASPOON KOSHER SALT, PLUS MORE TO TASTE

2 MEDIUM EGGS

1 EGG YOLK

1½ TEASPOONS CHOPPED FRESH CHIVES

BLACK PEPPER, TO TASTE

1. Preheat the oven to 325°F. Coat four 4-oz. ramekins with nonstick cooking spray and place them in a baking dish.

2. Place the butter in a medium saucepan and melt it over medium-low heat. Add the garlic and cook until it has softened, about 5 minutes.

3. Stir in the cream and the salt, raise the heat to medium, and bring the mixture to a simmer.

4. Remove the pan from heat and let the mixture stand for 10 minutes. Strain the custard into a bowl through a fine-mesh sieve.

5. Place the eggs and the yolk in a medium-size bowl and whisk until scrambled. Add the chives and whisk to combine.

6. Add the garlic mixture and whisk to combine. Season with salt and pepper and divide the mixture among the ramekins. Pour hot water into the baking dish until it goes halfway up the sides of the ramekins.

7. Place the baking dish in the oven and bake the custards until they are firm and a knife comes out clean when inserted into their centers. Remove the baking dish from the oven and chill the custard in the refrigerator for 1 hour before serving.

Garlic Mayonnaise

YIELD: ½ CUP | **ACTIVE TIME:** 5 MINUTES | **TOTAL TIME:** 5 MINUTES

½ CUP MAYONNAISE

2 GARLIC CLOVES, MINCED

1. Place all of the ingredients in a bowl, stir to combine, and use immediately or store in the refrigerator.

Tabasco Butter

YIELD: ½ CUP | **ACTIVE TIME:** 5 MINUTES | **TOTAL TIME:** 1 HOUR AND 5 MINUTES

½ CUP UNSALTED BUTTER, MELTED

1 TABLESPOON FRESH LEMON JUICE

¼ TEASPOON TABASCO

¼ TEASPOON CHOPPED FRESH PARSLEY

1. Place all of the ingredients in a bowl, stir to combine, and store the butter in the refrigerator for 1 hour before serving.

Kimchi

YIELD: 4 CUPS | **ACTIVE TIME:** 30 MINUTES | **TOTAL TIME:** 3 TO 7 DAYS

1 HEAD OF NAPA CABBAGE, CORE REMOVED, CUT INTO STRIPS

½ CUP KOSHER SALT

2 TABLESPOONS MINCED FRESH GINGER

4 GARLIC CLOVES, MINCED

1 TEASPOON SUGAR

5 TABLESPOONS RED PEPPER FLAKES

2 BUNCHES OF SCALLIONS, TRIMMED AND SLICED

FILTERED WATER, AS NEEDED

1. Place the cabbage and salt in a large bowl and stir to combine. Work the mixture with your hands, squeezing to remove as much liquid as possible. Let the mixture rest for 2 hours.

2. Add the remaining ingredients, except for the water. Stir the mixture until well combined and squeeze to remove as much liquid as possible.

3. Transfer the mixture to a container and press down so it is tightly packed. The liquid should be covering the mixture. If it is not, add water until the liquid covers the mixture.

4. Cover the jar and let the mixture sit at room temperature for 3 to 7 days, removing the lid daily to release the gas that has built up. When the taste is to your liking, store the kimchi in an airtight container in the refrigerator.

Wasabi Butter

YIELD: ½ CUP | **ACTIVE TIME:** 10 MINUTES | **TOTAL TIME:** 1 HOUR AND 10 MINUTES

½ CUP UNSALTED BUTTER

1 TEASPOON WASABI

½ TEASPOON KOSHER SALT

¼ TEASPOON SOY SAUCE

1. Place all of the ingredients in a saucepan and warm the mixture over medium heat. Cook for 5 minutes and then pour the mixture into a bowl. Store in the refrigerator for 1 hour before serving.

Chili & Lime Butter

YIELD: ⅔ CUP | **ACTIVE TIME:** 10 MINUTES | **TOTAL TIME:** 1 HOUR AND 10 MINUTES

½ CUP UNSALTED BUTTER

1 TABLESPOON LIME ZEST

2 TEASPOONS CHILI POWDER

1 TEASPOON FRESH LIME JUICE

½ TEASPOON KOSHER SALT

1. Place all of the ingredients in a saucepan and warm the mixture over medium heat. Cook for 5 minutes and then pour the mixture into a bowl. Store in the refrigerator for 1 hour before serving.

Lime Crema

YIELD: 1 CUP | **ACTIVE TIME:** 5 MINUTES | **TOTAL TIME:** 5 MINUTES

1 CUP CREMA (MEXICAN SOUR CREAM)

3 TABLESPOONS FRESH LIME JUICE

SALT, TO TASTE

1. Place all of the ingredients in a small bowl, stir to combine, and use immediately or store in the refrigerator.

Miso Butter

YIELD: ¾ CUP | **ACTIVE TIME:** 5 MINUTES | **TOTAL TIME:** 5 MINUTES

½ CUP UNSALTED BUTTER, SOFTENED

¼ CUP MISO

ZEST OF 1 LIME

1. Place the butter, miso, and lime zest in a bowl, stir to combine, and use immediately or store in the refrigerator.

Lime Crema
SEE PAGE 505

Turmeric Cream

YIELD: ½ CUP | **ACTIVE TIME:** 5 MINUTES | **TOTAL TIME:** 5 MINUTES

½ CUP HEAVY CREAM
½ TEASPOON TURMERIC
PINCH OF KOSHER SALT

1. Place the heavy cream in the work bowl of a stand mixer fitted with the whisk attachment and whip until the cream holds medium peaks.

2. Stir in the turmeric and salt and use immediately or store in the refrigerator until ready to use.

Preserved Limes with Chile de Àrbol & Spices

YIELD: 2 CUPS | **ACTIVE TIME:** 25 MINUTES | **TOTAL TIME:** 2 WEEKS TO 1 MONTH

7 LIMES

2 TABLESPOONS CARDAMOM SEEDS, GROUND

2 TABLESPOONS SMOKED PAPRIKA

2 TABLESPOONS TURMERIC

1½ TEASPOONS CUMIN SEEDS, TOASTED AND GROUND

3 TABLESPOONS KOSHER SALT

5 DRIED CHILES DE ÀRBOL, STEMS AND SEEDS REMOVED, GROUND

1. Juice the limes into a large bowl and save the spent halves. Add all of the remaining ingredients to the bowl and stir until the mixture is a paste.

2. Put on gloves, add the spent lime halves, and work the mixture with your hands until well combined.

3. Transfer the mixture to an airtight container and gently press down on it to make sure there are no pockets that air can get into. Seal the container and store it at room temperature or chill in the refrigerator until the lime halves are tender. This will take about 2 weeks at room temperature, and a month in the refrigerator.

4. Mince the limes and use immediately or store in the refrigerator.

Fall Spiced Cream

YIELD: ½ CUP | **ACTIVE TIME:** 5 MINUTES | **TOTAL TIME:** 5 MINUTES

½ CUP HEAVY CREAM

½ TEASPOON FRESHLY GRATED NUTMEG

PINCH OF SALT

1. Place the heavy cream in the work bowl of a stand mixer fitted with the whisk attachment and whip until the cream holds medium peaks.

2. Stir in the nutmeg and salt and use immediately or store in the refrigerator until ready to use.

Chiles Toreados

YIELD: 1 CUP | **ACTIVE TIME:** 20 MINUTES | **TOTAL TIME:** 1 HOUR

10 SERRANO CHILE PEPPERS

1 SMALL WHITE ONION, QUARTERED

3 GARLIC CLOVES, UNPEELED

½ CUP SOY SAUCE

½ CUP FRESH LIME JUICE

2 TABLESPOONS MAGGI SEASONING SAUCE

1. Warm a cast-iron skillet over high heat. Place the chiles in the pan and toast until they are very charred all over, turning them as necessary. Remove the chiles from the pan and let them cool.

2. Place the onion and garlic cloves in the pan and toast them until lightly charred, turning them as necessary. Remove them from the pan and let them cool.

3. Peel the garlic cloves, mince them, and place them in a bowl. Julienne the onion and place it in the bowl.

4. Remove all but one-quarter of the charred skin from the chiles. Remove the stems and seeds and finely chop the remaining flesh. Add it to the garlic mixture along with the remaining ingredients and stir until combined.

5. Let the mixture steep for 30 minutes before serving.

Cashew Butter

YIELD: 2½ CUPS | **ACTIVE TIME:** 5 MINUTES | **TOTAL TIME:** 30 MINUTES

2 CUPS UNSALTED RAW CASHEWS

½ CUP AVOCADO OIL

½ TEASPOON KOSHER SALT

1. Preheat the oven to 350°F. Place the cashews on a baking sheet and place them in the oven. Roast the cashews, stirring occasionally, until they are golden brown, about 10 minutes. Remove the cashews from the oven and let them cool.

2. Place the cashews and remaining ingredients in a food processor, blitz until smooth, and use immediately or store in the refrigerator.

Cashew Butter
SEE PAGE 511

Paprika Butter

YIELD: ¼ CUP | **ACTIVE TIME:** 5 MINUTES | **TOTAL TIME:** 1 HOUR AND 5 MINUTES

4 TABLESPOONS UNSALTED
BUTTER, SOFTENED

2 TEASPOONS PAPRIKA

1. Place the ingredients in a bowl and stir until combined. Place the butter on a piece of plastic wrap and roll it into a log. Chill the butter in the refrigerator for 1 hour before serving.

Juniper Cream

YIELD: 1 CUP | **ACTIVE TIME:** 5 MINUTES | **TOTAL TIME:** 20 MINUTES

½ CUP HEAVY CREAM

4 SHALLOTS, MINCED

8 JUNIPER BERRIES

1. Place the cream, shallots, and juniper berries in a saucepan and warm the mixture over low heat for 2 minutes.

2. Remove the pan from heat and let the mixture steep for 15 minutes. Strain before using or storing in the refrigerator.

Lime & Cilantro Sour Cream

YIELD: 2 CUPS | **ACTIVE TIME:** 5 MINUTES | **TOTAL TIME:** 5 MINUTES

½ CUP CHOPPED FRESH CILANTRO

¼ CUP FRESH LIME JUICE

1¼ CUPS SOUR CREAM

1½ TEASPOONS KOSHER SALT

½ TEASPOON BLACK PEPPER

1. Place all of the ingredients in a bowl, stir to combine, and use immediately or store in the refrigerator.

Herb Butter

YIELD: ¾ CUP | **ACTIVE TIME:** 10 MINUTES | **TOTAL TIME:** 40 MINUTES

½ CUP UNSALTED BUTTER, SOFTENED

1 TABLESPOON EXTRA-VIRGIN OLIVE OIL

1 SMALL SHALLOT, MINCED

1 TEASPOON FRESH LEMON JUICE

2 TEASPOONS CHOPPED FRESH PARSLEY

1 TEASPOON CHOPPED FRESH TARRAGON

1 TEASPOON CHOPPED FRESH CHIVES

1 TEASPOON CHOPPED FRESH MARJORAM

SALT AND PEPPER, TO TASTE

1. Place the butter in the work bowl of a stand mixer fitted with the paddle attachment and beat until it is fluffy. Set it aside.

2. Place the olive oil in a small skillet and warm it over medium heat. Add the shallot and cook, stirring occasionally, until it is translucent, about 3 minutes. Stir in the lemon juice, remove the pan from heat, and let the mixture cool completely.

3. Add the shallot and the fresh herbs to the butter and stir to combine. Season the butter with salt and pepper and chill in the refrigerator for 30 minutes before serving.

Garlic & Chive Butter

YIELD: ⅔ CUP | **ACTIVE TIME:** 10 MINUTES | **TOTAL TIME:** 1 HOUR AND 10 MINUTES

½ CUP UNSALTED BUTTER

2 GARLIC CLOVES, MINCED

1 TABLESPOON CHOPPED FRESH CHIVES

½ TEASPOON KOSHER SALT

1. Place all of the ingredients in a saucepan and warm the mixture over medium heat. Cook for 5 minutes and then pour the mixture into a bowl. Store in the refrigerator for 1 hour before serving.

Rosemary & Lemon Butter

YIELD: ½ CUP | **ACTIVE TIME:** 10 MINUTES | **TOTAL TIME:** 1 HOUR AND 10 MINUTES

½ CUP UNSALTED BUTTER

1 TEASPOON LEMON ZEST

1 TEASPOON FRESH LEMON JUICE

½ TEASPOON KOSHER SALT

½ TEASPOON CHOPPED FRESH ROSEMARY

1. Place all of the ingredients in a saucepan and warm the mixture over medium heat. Cook for 5 minutes and then pour the mixture into a bowl. Store in the refrigerator for 1 hour before serving.

Maître'd Butter

YIELD: ½ CUP | **ACTIVE TIME:** 10 MINUTES | **TOTAL TIME:** 1 HOUR AND 10 MINUTES

½ CUP UNSALTED BUTTER

½ TEASPOON CHOPPED FRESH ROSEMARY

½ TEASPOON CHOPPED FRESH TARRAGON

½ TEASPOON CHOPPED FRESH CHIVES

½ TEASPOON CHOPPED FRESH THYME

1. Place all of the ingredients in a saucepan and warm the mixture over medium heat. Cook for 5 minutes and then pour the mixture into a bowl. Store in the refrigerator for 1 hour before serving.

Lemon & Herb Butter

YIELD: ½ CUP | **ACTIVE TIME:** 5 MINUTES | **TOTAL TIME:** 5 MINUTES

4 TABLESPOONS UNSALTED BUTTER, CHOPPED AND SOFTENED

JUICE OF 1 LEMON

¼ CUP CHOPPED FRESH BASIL OR PARSLEY

1. Place all of the ingredients in a bowl, stir to combine, and use immediately or store in the refrigerator.

Habanero Honey

YIELD: 1 CUP | **ACTIVE TIME:** 10 MINUTES | **TOTAL TIME:** 2 HOURS

4 HABANERO CHILE PEPPERS, PIERCED

1 CUP HONEY

1. Place the chiles and honey in a saucepan and bring to a very gentle simmer over medium-low heat. Reduce the heat to lowest possible setting and cook for 1 hour.

2. Remove the saucepan from heat and let the mixture infuse for another hour.

3. Remove the peppers. Transfer the honey to a container, cover, and chill in the refrigerator until ready to serve.

Lemon & Herb Butter

SEE PAGE 519

Lemon & Garlic Butter

YIELD: 1¼ CUPS | **ACTIVE TIME:** 5 MINUTES | **TOTAL TIME:** 5 MINUTES

1 CUP UNSALTED BUTTER, SOFTENED

1½ TEASPOONS FRESH LEMON JUICE

2 GARLIC CLOVES, MINCED

3 TABLESPOONS CHOPPED FRESH PARSLEY

SALT AND PEPPER, TO TASTE

1. Place the butter in the work bowl of a stand mixer fitted with the paddle attachment and beat until it is light and fluffy.

2. Add the remaining ingredients, beat to combine, and use immediately or store in the refrigerator.

Chile Toreado Mayonnaise

YIELD: 1½ CUPS | **ACTIVE TIME:** 20 MINUTES | **TOTAL TIME:** 20 MINUTES

2 SERRANO CHILE PEPPERS

2 TABLESPOONS SOY SAUCE

2 TABLESPOONS FRESH
LIME JUICE

1 CUP MAYONNAISE

1. Warm a large cast-iron skillet over high heat. Add the serrano peppers and cook until charred all over, turning as necessary. Transfer the charred peppers to a bowl and add the soy sauce and lime juice. Let the mixture steep for 15 minutes.

2. Remove the peppers from the liquid, place them in a bowl, and mash until smooth. Add the mayonnaise and stir to combine. Incorporate the soy-and-lime mixture a little bit at a time until the taste of the mayo is to your liking. Use immediately or store in the refrigerator.

Salata Mechouia

YIELD: 2 CUPS | **ACTIVE TIME:** 20 MINUTES | **TOTAL TIME:** 1 HOUR AND 15 MINUTES

1 JALAPEÑO CHILE PEPPER

6 LARGE PLUM TOMATOES

3 GREEN BELL PEPPERS

2 GARLIC CLOVES, UNPEELED

1 TEASPOON KOSHER SALT

¼ TEASPOON BLACK PEPPER

¼ CUP FRESH LEMON JUICE

3 TABLESPOONS EXTRA-VIRGIN OLIVE OIL

1. Preheat the oven to 375°F. Use a knife to poke a small slit in the jalapeño.

2. Place the tomatoes, bell peppers, jalapeño, and garlic on an aluminum foil–lined baking sheet. Place it in the oven and roast until the vegetables are well browned and just tender, about 30 minutes for the garlic and 1 hour for the peppers and tomatoes.

3. Remove the vegetables from the oven. Place the garlic cloves on a plate and let them cool. Place the other roasted vegetables in a large bowl and cover it with plastic wrap. Let them rest for about 15 minutes.

4. Peel the garlic cloves and set them aside. Remove the charred skins from the other vegetables, place the vegetables in a colander, and let them drain.

5. Using a fork, mash the roasted garlic.

6. Transfer the drained vegetables to a cutting board. Remove the seeds from the bell peppers and the jalapeño. Finely chop all of the vegetables and place them in a mixing bowl. Add the mashed garlic, salt, pepper, lemon juice, and olive oil, stir until well combined, and use immediately.

Roasted Bone Marrow

YIELD: ¼ CUP | **ACTIVE TIME:** 5 MINUTES | **TOTAL TIME:** 20 MINUTES

4 MARROW BONES

1. Preheat the oven to 450°F. Place the marrow bones upright on a baking sheet, place them in the oven, and roast for 15 minutes.

2. Remove the bones from the oven, scrape the marrow out of them, and use immediately.

Sweet Potato & Tahini Spread

YIELD: 1 CUP | **ACTIVE TIME:** 15 MINUTES | **TOTAL TIME:** 1 HOUR

EXTRA-VIRGIN OLIVE OIL, AS NEEDED

1 SWEET POTATO, HALVED

1 YELLOW ONION, QUARTERED

2 LARGE GARLIC CLOVES

¼ CUP TAHINI PASTE

1 TEASPOON FRESH LEMON JUICE

½ TEASPOON KOSHER SALT

2 TABLESPOONS HONEY

½ TEASPOON ANCHO CHILE POWDER

1 TABLESPOON MINCED PISTACHIOS, FOR GARNISH

1. Preheat the oven to 400°F and coat a baking sheet with olive oil. Place the sweet potato, cut side down, and the onion on the baking sheet. Place the garlic cloves in a small piece of aluminum foil, sprinkle a few drops of oil on them, wrap them up, and place them on the baking sheet.

2. Place the baking sheet in the oven and roast for approximately 20 minutes, then remove the garlic. Roast the sweet potato and onion until the sweet potato is very tender, another 10 minutes or so. Remove them from the oven and let them cool.

3. Scoop the sweet potato's flesh into a food processor. Add the roasted onion, garlic, tahini, lemon juice, and salt. Pulse until the mixture is a smooth paste. Taste and adjust the seasoning as necessary.

4. Place the honey in a very small pot and warm it over low heat. Add the ancho chile powder, remove the pan from heat, and let it sit for a few minutes.

5. Place the puree in a shallow bowl and make a well in the center. Pour some of spiced honey in the well, garnish with the chopped pistachios, and enjoy.

Pea & Parmesan Spread

YIELD: 2 CUPS | **ACTIVE TIME:** 10 MINUTES | **TOTAL TIME:** 20 MINUTES

SALT AND PEPPER, TO TASTE

3 CUPS PEAS

1 CUP WATER

3 TABLESPOONS PINE NUTS

1 CUP FRESHLY GRATED PARMESAN CHEESE

1 GARLIC CLOVE, MINCED

½ CUP FRESH BASIL, CHIFFONADE

1. Bring water to a boil in a large saucepan. Add salt and the peas and cook until the peas are bright green and warmed through, about 2 minutes.

2. Transfer half of the peas to a food processor. Add the water, pine nuts, Parmesan, and garlic and blitz until pureed.

3. Place the puree in a serving dish, add the remaining peas and the basil, and fold to incorporate. Season the dip with salt and pepper and chill in the refrigerator until ready to serve.

Roasted Bone Marrow

SEE PAGE 526

Sweet & Spicy Yogurt

YIELD: 1 CUP | **ACTIVE TIME:** 5 MINUTES | **TOTAL TIME:** 5 MINUTES

1 CUP FULL-FAT GREEK YOGURT

½ TEASPOON CAYENNE PEPPER

4 TEASPOONS HONEY

SALT AND PEPPER, TO TASTE

1. Place all of the ingredients in a mixing bowl, stir to combine, and use immediately or store in the refrigerator.

Hummus

YIELD: 6 CUPS | **ACTIVE TIME:** 1 HOUR | **TOTAL TIME:** 24 HOURS

2 LBS. DRIED CHICKPEAS

1 TABLESPOON BAKING SODA

12 CUPS ROOM-TEMPERATURE WATER

12 CUPS VEGETABLE STOCK (SEE PAGE 303)

1 CUP TAHINI PASTE

2 TABLESPOONS ZA'ATAR (SEE PAGE 68)

2 TABLESPOONS SUMAC

2 TABLESPOONS CUMIN

2 TABLESPOONS KOSHER SALT

2 TABLESPOONS BLACK PEPPER

2 GARLIC CLOVES, GRATED

½ BUNCH OF FRESH CILANTRO, CHOPPED

1 CUP EXTRA-VIRGIN OLIVE OIL

1 CUP SESAME OIL

1 CUP ICE WATER

½ CUP FRESH LEMON JUICE

1. Place the chickpeas, baking soda, and water in a large saucepan, stir, and cover. Let the chickpeas soak overnight at room temperature.

2. Drain the chickpeas and rinse them. Place them in a large saucepan, add the stock, and bring to a steady simmer. Cook until the chickpeas are quite tender, about 1 hour.

3. In a blender or food processor, combine all of the remaining ingredients and puree until achieving a perfectly smooth, creamy sauce; the ice water is the key to getting the correct consistency.

4. Add the warm, drained chickpeas to the tahini mixture and blend until the hummus is perfectly smooth and not at all grainy, occasionally stopping to scrape down the sides of the bowl. This blending process may take 3 minutes; remain patient and keep going until the mixture is very creamy and fluffy, adding water as necessary to get the right consistency.

5. Taste, adjust the seasoning as necessary, and enjoy.

Meyer Lemon Marmalade

YIELD: 2 CUPS | **ACTIVE TIME:** 45 MINUTES | **TOTAL TIME:** 2 HOURS

5 MEYER LEMONS

2 FRESNO CHILE PEPPERS, STEMS AND SEEDS REMOVED, DICED

4 GARLIC CLOVES, MINCED

1 TABLESPOON KOSHER SALT

1 TEASPOON BLACK PEPPER

1 CUP WATER

1 CUP WHITE VINEGAR

2 CUPS SUGAR

1. Cut the lemons, rind and all, into ½-inch chunks.

2. Place all of the ingredients in a saucepan and bring the mixture to a boil over high heat. Reduce the heat to medium-high and simmer, stirring occasionally, until everything has softened, about 45 minutes.

3. Raise the heat back to high and cook until the mixture reaches 220°F.

4. Remove the pan from heat and let it cool completely before using or storing in the refrigerator.

Guacamole

YIELD: 2 CUPS | **ACTIVE TIME:** 15 MINUTES | **TOTAL TIME:** 25 MINUTES

1 LARGE TOMATO, FINELY DICED

2 SERRANO CHILE PEPPERS, STEMS AND SEEDS REMOVED, FINELY DICED

½ ONION, FINELY DICED

1 GARLIC CLOVE, MASHED

4 LARGE AVOCADOS, PITTED AND DICED

6 TABLESPOONS FRESH LIME JUICE

SALT, TO TASTE

½ CUP FRESH CILANTRO, CHOPPED

1. Combine the tomato, serrano peppers, and onion in a bowl. Place the garlic clove in a separate bowl.

2. Add the avocados to the bowl containing the garlic and stir until well combined. Stir in the lime juice and season with salt.

3. Add the tomato mixture and stir until it has been incorporated. Add the cilantro and stir to combine. Taste and adjust the seasoning as necessary.

Thai Chili Jam

YIELD: 2 CUPS | **ACTIVE TIME:** 45 MINUTES | **TOTAL TIME:** 1 HOUR AND 30 MINUTES

8 DRIED THAI CHILI PEPPERS, STEMS AND SEEDS REMOVED

1½ CUPS CANOLA OIL, PLUS MORE AS NEEDED

1 CUP THINLY SLICED GARLIC

4 SHALLOTS, SLICED THIN

¼ CUP DRIED SHRIMP

1 TABLESPOON SHRIMP PASTE

3 TABLESPOONS SEEDLESS TAMARIND PASTE

3 CUPS BOILING WATER

⅓ CUP COCONUT OR PALM SUGAR

2 TABLESPOONS FISH SAUCE

1 TEASPOON KOSHER SALT

1. Place the chiles in a dry skillet and toast them over medium heat for 5 to 8 minutes, making sure not to burn them. Transfer the toasted chiles to a plate.

2. Add 1 cup of the canola oil and the garlic to the hot skillet and fry the garlic until it is light brown and crispy, about 6 minutes. Use a slotted spoon to transfer the garlic to a paper towel–lined plate.

3. Add the shallots and dried shrimp and fry until lightly golden brown, about 4 minutes. Transfer the mixture to the paper towel–lined plate.

4. Place the chiles, garlic, shallots, dried shrimp, and shrimp paste in a food processor and blitz until the mixture is a thick paste. Set the mixture aside.

5. Break the tamarind paste into chunks, place them in a bowl, and cover with the boiling water. Cover the bowl and let the tamarind steep for 30 minutes.

6. Using your hands or a masher, break the tamarind down further. Let the tamarind steep for another 15 minutes.

7. Strain the mixture through a fine mesh sieve and scrape the pulp from the underside of the sieve into the bowl. Discard the stringy material, stir the juice and pulp until combined, and set the tamarind water aside.

8. Place the paste, sugar, ⅓ cup of the tamarind water, fish sauce, and salt in a clean saucepan and cook over medium heat, stirring occasionally, until the mixture is jammy, 15 to 20 minutes.

9. Transfer the jam to a mason jar and let it cool completely before using or storing in the refrigerator. To can this jam, see page 486. You can store this jam in the refrigerator for up to 1 month.

Raspberry Jam

YIELD: 2 CUPS | **ACTIVE TIME:** 30 MINUTES | **TOTAL TIME:** 3 HOURS

1 LB. FRESH RASPBERRIES

1 LB. SUGAR

ZEST AND JUICE OF 1 LEMON

1. Place the ingredients in a large saucepan fitted with a candy thermometer and cook it over medium-high heat until the mixture is 220°F. Stir the jam occasionally as it cooks.

2. Pour the jam into jars and let it cool completely before using or storing in the refrigerator. To can this jam, see page 486.

Tzatziki

YIELD: 2 CUPS | **ACTIVE TIME:** 5 MINUTES | **TOTAL TIME:** 1 HOUR AND 5 MINUTES

1 CUP PLAIN FULL-FAT YOGURT

¾ CUP SEEDED AND MINCED CUCUMBER

1 GARLIC CLOVE, MINCED

JUICE FROM 1 LEMON WEDGE

SALT AND WHITE PEPPER, TO TASTE

FRESH DILL, FINELY CHOPPED, TO TASTE

1. Place the yogurt, cucumber, garlic, and lemon juice in a mixing bowl and stir to combine. Taste and season with salt and pepper. Stir in the dill.

2. Place the tzatziki in the refrigerator and chill for 1 hour before serving.

Red Pepper Feta & Ricotta

YIELD: 1½ CUPS | **ACTIVE TIME:** 5 MINUTES | **TOTAL TIME:** 5 MINUTES

4 OZ. FETA CHEESE

2 OZ. RICOTTA CHEESE

1 CUP CHOPPED ROASTED
RED PEPPERS

¼ CUP EXTRA-VIRGIN OLIVE
OIL

1 TABLESPOON FRESH
LEMON JUICE

1. Place all of the ingredients in a food processor, blitz until smooth, and use immediately or store in the refrigerator.

Green Tomato Jam

YIELD: 2 CUPS | **ACTIVE TIME:** 35 MINUTES | **TOTAL TIME:** 5 TO 7 HOURS

¾ LB. GREEN TOMATOES, DICED

¼ LARGE ONION, DICED

½-INCH PIECE OF FRESH GINGER, PEELED AND MINCED

2 GARLIC CLOVES, CHOPPED

1 TEASPOON MUSTARD SEEDS

1 TEASPOON CUMIN

1 TEASPOON CORIANDER

2 TEASPOONS KOSHER SALT

½ CUP HONEY OR MAPLE SYRUP

1 CUP APPLE CIDER VINEGAR

1 CUP RAISINS

1. Place all the ingredients in a large saucepan and bring to a boil. Reduce the heat so that the mixture simmers and cook, stirring occasionally, until the onions and tomatoes are tender and the juices have thickened, 20 to 30 minutes. If a smoother jam is desired, mash the mixture with a wooden spoon as it simmers.

2. Remove the pan from heat and let it cool completely before using or storing in the refrigerator. To can this jam, see page 486.

Blueberry & Basil Jam

YIELD: 3½ CUPS | **ACTIVE TIME:** 10 MINUTES | **TOTAL TIME:** 1 HOUR AND 30 MINUTES

3 QUARTS OF FRESH
BLUEBERRIES

LEAVES FROM 1 BUNCH OF
BASIL, FINELY CHOPPED

2 TEASPOONS FRESH
LEMON JUICE

2 CUPS SUGAR

½ CUP WATER

1. Place all of the ingredients in a large saucepan and bring to a boil, while stirring frequently, over medium-high heat.

2. Once the mixture has come to a boil, reduce the heat so that it simmers and cook, stirring frequently, until the mixture has reduced by half and is starting to thicken, about 1 hour. Remove the jam from heat and let it thicken and set as it cools. If the jam is still too thin after 1 hour, continue to simmer until it is the desired consistency. Let it cool completely before using or storing in the refrigerator. To can this jam, see page 486.

Sweet Corn & Pepita Guacamole

YIELD: 3 CUPS | **ACTIVE TIME:** 15 MINUTES | **TOTAL TIME:** 30 MINUTES

1 EAR OF YELLOW CORN, WITH HUSK ON

1 OZ. PUMPKIN SEEDS

1 OZ. POMEGRANATE SEEDS

FLESH OF 3 AVOCADOS

½ RED ONION, CHOPPED

½ CUP FRESH CILANTRO, CHOPPED

1 TEASPOON FRESH LIME JUICE

SALT AND PEPPER, TO TASTE

1. Preheat a gas or charcoal grill to medium-high heat (about 450ºF). Place the corn on the grill and cook until it is charred all over and the kernels have softened enough that there is considerable give in them.

2. Remove the corn from the grill and let it cool. When cool enough to handle, husk the corn and cut off the kernels.

3. Combine the corn, pumpkin seeds, and pomegranate seeds in a small bowl. Place the avocados in a separate bowl and mash until it is just slightly chunky. Stir in the corn mixture, onion, cilantro, and lime juice, season the mixture with salt and pepper, and work the mixture until the guacamole is the desired texture.

Mostarda

YIELD: 1 CUP | **ACTIVE TIME:** 5 MINUTES | **TOTAL TIME:** 15 MINUTES

4 OZ. DRIED APRICOTS, CHOPPED

¼ CUP CHOPPED DRIED CHERRIES

1 SHALLOT, MINCED

1½ TEASPOONS MINCED CRYSTALLIZED GINGER

½ CUP DRY WHITE WINE

3 TABLESPOONS WHITE WINE VINEGAR

3 TABLESPOONS WATER

3 TABLESPOONS SUGAR

1 TEASPOON DRY MUSTARD

1 TEASPOON DIJON MUSTARD

1 TABLESPOON UNSALTED BUTTER

1. Place the apricots, cherries, shallot, ginger, wine, vinegar, water, and sugar in a saucepan and bring to a boil over medium-high heat. Cover, reduce the heat to medium, and cook until all the liquid has been absorbed and the fruit is soft, about 10 minutes.

2. Uncover the pot and stir in the dry mustard, mustard, and butter. Simmer until the mixture is jam-like, 2 to 3 minutes. Remove the pan from heat and let the mostarda cool slightly before serving. The mostarda will keep in the refrigerator for up to 1 week.

Apricot & Chile Jam

YIELD: 8 CUPS | **ACTIVE TIME:** 20 MINUTES | **TOTAL TIME:** 1 HOUR AND 30 MINUTES

2 LBS. APRICOTS, HALVED, PITTED, AND CHOPPED

ZEST AND JUICE OF 1 LEMON

2 LBS. SUGAR

1 CUP WATER

3 RED CHILE PEPPERS, STEMS AND SEEDS REMOVED, MINCED

1 TABLESPOON UNSALTED BUTTER

1. Place all of the ingredients, except for the butter, in a saucepan and bring to a gentle boil over medium heat, stirring to help the sugar dissolve. Boil the mixture for about 5 minutes.

2. Reduce the heat and simmer for 15 minutes, stirring frequently. If you prefer a smoother jam, mash the mixture with a wooden spoon as it cooks.

3. When the jam has formed a thin skin, remove the pan from heat. Add the butter and stir to disperse any froth. Let the jam cool completely before using or storing in the refrigerator. To can this jam, see page 486.

Sriracha & Honey Mayonnaise

YIELD: ½ CUP | **ACTIVE TIME:** 5 MINUTES | **TOTAL TIME:** 15 MINUTES

½ CUP MAYONNAISE

2 TABLESPOONS HONEY

1 TABLESPOON SRIRACHA

1. Place all of the ingredients in a small bowl and stir until thoroughly combined.

2. Chill the mayonnaise in the refrigerator for 10 minutes before serving.

Coconut & Cilantro Chutney

YIELD: ½ CUP | **ACTIVE TIME:** 5 MINUTES | **TOTAL TIME:** 5 MINUTES

1 BUNCH OF FRESH CILANTRO

¼ CUP GRATED FRESH COCONUT

15 FRESH MINT LEAVES

1 TABLESPOON MINCED CHILE PEPPER

1 GARLIC CLOVE

1 TEASPOON GRATED GINGER

1 PLUM TOMATO, CHOPPED

1 TABLESPOON FRESH LEMON JUICE

WATER, AS NEEDED

SALT, TO TASTE

1. Place all of the ingredients, except for the water and salt, in a food processor and puree until smooth, adding water as needed to get the desired consistency.

2. Taste, season with salt, and use immediately or store in the refrigerator.

Raspberry & Chia Jam

YIELD: 2 CUPS | **ACTIVE TIME:** 20 MINUTES | **TOTAL TIME:** 1 HOUR AND 30 MINUTES

2 CUPS RASPBERRIES

2 TABLESPOONS WATER

1 TABLESPOON FRESH LEMON JUICE

3 TABLESPOONS CHIA SEEDS

3 TABLESPOONS HONEY

1. Place the raspberries and water in a saucepan and cook the mixture over medium heat for 2 minutes.

2. Stir in the remaining ingredients and cook until the mixture has thickened and acquired a jammy consistency. Remove the pan from heat and let the jam cool completely before using or storing in the refrigerator. To can this jam, see page 486.

Cranberry Relish

YIELD: 2 CUPS | **ACTIVE TIME:** 5 MINUTES | **TOTAL TIME:** 1 HOUR

¾ LB. CRANBERRIES

1 GRANNY SMITH APPLE, CORED AND DICED

½ ORANGE, PEELED, MEMBRANE REMOVED

1 CUP SUGAR

1. Place the cranberries in a food processor and pulse for 1 minute. Add the apple and orange and pulse until combined. Add the sugar and pulse until incorporated.

2. Transfer the mixture to a bowl and let it steep for at least 1 hour before serving.

Orange Marmalade

YIELD: 2 CUPS | **ACTIVE TIME:** 30 MINUTES | **TOTAL TIME:** 4 HOURS

2 ORANGES, SLICED

2 LEMONS, SLICED

4 CUPS WATER

4 CUPS SUGAR

1. Place all of the ingredients in a large saucepan fitted with a candy thermometer. Cook over medium-low heat, stirring occasionally, until the mixture reaches 220ºF, about 2 hours.

2. Pour the marmalade into a mason jar and let it cool completely before serving.

Raspberry & Chia Jam
SEE PAGE 546

Rhubarb Jam

YIELD: 4 CUPS | **ACTIVE TIME:** 20 MINUTES | **TOTAL TIME:** 2 HOURS AND 30 MINUTES

4 CUPS CHOPPED RHUBARB

1 CUP WATER

¾ CUP SUGAR

½ TEASPOON KOSHER SALT

1 TEASPOON PECTIN

1. Place the rhubarb, water, sugar, and salt in a saucepan and cook the mixture over high heat, stirring occasionally, until the rhubarb is very tender and nearly all of the liquid has evaporated, about 25 minutes.

2. Add the pectin and stir the mixture for 1 minute.

3. Transfer the jam to a mason jar and let it cool completely before using or storing in the refrigerator. To can this jam, see page 486.

Cucumber, Tomato & Mango Relish

YIELD: 10 CUPS | **ACTIVE TIME:** 10 MINUTES | **TOTAL TIME:** 10 MINUTES

3 CUPS HALVED HEIRLOOM CHERRY TOMATOES

2 CUPS DESEEDED AND DICED PERSIAN CUCUMBERS

1 SMALL MANGO, PITTED AND DICED

½ CUP DICED RED ONION

1 TABLESPOON RED WINE VINEGAR

2 TABLESPOONS FRESH LEMON JUICE

1 TABLESPOON ZA'ATAR (SEE PAGE 68)

1 TABLESPOON SUMAC

2 TABLESPOONS FINE SEA SALT

1 TABLESPOON BLACK PEPPER

¼ CUP CHOPPED FRESH DILL

¼ CUP EXTRA-VIRGIN OLIVE OIL

1. Place all of the ingredients in a large mixing bowl and stir until combined.

2. Taste, adjust the seasoning as necessary, and use immediately or store in the refrigerator.

Red Zhug

YIELD: 3 CUPS | **ACTIVE TIME:** 10 MINUTES | **TOTAL TIME:** 10 MINUTES

4 FRESNO CHILE PEPPERS, STEMS REMOVED, CHOPPED

2 CUPS FRESH PARSLEY LEAVES

1 ONION, CHOPPED

5 GARLIC CLOVES

JUICE OF 1 LEMON

1 TABLESPOON KOSHER SALT

1 TEASPOON CAYENNE PEPPER

1 TABLESPOON CUMIN

2 TABLESPOONS PAPRIKA

¾ CUP EXTRA-VIRGIN OLIVE OIL

¼ CUP WATER

1. Place the chiles, parsley, onion, garlic, and lemon juice in a food processor and pulse until the mixture is roughly chopped.

2. Add the salt, cayenne, cumin, and paprika, and, with the food processor running on high, add the olive oil in a slow stream. Add the water as needed until the mixture is smooth.

3. Taste, adjust the seasoning as necessary, and serve.

Beet Relish

YIELD: 3 CUPS | **ACTIVE TIME:** 15 MINUTES | **TOTAL TIME:** 1 HOUR

4 RED BEETS, TRIMMED AND RINSED WELL

1 LARGE SHALLOT, MINCED

2 TEASPOONS WHITE WINE VINEGAR

SALT AND PEPPER, TO TASTE

1 TABLESPOON RED WINE VINEGAR

2 TABLESPOONS EXTRA-VIRGIN OLIVE OIL

1. Preheat the oven to 400°F. Place the beets in a baking dish, add a splash of water, cover the dish with aluminum foil, and place it in the oven. Roast the beets until they are so tender that a knife easily goes to the center when poked, 45 minutes to 1 hour. Remove the beets from the oven, remove the foil, and let the beets cool.

2. While the beets are in the oven, place the shallot and white wine vinegar in a mixing bowl, season the mixture with salt, and stir to combine. Let the mixture marinate.

3. Peel the beets, dice them, and place them in a mixing bowl. Add the remaining ingredients and the shallot mixture, season to taste, and serve.

Bacon Jam

YIELD: ½ CUP | **ACTIVE TIME:** 20 MINUTES | **TOTAL TIME:** 1 HOUR

½ LB. BACON

½ WHITE ONION, MINCED

1 GARLIC CLOVE, MINCED

2 TABLESPOONS APPLE CIDER VINEGAR

2 TABLESPOONS BROWN SUGAR

1 TABLESPOON MAPLE SYRUP

1. Preheat the oven to 350°F. Set a wire rack in a rimmed baking sheet, place the bacon on the rack, and place the sheet in the oven. Bake the bacon until it is crispy, about 10 minutes.

2. Remove the bacon from the oven and transfer it to a paper towel–lined plate to drain. Reserve the bacon fat. When the bacon is cool enough to handle, chop it into small pieces.

3. Place the reserved bacon fat in a large skillet and warm it over medium heat. Add the onion and cook, stirring frequently, until it has softened, about 5 minutes.

4. Stir in the bacon and the remaining ingredients, bring the mixture to a simmer, and cook until it has thickened slightly. Transfer the mixture to a bowl and let it chill in the refrigerator before serving.

Passion Fruit Emulsion

YIELD: 1 CUP | **ACTIVE TIME:** 5 MINUTES | **TOTAL TIME:** 5 MINUTES

1 SHALLOT, CHOPPED

1 CUP PASSION FRUIT PUREE

1 CUP CANOLA OIL

1. Place the shallot and passion fruit puree in a blender and puree on medium until smooth.

2. Reduce the speed to low and slowly drizzle in the canola oil until it has emulsified. Use immediately or store in the refrigerator.

Gremolata

YIELD: ½ CUP | **ACTIVE TIME:** 5 MINUTES | **TOTAL TIME:** 5 MINUTES

8 GARLIC CLOVES, MINCED

ZEST OF 8 LEMONS

¼ CUP CHOPPED FRESH PARSLEY

1. Place all of the ingredients in a bowl, stir to combine, and use immediately or store in the refrigerator.

Black Currant Compote

YIELD: 1 CUP | **ACTIVE TIME:** 10 MINUTES | **TOTAL TIME:** 20 MINUTES

1 CUP FRESH BLACK CURRANTS

1 TABLESPOON SUGAR

ZEST AND JUICE OF 2 LEMONS

1 TABLESPOON CHOPPED FRESH PARSLEY

1 TABLESPOON CRÈME DE CASSIS

1. Place all of the ingredients in a saucepan and bring the mixture to a simmer over medium heat. Cook for 5 minutes, occasionally stirring and mashing the currants with a fork.

2. Remove the pan from heat and let the compote cool before using or storing in the refrigerator.

Bacon Jam
SEE PAGE 552

Olive Relish

YIELD: 1 CUP | **ACTIVE TIME:** 10 MINUTES | **TOTAL TIME:** 10 MINUTES

¼ CUP EXTRA-VIRGIN OLIVE OIL

1 TABLESPOON DRIED OREGANO

2 TABLESPOONS RED WINE VINEGAR

½ ONION, FINELY DICED

2 TEASPOONS DIJON MUSTARD

2 TABLESPOONS MINCED KALAMATA OLIVES

2 TABLESPOONS MINCED GREEN OLIVES

1 TABLESPOON MINCED CAPERS

1 TABLESPOON CHOPPED FRESH PARSLEY

SALT AND PEPPER, TO TASTE

1. Place the olive oil in a small saucepan and warm it over low heat. Add the oregano, remove the pan from heat, and cover it. Let the mixture steep for 5 minutes.

2. Add the vinegar, onion, mustard, olives, capers, and parsley, season the relish with salt and pepper, and stir to combine. Use immediately or store in the refrigerator.

Red Pepper Mayonnaise

YIELD: 1 CUP | **ACTIVE TIME:** 5 MINUTES | **TOTAL TIME:** 50 MINUTES

3 RED BELL PEPPERS

½ CUP MAYONNAISE

1. Preheat the oven to 400°F. Place the red peppers on a baking sheet, place them in the oven, and roast, turning them occasionally, until the peppers are blistered all over, 35 to 40 minutes. Remove them from the oven and let them cool. When cool enough to handle, remove the skins and seeds from the peppers.

2. Place the roasted peppers and mayonnaise in a food processor, blitz until smooth, and use immediately or store in the refrigerator.

Green Zhug

YIELD: 2½ CUPS | **ACTIVE TIME:** 10 MINUTES | **TOTAL TIME:** 10 MINUTES

4 JALAPEÑO CHILE PEPPERS, STEMS AND SEEDS REMOVED, CHOPPED

2 CUPS FRESH PARSLEY

¼ CUP FRESH CILANTRO

6 FRESH MINT LEAVES

1 ONION, QUARTERED

5 GARLIC CLOVES

JUICE OF 1 LEMON

1 TABLESPOON KOSHER SALT

½ CUP EXTRA-VIRGIN OLIVE OIL

1. Place the jalapeños, parsley, cilantro, mint, onion, garlic, lemon juice, and salt in a food processor and pulse until combined.

2. With the food processor running, add the olive oil in a slow stream until it has emulsified. Use immediately or store in the refrigerator.

Red Pepper & Garlic Honey

YIELD: ½ CUP | **ACTIVE TIME:** 5 MINUTES | **TOTAL TIME:** 5 MINUTES

1 TEASPOON RED PEPPER FLAKES

1 GARLIC CLOVE, MINCED

1 TABLESPOON EXTRA-VIRGIN OLIVE OIL

2 TABLESPOONS FRESH LEMON JUICE

SALT, TO TASTE

6 TABLESPOONS HONEY

1. Using a spice grinder or a mortar and pestle, grind the red pepper flakes until they are reduced to a fine powder.

2. Place the powder in a bowl, add the remaining ingredients, and stir to combine. Use immediately or store in an airtight container.

Pistachio Gremolata

YIELD: 2 CUPS | **ACTIVE TIME:** 5 MINUTES | **TOTAL TIME:** 5 MINUTES

1½ CUPS FRESH MINT LEAVES

½ CUP ROASTED, SALTED PISTACHIOS, SHELLS REMOVED

2 GARLIC CLOVES

2 TEASPOONS LEMON ZEST

¼ TEASPOON KOSHER SALT

⅛ TEASPOON BLACK PEPPER

2 TABLESPOONS EXTRA-VIRGIN OLIVE OIL

1. Place the mint, pistachios, garlic, lemon zest, salt, and pepper in a food processor and pulse until the mixture is combined and coarsely chopped.

2. Add the olive oil in a slow stream and pulse until the mixture is just combined, making sure not to overprocess the gremolata—you want it to have some texture. Use immediately or store in an airtight container.

Spicy Honey Mayonnaise

YIELD: ½ CUP | **ACTIVE TIME:** 5 MINUTES | **TOTAL TIME:** 15 MINUTES

½ CUP MAYONNAISE

2 TABLESPOONS HONEY

1 TABLESPOON SRIRACHA

1. Place all of the ingredients in a small bowl and stir until thoroughly combined.

2. Chill the mayonnaise in the refrigerator for 10 minutes before serving.

Tahini Mayonnaise

YIELD: 1 CUP | **ACTIVE TIME:** 10 MINUTES | **TOTAL TIME:** 10 MINUTES

2 EGG YOLKS

¼ CUP TAHINI PASTE

3 TABLESPOONS FRESH LEMON JUICE

1 TABLESPOON WATER

1 TEASPOON KOSHER SALT

½ CUP EXTRA-VIRGIN OLIVE OIL

1. Place the egg yolks, tahini, lemon juice, water, and salt in a food processor and blitz until the mixture is combined.

2. With the food processor running, add the olive oil in a slow stream and blitz until the mayonnaise is extremely thick and velvety. Use immediately or store in the refrigerator.

Spiced Crème Fraîche

YIELD: 1 CUP | **ACTIVE TIME:** 5 MINUTES | **TOTAL TIME:** 5 MINUTES

1 CUP CRÈME FRAÎCHE

½ TEASPOON CINNAMON

⅛ TEASPOON FRESHLY GRATED NUTMEG

⅛ TEASPOON GROUND CLOVES

1 TABLESPOON REAL MAPLE SYRUP

1. Place all of the ingredients in a bowl, stir to combine, and use immediately or store in the refrigerator.

Tahini Mayonnaise
SEE PAGE 559

METRIC CONVERSION CHART

U.S. Measurement	Approximate Metric Liquid Measurement	Approximate Metric Dry Measurement
1 teaspoon	5 ml	—
1 tablespoon or ½ ounce	15 ml	14 g
1 ounce or ⅛ cup	30 ml	29 g
¼ cup or 2 ounces	60 ml	57 g
⅓ cup	80 ml	—
½ cup or 4 ounces	120 ml	113 g
⅔ cup	160 ml	—
¾ cup or 6 ounces	180 ml	—
1 cup or 8 ounces or ½ pint	240 ml	227 g
1½ cups or 12 ounces	350 ml	—
2 cups or 1 pint or 16 ounces	475 ml	454 g
3 cups or 1½ pints	700 ml	—
4 cups or 2 pints or 1 quart	950 ml	—

Miso Dressing, 446

Olive & Whole Lemon Vinaigrette, 464

Orange Vinaigrette, 463

Oregano Vinaigrette, 417

Pomegranate & Mint Vinaigrette, 462

Pomegranate Vinaigrette, 465

Preserved Lemon Vinaigrette, 424

Ranch Dressing, 471

Red Wine & Chile Dressing, 434

Red Wine & Maple Vinaigrette, 434

Shallot, Honey & Herb Vinaigrette, 453

Soy & Sesame Dressing, 464

Spicy Honey Vinaigrette, 463

Tahini Dressing, 445

Thai Chili Dressing, 431

Thousand Island Dressing, 474

White Balsamic Vinaigrette, 450

White Wine Vinaigrette, 418

Yuzu Vinaigrette, 459

Dukkah, 59

Dukkah, Walnut, 52

Dzikil P'aak, 378

E

eggplants

Eggplant & Pine Nut Ragout, 390

Tomato & Eggplant Sauce alla Norma, 408

eggs

Agristrada Sauce, 310

Aioli, 298

Béarnaise Sauce, 318

Blender Hollandaise, 247

Classic Caesar Dressing, 470

Cumin & Cilantro Vinaigrette, 453

Garlic Custard, 502

Roasted Garlic Aioli, 288

Smoked Egg Aioli, 284

Sunchoke Aioli, 206

Tahini Mayonnaise, 559

Thousand Island Dressing, 474

epazote/epazote leaves

Epazote Oil, 425

Mojo de Ajo, 254

Mole Verde, 394

Pipian Verde, 256

espresso beans

Colombian Gold Rub, 31

see also coffee

Everything Seasoning, 46

extra-virgin olive oil, about, 14

F

Fall Spiced Cream, 510

fennel

Fennel & Lemon Gremolata, 492

Mole Blanco, 267

Pernod Cream, 499

fennel pollen, about, 10

fennel seeds

about, 10

BBQ Poultry Rub, 22

Chinese Five-Spice Rub, 89

Everything Seasoning, 46

Five-Alarm Rub, 89

Laksa Curry Paste, 45

Lemon & Herb Marinade, 147

Mole Blanco, 267

Pernod Cream, 499

Pomegranate & Fennel Glaze, 104

Toasted Fennel Seed Rub, 85

Fermented Chile Adobo

Maple & Chipotle Glaze, 123

recipe, 371

Fermented Hot Sauce, 209

feta cheese

about, 15

Red Bell Pepper & Shallot Pesto, 250

Red Pepper Feta & Ricotta, 538

Fig Vinaigrette, 465

Five-Alarm Rub, 89

Five-Spice Marinade, 163

five-spice powder

about, 12

Char Siu Marinade, 152

Five-Spice Marinade, 163

Marley's Collie, 130

Fontina cheese

about, 15

Fontina Sauce, 237

Furikake, 50

G

galangal root

Red Thai Curry Paste, 44

Tom Yum Paste, 27

Garam Masala

Masala Rub, 27

recipe, 39

garlic powder

Acapulco Gold Rub, 31

Agave & Sriracha Glaze, 134

Balsamic Ranch Dressing, 414

BBQ Poultry Rub, 22

BBQ Shrimp Rub, 95

Blackening Spice, 47

Buffalo Dry Rub, 93

Cajun Seafood Rub, 46

Cajun Turkey Rub, 37

Carne Asada, 160

Chinese Five-Spice Rub, 89

Classic Seafood Rub, 61

Coffee & Bourbon BBQ Sauce, 349

Colombian Gold Rub, 31

Donair Sauce, 207

Five-Alarm Rub, 89

Lemon-Pepper Poultry Rub, 23

Nashville Hot Chicken Rub, 30

Pastrami Rub, 90

Red Wine & Chile Dressing, 434

Salsa Chipotle de Adobo, 367

Salt & Vinegar Marinade, 169

San Sebastian Rub, 23

Sazón, 76

Smoky Cajun Rub, 77

Smoky St. Louis Rub, 77

Spicy Coffee Rub, 80

Spicy Steak Rub, 94

St. Louis Rub, 60

Surefire Steak Rub, 71

Sweet & Spicy Rub, 26

Taco Seasoning Blend, 76

Three-Pepper Rub, 18

Universal BBQ Sauce, 353

Za'atar, 68

General Tso Sauce, 239

gherkins

Tartar Sauce, 331

ginger, crystallized

Mostarda, 544

ginger, ground

Acapulco Gold Rub, 31

Bay Blend Marinade, 134

Chinese Five-Spice Rub, 89

Crayfish Boil Blend, 45

Five-Alarm Rub, 89

Indian Kush Rub, 39

Madras Curry Blend, 82

Mole Rub, 38

Pomegranate & Honey Glaze, 112

Pomegranate Sauce, 383

Ras el Hanout, 55

Smoky St. Louis Rub, 77

St. Louis Rub, 60

Togarashi, 44

ginger juice

Gochujang & Scallion Sauce, 266

Gingery Red Pepper Sauce, 196

glazes

Agave & Sriracha Glaze, 134

Apple Cider & Honey Glaze, 127

Apple Glaze, 115

Balsamic Glaze, 108

BBQ Glaze, 109

Bourbon & Brown Sugar Glaze, 109

Harissa Glaze, 123

Maple & Chipotle Glaze, 123

Orange & Buckwheat Honey Glaze, 106

Pomegranate & Fennel Glaze, 104

Pomegranate & Honey Glaze, 112

Sweet Cilantro Glaze, 145

Sweet Maple BBQ Glaze, 116

gochugaru

Beef Bulgogi Marinade, 151

Nakji Sauce, 312

gochujang

Gochujang & Scallion Sauce, 266

Korean BBQ Sauce, 354

Nakji Sauce, 312

South Asian BBQ Marinade, 108

Gooseberry Vinaigrette, 441

Gorgonzola Cream Sauce, 254

grapefruit juice

Al Pastor Marinade, 181

Recado Rojo, 132

Spicy Honey Vinaigrette, 463

Greek yogurt, about, 15

Green Goddess Dressing, 422

Green Tomato Chutney, 496

Green Tomato Jam, 541

Green Zhug

recipe, 557

Spiced Yogurt Sauce, 390

Gremolata, 553

Grilled Corn & Jalapeño Salsa, 310

Grilled Poultry Marinade, 140

Grilled Seafood Marinade, 162

Gruyère, about, 15

Guacamole, 531

Guinness

Smoky Stout BBQ Sauce, 350

H

Habanero, Calabrian Chile & Pineapple Hot Sauce, 219

Habanero Honey, 519

Ham Sauce, Broccoli Rabe &, 200

Harissa Sauce

Harissa & Dijon Vinaigrette, 462

recipe, 285

harissa/harissa paste

Harissa Glaze, 123

ABOUT CIDER MILL PRESS BOOK PUBLISHERS

Good ideas ripen with time. From seed to harvest, Cider Mill Press brings fine reading, information, and entertainment together between the covers of its creatively crafted books. Our Cider Mill bears fruit twice a year, publishing a new crop of titles each spring and fall.

"Where Good Books Are Ready for Press"

Visit us online at
cidermillpress.com
or write to us at
501 Nelson Place
Nashville, TN 37214